W9-BCN-289

FREUD AND HIS APHASIA BOOK

CORNELL STUDIES IN THE HISTORY OF PSYCHIATRY

EDITED BY SANDER L. GILMAN AND GEORGE J. MAKARI

FREUD AND HIS APHASIA BOOK

LANGUAGE AND THE
SOURCES OF PSYCHOANALYSIS

VALERIE D. GREENBERG

CORNELL UNIVERSITY PRESS

ITHACA AND LONDON

First published 1997 by Cornell University Press.

Printed in the United States of America

Cornell University Press strives to utilize environmentally responsible suppliers and materials to the fullest extent possible in the publishing of its books. Such materials include vegetable-based, low-VOC inks and acid-free papers that are also either recycled, totally chlorine-free, or partly composed of nonwood fibers.

Library of Congress Cataloging-in-Publication Data
Greenberg, Valerie D.
Freud and his aphasia book : language and the sources of psychoanalysis /
Valerie D. Greenberg.
p.   cm. — (Cornell studies in the history of psychiatry)
Includes bibliographical references and index.
ISBN 0-8014-3284-7 (alk. paper)
1. Freud, Sigmund, 1856–1939—Contributions in psycholinguistics.
2. Freud, Sigmund, 1856–1939—Contributions in aphasia. I. Title. II. Series.
BF109.F   G   1997
616.85′52—dc21   97-18277

Cloth printing   10   9   8   7   6   5   4   3   2   1

Dedicated to Sander L. Gilman

CONTENTS

ACKNOWLEDGMENTS

Once again, I was able to rely on the assistance of my helper and partner, my husband, Bob Greenberg, who knows how grateful I am.

I am deeply grateful to the John Simon Guggenheim Memorial Foundation for its generous support for a year of work on the project.

My initial interest in the "early Freud" was stimulated by the opportunity to work at the Freud Museum in London in 1991 as a member of a National Endowment for the Humanities Summer Seminar led by Sander Gilman. I thank the NEH for having provided this opportunity.

Thanks are due to Michael Molnar, Director of Research at the Freud Museum, who shared his lectures on Freud when I needed them. Eleanor Elder, science librarian at the Howard-Tilton Library of Tulane University, has assisted me with good humor and great expertise.

Special colleagues in New Orleans—Felicia McCarren and Vann Spruiell—shared their ideas on psychoanalysis and science and on many other topics. I am grateful to them for expanding my intellectual horizons. Timothy Bahti, who read the introduction, made a valuable suggestion.

Finally, I want to express my appreciation to anonymous readers at Cornell University Press, and to Janet Mais for the exceptional quality of her work as copyeditor.

V. D. G.

FREUD AND HIS APHASIA BOOK

INTRODUCTION

I nterest in the "early Freud" has been growing, particularly among
analysts; but significant gaps remain, partly because translation of
his early writings is only beginning. This book is intended to help
fill the gaps. It is an analysis of Freud's *On Interpretation of the Aphasias: A Critical Study* (1891)[1] as a meeting ground for two strains of
inquiry: one having to do with Freud's early neurological writing and
career as a research scientist, the other having to do with the origins of
psychoanalysis in late-nineteenth-century intellectual culture, particularly
in the preoccupation with language. Freud's aphasia study is positioned at
the intersection of several disciplines in various stages of development in
the late nineteenth century and at a meeting point of British and Conti-
nental theorizing on aphasia.[2] Although it is the first book of which
he was sole author, and has been recognized as a central document in
the development of psychoanalysis, it has received relatively little attention compared with Freud's later works. There is no doubt that it repre-

---

1. Sigmund Freud, *Zur Auffassung der Aphasien: Eine kritische Studie* (Leipzig: Franz Deuticke, 1891), referred to hereafter as *AA*. There is a revised edition: ed. Paul Vogel and
Ingeborg Meyer-Palmedo, intro. Wolfgang Leuschner (Frankfurt am Main: S. Fischer,
1992). The only translation is Erwin Stengel, *On Aphasia* (New York: International Universities Press, 1953).
2. The term *aphasia* was coined by Armand Trousseau in 1864.

sented an emancipatory gesture that helped to define the Sigmund Freud of 1891.

At the age of thirty-five, Freud had to his credit a series of distinguished publications on histology (the first as a twenty-two-year-old student in 1877) and neurology, important studies of the nervous system (for example, a monograph on childhood cerebral palsy written with Oscar Rie), and he had begun to see the first of the later-famous patients afflicted with hysteria. Although he was moving toward a clinical practice in psychiatry, he nevertheless still identified himself on the title page of the aphasia book as "Dr. Sigm. Freud, lecturer in neuropathology at the University of Vienna." His study of language disorders that result from brain lesions (usually caused by stroke, injury, tumors, or other brain damage) shows Freud as a bold investigator who encounters, in the sources he uses, some of the most important ideas that are later to evolve into psychoanalysis. In addition, the aphasia book marks the flowering of his characteristic research methods and his rhetorical mastery. It reveals him as an active participant in an international network of cross-disciplinary researchers united by their fascination with patients whose striking deficits challenged the limits of science.

The aphasia book would be worthy of close scrutiny, however, even if someone other than Freud had written it—that is, if it were divorced from the origins of psychoanalysis. It was a rarity among medical treatises of its time for its combination of self-conscious composition, rigorous argument, and pointed rhetorical effects, as well as for the audacity of its agenda. It contributed to aphasia studies ideas that proved to be prescient, although Freud's contribution is hardly acknowledged today. Aphasia studies flourished in the late nineteenth century when aphasia was the focus of efforts to understand and minister to patients whose problems lent themselves to explanation in neurological, psychological, and linguistic terms. Today, aphasia is once again of great interest; for advances in medical imaging technology have given access to new information about language in the brain. When one enters the world of aphasia studies, one enters a sphere that encompasses inquiry into language, brain, consciousness, and ultimately, the entire question of mind-body relations. Thus Freud's aphasia study both represents its time and reaches out to ours, stands both for late-nineteenth-century disciplinary ferment and for later twentieth-century neurological discovery.

At the time of Freud's writing, a large circle of aphasiologists in France, England, the United States, Germany, and the Austro-Hungarian Empire were reading one another's work, quoting one another regularly, and using one another's clinical reports. Antonio Damasio calls late nineteenth-century aphasia studies "the intellectual and practical center of neurology but also the focus for scientists and philosophers interested in the field that was to become psychology."[3] He points out that by the early twentieth century "both subject and theory had largely lost their influence," mainly because of the limitations on brain research owing to lack of noninvasive techniques. Late-twentieth-century progress in medical technology has brought new insights, although the interpretive space in which Freud wrote remains contested territory. According to Damasio, for present-day "psychologists, linguists, computational scientists, and philosophers," aphasia serves as a "testing ground for theories of mind and brain" (531).

Freud's purposes in 1891 were to refute prevailing theories and to propose one of his own. An aphasia theory of his own would necessarily require some explicit or implicit theory of language. Walther Riese writes, "Each theory of aphasia implies a theory of language adopted by its author, willingly or not."[4] The theories Freud wanted to refute are: (1) that there is a distinction between aphasia caused by destruction of nerve centers and aphasia caused by destruction of neural pathways and (2) that the functions of the nervous system are restricted to anatomically definable areas, or localized. The leading researchers drew diagrams of nerve "centers" in the brain, damage to which would mean massive injury, and lines radiating to and from these centers, damage to which would cause a specific, local, and lesser form of aphasia. Freud argued for a "functional" explanation beyond the localizing one. He believed the damage caused by a brain lesion could affect areas of the brain at remove from the lesion site. Therefore the many complex subvarieties of aphasic disturbances could not necessarily be accurately predicted by the site of, for example, a brain tumor.

Freud's proposal for a theory of aphasia adds the quality of indeterminacy to his own certainty of the character of neurological organization as derived from clinical reports, information on brain physiology, and postmortem findings. Freud's theory in its full elaboration, but also his method, that is, how he marshals his argument, including the gaps in explanation and meanings left unexplored, suggest that it is already possible in this early text to tease out the play of transformative memory versus recollection, of interpretation versus reproduction. In the aphasia study

3. Antonio Damasio, "Aphasia," review article, *New England Journal of Medicine* 326 (February 20, 1992): 531–539, here 532.
4. Walther Riese, "Freudian Concepts of Brain Function and Brain Disease," *Journal of Nervous and Mental Disease* 127 (October 1958): 287–307, here 299.

Freud believes he knows "what really happened" in the brain, but at the same time he suggests that the story of nervous structures is a narrative of transformation.

The importance of aphasic syndromes for psychoanalysis lies in the apparent similarities between communication disorders caused by brain damage and those resulting from disturbances of the psyche. For example, aphasia may duplicate symptoms exhibited by hysterical patients, or it may produce types of errors, breakdowns, and reassemblings in grammar and word choice like those that appear in Freud's later investigations of dreams, jokes, and parapraxia in everyday life. To deal with aphasic patients, or even, as Freud did, only with the clinical reports, one had, first of all, to measure intelligibility and theorize the production of meaning. Only an insightful and intuitive reader had any chance of "reading" and understanding patients with severe disorders.

Mark Solms and Michael Saling, writing from a neurological perspective, maintain that the aphasia book is Freud's "first account of the dynamics of mental process," that it "contains a detailed model of the speech apparatus" (central in "the talking cure") and "the germs of the theory of regression and the genetic point of view in psychoanalysis" as well as "the beginning of a new attitude toward brain functioning which became the conceptual framework within which psychoanalysis could develop."[5] Some researchers see the book as a bridge between Freud's neurological thinking and his psychological thinking; others consider it his attempt to impose the categories of psychology on neurological phenomena; some interpret it as revolutionary, others as the same old nineteenth-century stuff clothed in a somewhat different discourse. The aphasia text and Freud's contribution thus appear in various lights with changing interpretation through the years.

I see it as also the story of how Freud positioned himself at a time of great intellectual ferment in the sciences. Neurology was in its infancy, its vocabulary being worked out and brain study limited by relatively crude methods. Psychology was in the throes of becoming an experimental science under the leadership of Wilhelm Wundt and replacing philosophy as a methodological model for the field of philology. One of Freud's important sources, James Ross, a British physician whom today we might

---

5. Mark Solms and Michael Saling, "On Psychoanalysis and Neuroscience: Freud's Attitude to the Localizationist Tradition," *International Journal of Psycho-Analysis* 67 (1986): 397–416, here 399.

call a neurologist or a neuropathologist, called himself and other aphasiologists "psychologists." Terms were not at all fixed; their meanings were evolving. Psychoanalysis as such had not yet been born. Only physics had an established and legitimating discourse. *On Interpretation of the Aphasias* stands at this confluence.

Freud concurred with the argument of the British neurologist John Hughlings Jackson that physiological and psychological processes were parallel but did not intersect; that is, an individual psychological state could not be attributed to an immediate "cause" in the nervous system. Jackson's view provided Freud with a neurological explanation for the notion that there could be such a thing as, for example, hysterical paralysis —a psychic disturbance not associated with a physical finding. Hughlings Jackson was also Freud's main source for the theory of how language was lost in cases of aphasia. Influenced by the evolutionary theories of his teacher Herbert Spencer and by observing his own patients, Jackson had developed the theory of "dissolution," one example of which is his observation that in aphasia a later-acquired language tends to be lost before a patient's native language. In more general terms, Jackson believed that the last-acquired, most advanced, and thus least organized capacities were lost before the earliest-acquired, more organized (i.e., habitual) ones. Freud's theory of regression is often attributed to the influence of Jackson's ideas. Freud's intersection—via Jackson—with the thinking of the founder of British associationist psychology, Herbert Spencer, and the example of Jackson himself illustrate the profound influence of British aphasiology on Freud's work. Despite occasional clear disagreement, Freud did not try to refute his British sources. The authorities he set out to refute in the aphasia book belonged exclusively to the German-speaking world.

Freud shared with his British sources the influence of Darwin *and* Lamarck (the inheritance of acquired characteristics); associationist philosophy (via Spencer and John Stuart Mill, the only philosopher to whom Freud refers in the aphasia book); and the view of contemporary philology (or historical linguistics) which held that the history of a language inscribes the history of a culture and a people as well as of individual development. The study of historical development as a means of understanding individual psychology entailed in today's parlance, anthropology, archaeology, and psycholinguistics. Add brain anatomy, physiology, pathology, and clinical experience, and we can see Freud's aphasia study as a narrative of nineteenth-century European intellectual culture. As the neurologist Richard M. Restak writes, "Each generation's thinking about the brain borrows from the social, political, and technological climate of the period."[6] "In the space of one generation," he points out, "theories about the brain moved from analogies drawn from theology and philosophy to analogies drawn from politics and social science" (22–23).

One of Restak's examples is the work of John Hughlings Jackson:

> His thinking was a blend of evolution and class consciousness appropriate for an age deeply influenced and yet haunted by revolutions and insurrections. Jackson spoke of "control" and "release," "dissolution" and the consequent "welling up" of "primitive brain levels" after injury to "higher" centers. Indeed brain injury, whether due to stroke or tumor or by other means, involved a reversal of the evolutionary process and the ascendence of lower, more "atavistic" forces.

Restak believes that Freud "incorporated Jackson's hierarchical organization in his theories about mental illness" (22). There is no doubt that the discourses of the sciences, like those of other disciplines, are shaped by a culture's dominant metaphors, just as theory formation reflects ideological imperatives. Nevertheless, if it were true that Freud simply "incorporated" a scheme from Hughlings Jackson into his own theories, there would be no accounting for change. There must be a means of accounting for that point at which theory veers from that which has come before.

At any given time, multiple discourses coexist, from which each user, depending on inclination or creativity, may make choices and combinations within certain boundaries, which themselves are always shifting. No theory is independent of choice of discursive environment, and within those environments, dominant metaphors may be adopted or not, modified to a greater or lesser degree, or even critically recast or subverted. Hughlings Jackson, for example, started out to be a writer or philosopher and became a scientist whose neurological writings, perhaps because of those early interests, include subversive interventions in prevailing discourses whose metaphors he found misleading and detrimental. New "languages" constantly develop, and they, in turn, work on prevailing ideologies that rework and reproduce yet further versions of "languages." In technologically advanced parts of the world at the close of the twentieth century, this complex feedback process has reached a fever pitch. It seems both worthwhile and necessary to wonder how and to what extent Freud's writing is both the product and the generator of tensions with discursive conventions and dominant metaphors.

6. Richard M. Restak, *The Modular Brain* (New York: Scribner's, 1994), 23.

I have taken Freud's aphasia book as a point of departure for branching out in several directions. By tracing Freud's references to his sources, I was able to reconstitute at least part of the intellectual network within which he was operating and arrive at some suggestive conclusions about how he may have read and thought, his evolving views on language, how the aphasia text connects to the development of psychoanalysis, and why the text and its fate tell us something about the history of science. Naturally it would be foolhardy to claim exhaustive coverage of the meanings in Freud's texts, let alone the strains of thought he took into consideration. I hope only to open some windows on qualities of the text and on his thought at a particular time and within a continuum over time. My reading of the aphasia book looks to what came before and what came after. Not only was Freud immersed in what had already been written on his subject, but also, deliberately or not, he was engaged, beyond his announced critique of the dominant theory of aphasia, in developing the theoretical framework for his future discipline. Wolfgang Leuschner, in his introduction to the new edition of the aphasia book (26), sees much of the edifice of psychoanalysis as built around the "word-presentation" and "object-presentation" relationship that Freud first theorized in the aphasia book. James Strachey had anticipated this line of reasoning when he detected the roots of Freud's "The Unconscious" (1915) in the aphasia book and, for that reason, translated relevant pages as an appendix to his *Standard Edition* translation of the paper.[7]

An interdisciplinary reexamination of Freud's work requires threading one's way among competing discourses, each with its own "Freud." The discourse of psychoanalysis, naturally the most pervasive, incorporates Freud into a narrative of development characterized by terminology, in English, that originated with James Strachey and others in the *Standard Edition* and was supplemented by later analytic schools and directions. That narrative's stress on clinical activity must give way to an emphasis on theory when interpreting the aphasia book, in which Freud presents no case histories of his own. Its coherent, identifiably scientific narrative arises out of conventional data and generally accepted constructs (e.g., of the foundations of language) but also out of images, argument, opinion, personal experience, and private motives.

7. *The Standard Edition of the Complete Psychological Works of Sigmund Freud*, ed. and trans. James Strachey, with Anna Freud, Alix Strachey, and Alan Tyson, 24 vols. (London: Hogarth, 1955–1974), 14:206–215. The *Standard Edition* is referred to hereafter as *SE*.

Yet reading Freud is always a loaded act. As field theory has taught us, one cannot help reading Freud from a vantage point that is already contained *by* Freud. The culture "speaks" Freud; the main tenets of psychoanalysis have become widespread assumptions. Thus we use instruments fashioned by Freud to dissect the toolmaker. There is no escape from that position. In addition, the Freud at the center of the investigation is always an invented figure who arises, genielike, from readings of his texts, including mine. At least two personas arise from any text: one a rhetorical construct of Freud's own making, the other assembled by the reader out of textual clues. Neither forms a coherent whole. From my perspective, closure on either of these constructs or on any reading of the aphasia text, mine included, is neither to be sought nor desired.

The other half of the reading equation is how Freud himself read. Ilse Grubrich-Simitis has gathered evidence from manuscripts of how he used his sources.[8] First of all, what features of the writers he read led Freud to accept only certain of them and integrate elements from their texts into his own thinking? Grubrich-Simitis quotes an extract from *Totem and Taboo* (1912–1913) in which Freud extols a researcher (W. Robertson Smith) for being "a man of many-sided interests, clear-sighted and liberal-minded," and praises his writing for its "lucidity and convincing force."[9] She also believes, however, that "Freud the innovator" was not especially interested in his intellectual ancestors and neighbors, which leads her to assume that via analogies and borrowed metaphors he incorporated into his psychoanalytic texts countless unacknowledged suggestions from sources. I believe that this is the manner in which any writer proceeds. Grubrich-Simitis (337) maintains that particularly in the context of his "intense searching" in the 1890s, Freud would have been looking, even in his private reading, for authors with whom he felt a kinship and whose "textual gestures and figures of thought" he found stimulating. She describes some of the features that appear to have led Freud to find congenial the rather idiosyncratic array of sources in his aphasia book.

Once his thinking had been stimulated by a writer, how did Freud use this material? In her study of his notes, which often were mere scraps of paper, Grubrich-Simitis demonstrates that material would reappear in the context of something he was writing even decades later. It seems that his

---

8. Ilse Grubrich-Simitis, *Zurück zu Freuds Texten* (Frankfurt am Main: S. Fischer, 1993).
9. Ibid., 163; *SE* 13:132–133. The German text is to be found in Sigmund Freud, *Gesammelte Werke*, 19 vols., ed. Anna Freud, Marie Bonaparte, E. Bibring, W. Hoffer, E. Kris, and O. Isakower (Frankfurt am Main: S. Fischer, 1952–1987), 9:160–161. The *Gesammelte Werke* is referred to hereafter as *GW*.

mind may have stored and reworked ideas, testimony, arguments, even images until he felt the need to integrate them into a work in progress (or, alternatively, until they themselves jogged a new work into existence). This processing strategy helps us understand the conceptual paths from the aphasia book to important elements in psychoanalysis, though, with the exception of Hughlings Jackson, many of Freud's sources have not yet been examined for the connections they might have to some of those elements and to Freud's conception of language. My exploration extends the range of relevant sources but also expands prevailing views of the kinds of writers and texts Freud tended to subsume into his creative thought process. In *Moses and Monotheism* (1939), Freud advises reading the Bible for what has been suppressed or hidden at separate locations.[10] If we carry that prescription for reading back to the aphasia book in order to read Freud reading, we find that even at the very beginning of his career, when he was on a steep learning curve, Freud read texts the way he was later to read patients.

The term *sources* is inevitably vexed by its association with the discredited term *influences*. I have tried to avoid "influence" without really stating what I believe a "source" does. I have no doubt that there are "sources" of all kinds for all of us, but just how they achieve their effects is going to remain open to debate. Therefore tracing terms and ideas from the aphasia book to psychoanalysis and psychoanalytic texts is by necessity a highly speculative undertaking, even though some researchers quite confidently list terms and ideas as if meanings had not changed in the last hundred years or in the course of transmission from the German to the English language. By contrast, Wolfgang Leuschner (20–21) points out the change over time in, for example, the terms *function* and *physiology*, which play a central role in the aphasia book. Riese (287) does the same for *neuropathology*, which is particularly important in view of Freud's self-designation as a lecturer in neuropathology. There are other terminological problems, for example, "linguistics," which I often use in place of "philology," which would be correct for the time of the aphasia book.

Questions of terminology raise the question of translation, which is particularly problematic in the case of the aphasia book. Erwin Stengel's translation made the book accessible to an English-speaking public but at the cost of accuracy to Freud's text. Words, phrases, sentences are left out, and the final result, though careful on points of neuroanatomy, is in toto impressionistic, if not at points misleading. Thus I have found it necessary

10. *SE* 23:43; *GW* 16:144.

to provide my own translation of quoted passages, with the exception of the several pages translated by Strachey and published in the *Standard Edition*. More extensive quotation becomes necessary toward the end of my book, and I am hoping that by providing a version one stage closer to Freud's text, I have assisted any future, improved translation of the whole.

Let me mention two particularly difficult challenges to translation which are also central to the aphasia book. One is the unresolvable conflict between "speech" and "language." Both are rendered by *Sprache* in German, and it is difficult in individual instances to decide which Freud meant when he used *Sprache* and its compounds. Obviously, the distinction is important. My best judgment has led me to use "language" in cases where others have used "speech," because I believe Freud had the more encompassing meaning in mind. The result can only be informed speculation. Another challenge is the German term *Vorstellung*, translated as "presentation" in the *Standard Edition*. In addition to being particularly amorphous and mutable according to context, *Vorstellung* entails a complex of historical and philosophic meanings that make it impossible to find one English equivalent. It has been appropriately translated into English as, among other things, "representation," "image," "idea," "notion," and "concept." Strachey's "presentation" is a less suitable translation for the aphasia text. Freud's use of the term changes with context, so I have tried to indicate that while at the same time leaving the word in the German original or providing it parenthetically.

It is fortunate that the S. Fischer Verlag published its new German edition of *On Interpretation of the Aphasias*, edited by Ingeborg Meyer-Palmedo (who continued the work begun by Paul Vogel). This is an invaluable resource in view of the extreme scarcity of the original edition. There are, however, some differences from the original: spelling has been modernized; paragraph indentations have been removed; page numbering is changed; and Freud's running page titles have been deleted, although they are listed in the appendix. Thus the text has a different appearance from Freud's, and the reader is deprived of the possibility of following along with Freud's sense of the most important point on each page. In the bibliography there are several errors in page references to the text. Leuschner's excellent introduction, the helpful notes, and the appendix of sources outweigh these minor failings. Nevertheless, it remains necessary for research purposes to look at the original.

My first chapter opens with a review of literature on the aphasia book which raises some of the important issues concerning Freud's text. It concludes with an exploration of Freud's rhetorical posture and the evidence of his sympathy for England. To follow the development of Freud's argument and his rhetorical shifts, as well as to be able to weigh the positioning of his sources in the text, the next four chapters follow the order of chapters in Freud's book. I often loop backward or forward, however, to make comparisons or draw points together. I have found it necessary to take longish excursions into the work and person of Freud's most important sources, especially the three whose portraits are included in this volume: H. Charlton Bastian, Otto Heubner, and John Hughlings Jackson. They compose a trinity (triumvirate, troika, or simply trio) of intellectual protagonists whose effect on Freud's thinking can hardly be exaggerated. With tongue in cheek, I might see Jackson as a "father," or acknowledged authority figure; the pediatrician Heubner as a "son," in whose report Freud found a significance that Heubner himself neither recognized nor pursued; and Bastian as a spirit that infused Freud's text. In the course of my investigation, I naturally cover territory familiar to some readers while also striving to add new material to what has already been written about the aphasia book. In particular, I try to draw attention to hitherto neglected figures from Freud's scholarly past who seem to have played a noteworthy role in his development.

Because diagrams played a defining role in theories of aphasia,[11] I have included in Chapters 4 and 5 reproductions of line drawings by Freud and several contemporaneous aphasiologists, along with a critical excursion on diagrams in the scientific culture. Freud's diagrams stand in a relationship of unresolved tension to the diagrams of his predecessors and to his own text.

Finally, I turn in Chapter 6 to a 1993 monograph, *Understanding Aphasia*, by Harold Goodglass.[12] My purpose is to examine a remarkable coincidence of ideas and point of view between two researchers separated in time and place. Freud's ghostly and unacknowledged habitation of Goodglass's book is a case in point of transformation and indeterminacy in the history of science.

11. Proponents of localization theories were in fact given the derogatory name "diagram makers" by Henry Head in his *Aphasia and Kindred Disorders of Speech*, 2 vols., 1926 (reprint, New York: Hafner, 1963). The epithet has remained in use.
12. Harold Goodglass, *Understanding Aphasia* (San Diego: Academic Press, 1993).

1

FREUD AMONG THE DISCOURSES
ON APHASIA

I t is evident from Freud's remarks in letters to Wilhelm Fliess between 1891 and 1896 that the author thought highly of his aphasia
book.[1] Despite Freud's confidence in it, however, his work on aphasia did not receive the initial attention he had hoped for and began to
be appreciated only some years later.[2] The considerable commentary

1. The comments are to be found in the letters of May 2, 1891, May 21, 1894, and December 6, 1896, in *Sigmund Freud: Briefe an Wilhelm Fließ, 1887–1904*, ed. Jeffrey Moussaieff
Masson, German ed. Michael Schröter, transcription by Gerhard Fichtner (Frankfurt am
Main: S. Fischer, 1986), referred to hereafter as *FB*. The letters in English are in *The
Complete Letters of Sigmund Freud to Wilhelm Fliess, 1887–1904*, trans. and ed. Jeffrey Moussaieff Masson (Cambridge: Belknap Press of Harvard University Press, 1985), referred to
hereafter as *FL*.
2. Ernest Jones, in his biography of Freud, gives the history of the volumes: "Of the 850
copies printed, 257 were sold after nine years, when the rest were pulped." *The Life and
Work of Sigmund Freud*, vol. 1 (New York: Basic Books, 1953), 216. Jones also asserts that
there was no copy in any British library, which Leon Bloom has shown to be an incorrect
statement. Bloom's research does show, however, that there was no review of Freud's book
in the leading British journals from 1891 through 1896; see his "Ellenberger on Freud's
Aphasia: Fact and Method in the History of Science," *Psychoanalytic Review* 62 (winter 1975–
1976): 615–637. It was listed in a prominent position in the bibliography on aphasia in the
1896 edition of the *Index-Catalogue of the Library of the Surgeon-General's Office, United States
Army*, Authors and Subjects, 2 ser., vol. 1 (Washington: Government Printing Office). Otto
M. Marx lists authors who mentioned Freud's book in their publications in 1903, 1912, 1926,
1928, and 1948—a scanty list of five; see his "Freud and Aphasia: An Historical Analysis,"
American Journal of Psychiatry 124 (December 1967): 815–825, here 815. One reviewer of
the English translation wrote that the aphasia book "has remained quite unobtainable, mostly

published in the latter half of the twentieth century interprets the aphasia book primarily in terms of its key position in the development of psychoanalysis. While attending to this retrospective, developmental interpretation, I see the book as a key text in other ways as well: as a prescient neurological narrative and as a narrative about Freud himself and how he read and used his source texts. These perspectives give access to explicit and implicit theories of language in the aphasia text and to the multidisciplinary space in which language theory was constructed in Freud's time. On this basis the formation of a discipline—psychoanalysis—can be understood as the product of an intellectual culture preoccupied with language and of the rhetoric of that culture.

Freud's self-identification as a neuropathologist on the title page of the aphasia book, a reminder that neuropathology was still a central interest of his in 1891, casts a line of theory that reaches to Freud's "Project" of 1895 and indicates that investigation of the aphasias has to do with correlating language symptoms with specific insults to brain tissue, therefore requiring a theory or theories of language sites and function in the brain.[3] Another line runs between the dedication of the book to Josef Breuer "in friendship and respect"[4] for Breuer's seminal influence on psychoanalysis as evidenced in his contributions to the joint volume *Studies on Hysteria* (1895) and the effusive credit Freud gave Breuer in "The Unconscious" (1915), a work James Strachey has shown to have derived some of its basic concepts from the aphasia book.[5] Thus we have on the title page and in the dedication two areas of endeavor—the neurological and the psychological—which some commentators on Freud have separated for the sake of severing the early laboratory researcher and scientist-scholar from the Freud who founded psychoanalysis. The aphasia book, which indicates that these "two" are in reality of whole cloth, demonstrates that the early work nourished and shaped Freud's ideas and informed the directions of his later work.

---

unread, and nearly always overlooked in discussions of neurological problems." Joseph Zinkin, *Psychoanalytic Review* 41 (October 1954): 377–378, here 377. Another wrote that it had "received little or no attention although many of its conclusions were accepted." Charles Davison, *Psychoanalytic Quarterly* 24 (1955): 115–119, here 119.

3. Walther Riese draws attention to an important consideration: "The term neuropathology was used in Freud's days and in German speaking countries in a sense quite different from the meaning the term finally assumed in our days and particularly in the United States. In Freud's own days and in his own country neuropathology was not understood to be merely a section of pathology, i.e. the investigation of altered nervous tissue; its primary purpose was rather to investigate sites and types of brain lesions with the final intention to *correlate* them with disturbed functions and behavior." "Freudian Concepts of Brain Function," 287.

4. "Herrn Dr. Josef Breuer in freundschaftlicher Verehrung."

5. *SE* 14:206–215.

One way to approach the aphasia monograph is to examine some of the aforementioned commentary that has grown up around it—commentary that sometimes illuminates the text and in other cases serves to obscure it but that always forms a discursive environment, a kind of intertextual setting, that tells us some things about Freud and his text and also something about the history of a set of intellectual concerns and the times in which they were addressed.

Ernest Jones calls the aphasia book "the most valuable of [Freud's] neurological writings, . . . a radical and revolutionary criticism" of the prevailing doctrine on aphasia . . . [and] the first to level such criticism" (213). In a lucid summary, Jones explains that the complexity of diagrams drawn up to explain the "bewildering combinations" of speech disturbances associated with aphasia had become a "Ptolemy-like situation [that] called for a Kepler to simplify it" and that Freud did so by casting doubt on the prevailing view that aphasias could be explained by lesions in associative pathways. Freud suggested that the multiple "subvarieties" of aphasia were explained by sympathetic involvement of areas subject to radiating effects from a damaged area (Jones 214). He disputed his teacher Theodor Meynert's theory that ideas and memories are attached to specific brain cells, and he showed the anatomic error on which Meynert's view was based— that the cortex contained projections of the parts of the body. Freud theorized that there was a "representation" of the organism on the cortex, but one "based on functional, rather than topographical groupings" (Jones 215).

In the 1950s a number of articles offered considered and suggestive examinations of the aphasia book. Stengel, translator of the aphasia volume, stresses "that Freud's anatomical, neurological, and psycho-analytical researches form a continuum and that they were strongly influenced by contemporary currents of thought."[6] Stengel reviews Freud's main contributions to aphasia theory and his introduction of "a number of terms which have become household words in psychoanalysis," in which he includes "projection," "cathexis" (Besetzung), and the concept of "overdetermination," concluding that "these instances illustrate how concepts of physiological dynamics were taken out of their original soil and transplanted into the field of psychodynamics" (86). In the introduction to his translation of the aphasia book, Stengel asserted that "the psychoanalyst

6. Erwin Stengel, "A Re-Evaluation of Freud's Book On Aphasia: Its Significance for Psycho-Analysis," International Journal of Psycho-Analysis 35, pt. 2 (1954): 85–89, here 85.

and psychiatrist will recognize it as the most significant forerunner of the author's later work."[7] In this generation of commentators on Freud, we find a full appreciation of the historical and cultural embeddedness of even a neurological study. After a discussion of Hughlings Jackson, whom Freud acknowledged as a primary influence on his theory of aphasia, Stengel concludes with an important nod to Freud's predilection for England: "It appears that Freud's direct contact with the evolutionary theories emanating from England was a highly significant event in the development of psychoanalysis. This book bears witness to that encounter" (xv).

In 1954, Richard L. Schoenwald also reviewed the aphasia book from the perspective of its place in Freud's development. He concludes: "In its pages rests the evidence of Freud's first extended wrestling with the relation to the psychological and the physiological. . . . Here, then is a real turning point. Leaving demands for absolutely anatomical-physiological explanations behind, at least for the time being, turning to the actuality of the behavior anatomy and physiology made possible, Freud managed to create a new conceptual scheme for everyday use in his own thinking and practice"[8]

What Paul Vogel considered most noteworthy in the aphasia study was its raising to prominence the role of the auditory element in language, thereby bringing "sensory aphasia into the centre of the system of aphasias." He also noted that "the word and speech psychology contained in the aphasia study" was continued and expanded in *The Ego and the Id* (1923).[9]

In "Freudian Concepts of Brain Function and Brain Disease," Walther Riese calls the aphasia book "a rare and brilliant piece of medical thought," stresses the continuity in Freud's thought between the neuropathologist and the psychoanalyst, and notes the book's "vigorous polemical element directed against the then very powerful doctrine of speech centers" (289). Riese reports Freud's view that "aphasia cannot be treated independently of a broad theory of cerebral activity," which made it necessary for Freud to address the doctrine of cerebral localization. Riese claims that "Freud's interpretation of the concept of localization as that of the restriction of nervous functions to anatomically definable areas still stands today as it did almost 70 years ago . . . [n]or did his argument lose anything of its

7. Stengel, *On Aphasia*, x.
8. Richard L. Schoenwald, "A Turning Point of Freud's Life: *Zur Auffassung der Aphasien*," *Osiris* 7:119–126, here 126.
9. Paul Vogel, "Zur Aphasielehre Sigmund Freuds," *Monatsschrift für Psychiatrie und Neurologie* 128 (1954): 256–264, here 264 and 263.

power and its justification" (291). Riese's interpretation of the aphasia book extends to include Wilhelm von Humboldt and Ernst Cassirer on philosophy of language, in an attempt to relate their theories to aphasia studies in general. He departs significantly from Freud, however, on a fundamental issue: the mind-brain relationship. Riese's view is strictly Cartesian; that is, he has no doubt of the separation of mind and brain. Thus he disagrees with Freud's view that the simultaneous appearance of two types of aphasia are a result of anatomic contiguity and faults Freud as an adherent of "the brain-materialistic views of his own century" (300). As indicated below, in the discussion of neurological theory today, it is, rather, Freud's "anti-Cartesian" thinking that is confirmed by the latest results in neurology.

The 1960s brought two major historical articles by Otto M. Marx, who takes a more critical position on Freud's book. In the first one,[10] he reviews the two main strains of thought that fed into aphasia studies: linguistic and medical. He demonstrates that the two strains developed independently with no crossover between the disciplines, with the one exception of Adolf Kussmaul (1822–1902), a physician who was influenced by the pioneering linguistic work of Heymann Steinthal (1823–1899). Steinthal, Marx tells us (348), saw psychology as a "method for examining the biological language capacity of man" and was the first of the linguists to examine the reports on aphasia, finding them insufficient because "they contained inadequate psychological descriptions and lacked a clear conception of language function. These deficiencies kept the work on aphasia from influencing or contributing to language theory." Marx speculates that the opposite case, the lack of attention to linguistics by aphasiologists, was so because "with localization of language as their chief goal and interest, most workers on aphasia had to limit their view of language capacity to a very simple function with a sensory and motor component" (349). Marx notes that the next contributors to language study were the anthropologists. He thus gives us an indication of the rich disciplinary mix that surrounded the topic of language in the latter half of the nineteenth century. In contrast to Marx, I propose that Freud's text demonstrates that very crossover among disciplines which Marx maintains did not happen.

The main conclusion in Marx's 1967 article "Freud and Aphasia: An Historical Analysis" is that Freud's book is "a final statement of 19th-century neurology" (824). This conclusion points up how Marx's concerns

10. Otto M. Marx, "Aphasia Studies and Language Theory in the Nineteenth Century," *Bulletin of the History of Medicine* 40 (1966): 328–349.

about categorization and historical boundaries of disciplines differ from a reading of Freud's text as a confluence disciplines. I see the permeability of boundaries, their sometime violation, and the mixing of disciplinary discourses as the hallmark of Freud's creativity. Marx points out that "in the 19th century, language 'revealed itself as the psychophysical problem par excellence,' "[11] and by the time Freud's monograph was published, "aphasia and the problems posed by its study had probably become the most publicized subject in neurology" (817). He quotes an article by Henry Maudsley[12] which, for researchers on aphasia, summarized the "central theoretical problem" of that time:

> that unknown region which lies between what we call mind and what we call matter, . . . [o]ur available methods of inquiry are indeed as completely divided as are the subject matters with which they deal: the objective or physiological method of direct observation is concerned with the clinical phenomena of aphasia and the pathological appearances which have been found to accompany it; the subjective or psychological method of introspection is applicable only to the observation of the mental processes, and to the part which words or names have in them. (Marx 818)

Maudsley would have been known to Freud through Charlton Bastian's critical discussion of Maudsley's ideas.[13] Bastian disagreed primarily with Maudsley's minimization of the role of language in the thinking process. Freud depended on Bastian but did not refer at all to Maudsley, so it may be that Freud did not accept the clear distinctions proposed in the quotation above between what is "objective" and what is "subjective" or the assignment of the latter to a position of lesser importance.

Although Marx (824) recognizes that Freud "reinterpreted and utilized the ideas of his predecessors in a way very much his own," he maintains that much of what Freud proposed remained within the established tenets of the time and, in particular, that Freud's concept of language did not offer anything new. I believe this argument rests on a failure to acknowledge the problematic nature of Freud's statements on language and Freud's own language use. From a later perspective, it is possible to bring to bear another kind of critique and, as a consequence, discover another concept

---

11. Marx, 824, quoting J. T. Merz, *History of European Thought in the Nineteenth Century* (Edinburgh: Blackwood, 1912), 536.
12. Henry Maudsley, "Concerning Aphasia," *Lancet*, November 28, 1868, 690–692.
13. H. Charlton Bastian, "On the Various Forms of Loss of Speech in Cerebral Disease," *British and Foreign Medico-Chirurgical Review* 43 (January–April 1869): 209–236 and 470–492.

of language in Freud's text. Marx (821) misreads Freud when he maintains that Freud's conclusions rest primarily on "introspection and formal philosophy," and he tends to forget Freud's training in the laboratory when accusing him of proposing a physiological model that is merely a restatement of what the psychological situation was thought to be. Despite differences in conclusions, Marx's work is the most closely related to my project, because he studied views on language with attention to problems of disciplinary categories and historical connections.

An article by Oswald Ulrich Kästle, which appeared in 1987, deals with medical dictionary entries of 1893 and 1894 by Freud on the topics of amnesia and aphasia and draws attention to several points of importance in relation to the aphasia monograph.[14] Kästle points out that speech disturbances were among the main symptoms of the hysterical patient "Emmy v.N," whose case and treatment Freud describes in *Studies on Hysteria*. This brings us to the connection between the aphasia study and Freud's clinical practice. As Kästle indicates, Freud draws on aphasia theory to assist in treatment (the case of "Miss Lucy R.") in *Studies on Hysteria*.[15] Kästle makes two more points of particular importance here. One is in reference to the social meaning of aphasia, or speech disturbances in general: "The significance of these speech disturbances can only really be understood when one takes into consideration the eminent social importance of speaking and of language in the upper classes in the nineteenth century."[16] The second is in reference to Freud's explication of his concept of "symbol." Kästle (518) argues that in the aphasia studies, Freud uses, as is customary in contemporary semiology and science, the concept of symbol as a sign. In the "Preliminary Communication" (1893) for the *Studies on Hysteria*, however, and from there onward, Freud uses the concept of symbol in the literary/cultural sense as an image, or a "metaphorical-metonymical presentation of complex subjective relationships."

Frank Heynick finds antecedents of dream theory in the concept of "functional retrogression" from the aphasia book. He writes that even if

14. Oswald Ulrich Kästle, "Einige bisher unbekannte Texte von Sigmund Freud aus den Jahren 1893/94 und ihr Stellenwert in seiner wissenschaftlichen Entwicklung," *Psyche* (Stuttgart) 41 (June 1987): 508–528.
15. *SE* 2:111–112; *GW* 1:169. On connections between the aphasia study and a theory of hysteria, John Forrester writes that although in the case of hysteria words "are both causative and curative of the symptoms . . ., what is general and common to both aphasia and hysteria is the attempt to find the general conditions involved in the malfunction of the speech apparatus." *Language and the Origins of Psychoanalysis* (London: Macmillan, 1980), 36.
16. "Die Bedeutung dieser Sprachstörungen läßt sich wohl nur dann richtig verstehen, wenn man den eminenten sozialen Stellenwert des Sprechens und der Sprache in den großbürgerlichen Schichten des 19. Jahrhunderts berücksichtigt" (Kästle, 513).

"The Project" had never been rediscovered, "one could still see how Freud's treatment of dream speech in 1900 might have been partly derived from his earlier neurological speculation on language pathology."[17]

Mark Solms and Michael Saling are researchers on Freud's neuroscientific work whose article "On Psychoanalysis and Neuroscience: Freud's Attitude to the Localizationist Tradition"[18] is a vigorous attack on the view that Freud's "Project" is of greater significance in the history of psychoanalysis than the aphasia book. They believe that the neurological model in "The Project" is actually based on the version of Hughlings Jackson's theories which Freud developed in *On Interpretation of the Aphasias*. Solms and Saling aim to disprove Peter Amacher's claim that psychoanalytic theory shows the influence of the outmoded brain theories of Freud's teachers.[19] Thus they correctly claim that *On the Aphasias* is "a scathing attack upon the neurological theories of Freud's teachers" and that it "signals Freud's radical departure from orthodox German neurology" (Solms and Saling 402).

On the occasion of the one-hundredth anniversary of the publication of *On the Aphasias*, Laurence Miller, whose field is psychiatric neuropsychology, published a commemorative article. I mention this instance of scientific interdisciplinarity because Miller stresses "the profound Freudian influence on both neuropsychology and psychodynamic personality theory articulated in such early works as *On Aphasia*."[20] Miller touches on the anticipations of *Studies on Hysteria, The Interpretation of Dreams, The Psychopathology of Everyday Life*, and "The Unconscious" but also on Freud's anticipations of modern neuropsychology.

A second anniversary article, by Victor W. Henderson, concentrates on the historical context of aphasia studies to which Freud's monograph was a response.[21] Henderson examines the theories of Carl Wernicke and Ludwig Lichtheim, which Freud's work is intended to refute, as well as

17. Frank Heynick, "Dream Dialogue and Retrogression: Neurolinguistic Origins of Freud's 'Replay Hypothesis,' " *Journal of the History of the Behavioral Sciences* 21 (October 1985): 321–341, here 321 and 325–326.
18. See above, Introduction, n. 5. Solms and Saling have also published their translation with commentary of two medical dictionary entries authored by Freud and published in 1888 —"Aphasia" and "Brain"—which provide useful background to Freud's book on aphasia; see their *A Moment of Transition: Two Neuroscientific Articles by Sigmund Freud* (London: Karnac, 1990).
19. Peter Amacher, *Freud's Neurological Education and Its Influence on Psychoanalytic Theory*, Monograph 16, *Psychological Issues* 4 (New York: International Universities Press, 1965).
20. Laurence Miller, "*On Aphasia* at 100: The Neuropsychodynamic Legacy of Sigmund Freud," *Psychoanalytic Review* 78 (fall 1991): 365–378, here 376.
21. Victor W. Henderson, "Sigmund Freud and the Diagram-Maker School of Aphasiology," *Brain and Language* 43 (1992): 19–41.

other predominant localizationist views on aphasia. He makes a thorough and careful study of Freud's views and those of his most important contemporaries in aphasia studies, drawing attention also to Freud's mentor at Ernst Brücke's institute, Sigmund Exner, to whom (along with Josef Paneth) Freud gave credit for the initial impetus for his aphasia theory. Henderson suggests that Freud's stance toward opposing theories—for example, his criticism even of Jean-Martin Charcot—had something to do with his defiant attitude toward authorities and that Freud's deference to the less well known (I would add, at least in German-speaking circles) Hughlings Jackson may be similarly explained: "It may be that Freud was more comfortable in acknowledging authoritative pronouncements by those who were not quite authority figures" (37). Henderson does not further explore this idea.

Between 1989 and 1993, Ana-Maria Rizzuto wrote four articles on the aphasia monograph.[22] The first one speculates that Freud's reason for writing the aphasia study was to understand the speech phenomena exhibited by three patients: Anna O. (Breuer's patient who coined the term *talking cure* for the therapeutic method that was to become psychoanalysis), Frau Emmy von N., and Frau Cäcilie. Rizzuto's "Proto-Dictionary of Psychoanalysis" takes terminology introduced in *On Interpretation of the Aphasias* and traces the path of those terms in the psychoanalytic vocabulary. The terms are association, divided attention, cathexis, complex, connection, physiological correlate, impulse to speak, memory-image, primary, representation, self-observation, spontaneous speech, and transference. Rizzuto's articles represent the psychoanalytic perspective, concerning themselves exclusively with the aphasia monograph as a source in the development of psychoanalytic theory and technique. Again, other writers do question the presumption that such terms can be transplanted essentially intact one hundred years later.

A second way to approach Freud's text is to see it as a remarkably intuitive preview—considering the limits of nineteenth-century brain study—of late twentieth-century theories of brain and language. Antonio Damasio's 1992 review article on aphasia gives Freud's aphasia study credit for criticism of oversimplified views on the organization of language in

---

22. Ana-Maria Rizzuto, "A Hypothesis about Freud's Motive for Writing the Monograph 'On Aphasia,' " *International Review of Psycho-Analysis* 16 (1989): 111–117; "The Origins of Freud's Concept of Object Representation ('Objektvorstellung') in His Monograph 'On Aphasia': Its Theoretical and Technical Importance," *International Journal of Psycho-Analysis* 71 (1990): 241–248; "A Proto-Dictionary of Psychoanalysis," ibid., 261–270; and "Freud's Speech Apparatus and Spontaneous Speech," ibid., 74 (1993): 113–127.

the brain.[23] Damasio's summary of the turns in aphasia theory—which have led in part to refutation, in part to confirmation, of some of the insights from Freud's time—shows how close to the mark, as seen from a contemporary neurological perspective, some of Freud's insights were. Historical echoes resonate in current theories. Damasio does not mention Freud's work, but theories he refers to as "the traditional view" are ones that Freud had opposed and refuted. Take, for example, one "traditional" notion with which Antonio and Hanna Damasio disagree: "We believe there are no permanently held 'pictorial' representations of objects or persons as was traditionally thought. Instead the brain holds, in effect, a record of the neural activity that takes place in the sensory and motor cortices during interaction with a given object."[24] In the course of his 1891 critique of Theodor Meynert's views on the reproduction of external images in the cortex, Freud put forth ideas not unlike the Damasios'. From a contemporary perspective, his thinking in the aphasia book is in basic agreement with what is now known as the "identity theory" of mind-brain relation. As an experienced neuropathologist and laboratory researcher steeped in brain anatomy, he moved into psychiatry with years of observations at his disposal, established patterns in his mind, and well-developed convictions about how the brain worked.[25] That background, modified and reworked, he brings to bear in his clinical sphere, making that activity seem an obvious outgrowth of those first scientific commitments. Damasio's *Descartes' Error*,[26] which presents the case for a comprehensive neuronal explanation of mind, reason, emotion, and behavior, is compatible with the aphasia book, in terms of both overall conviction and certain individual details, such as neural representation of the body.

Yet a third way to approach Freud's aphasia monograph is to see it as a forerunner of an integrative study of aphasia, such as Roman Jakobson's, that arrives at rhetorical and literary insights via the methodology of linguistics.[27] Jakobson's essay is a plea for the linguistic study of aphasia, not as a therapeutic tool but rather as a means of learning more about

23. Damasio, "Aphasia."
24. Antonio R. Damasio and Hanna Damasio, "Brain and Language," *Scientific American* 267 (September 1992): 88–95, here 91.
25. For a related discussion, see my "Tangled Patterns: Freud, Vienna, and the Brain," *International Journal of Psycho-Analysis*, 74 (1993): 1017–1026.
26. Antonio R. Damasio, *Descartes' Error: Emotion, Reason, and the Human Brain* (New York: Putnam's, 1994).
27. Roman Jakobson, "Two Aspects of Language and Two Types of Aphasic Disturbances," in *Language in Literature*, ed. Krystyna Pomorska and Stephen Rudy (Cambridge: Belknap Press of Harvard University Press, 1987); originally published as pt. 2 of *Fundamentals of Language*, written in collaboration with Morris Halle (The Hague: Mouton, 1956).

language.[28] His is a territorial move: he writes as an advocate for "the participation of professional linguists familiar with the patterning and functioning of language" (95). The first authority he evokes, however, is neurologist Hughlings Jackson, who played such a signal role in Freud's work. Jakobson's "verbal regression" and "dissolution" are direct borrowings from Jackson and are components of the same principles that influenced Freud. Freud's aphasia study and his concepts of "displacement" and "condensation" from *The Interpretation of Dreams* seem to be the main intellectual building blocks on which Jakobson has constructed his theory. The theory, however, is problematic for two reasons: (1) Jakobson's classification of the aphasias into two types—defects of "selection and substitution" versus those of "combination and contexture"—follows his trajectory toward the literary (the metaphorical and the metonymic), leaving neurology and the aphasic patient behind and departing from the interdisciplinary framework with which he had opened his arguments. (2) His conclusions spread out into diffuse generalizations, arriving at a universal binary: "The varieties of aphasia are numerous and diverse, but all of them lie between the two polar types just described" (109). This reduction leads to a reductiveness toward literary genres and periods ("Romanticism is closely linked with metaphor" [114]), to the notion of a "bipolar structure of language (or other semiotic systems)" (111), and finally to the conclusion that "the dichotomy discussed here appears to be of primal significance and consequence for all verbal behavior and for human behavior in general" (112). In contrast, neuroscientists in the 1990s acknowledge the contribution of linguistic theory and extend their speculations on brain function to the production of rhetoric and thus, by implication, literature. For example, the Damasios (91) posit that "because the brain categorizes perceptions and actions simultaneously along many different dimensions, symbolic representations such as metaphor can easily emerge from this architecture."

John Forrester devotes special attention to Freud's aphasia book, stressing aphasia theory as a nexus of multiple disciplines.[29] Forrester's definition —"aphasia was the consequence of the altered general functioning of the [language] systems *occasioned* by a cerebral lesion"—is broad enough to circumvent the views on precise localization that Freud was attempting to combat and to be compatible with Freud's work on hysteria: "In showing

28. He writes: "The application of purely linguistic criteria to the interpretation and classification of aphasic facts can substantially contribute to the science of language and language disturbances" (96).
29. Forrester, *Language and the Origins of Psychoanalysis*.

that, even where there is an organic lesion, the explanation of aphasic phenomena must be understood independently of the location of the lesion, Freud paved the way for the understanding of hysteria as the lesion of an idea" (30). Forrester asserts that psychoanalysis "bridges the gap between neurology and philology with its central concern, language" (207), and his response to the rhetorical question "Who were these philologically minded psychoanalysts?" is "At the head of the list we must place Freud" (194).[30]

Finally, an essay by Rachelle Smith Doody takes a broad historical perspective on changing relations between linguistic theory and aphasiology and raises questions about aphasia theory on the basis of the Sapir-Whorf hypothesis. She suggests that aphasiology "might constitute a 'universe of discourse' " as defined by Edward Sapir, meaning that there is a separation between its self-contained laws and principles and "real human experience."[31] She traces historical connections among linguists and aphasiologists, in particular the fact that the work of the philologist August Schleicher was known to Paul Broca (whose publication in 1861 of a post mortem determination of a left frontal brain site for "motor" or articulatory aphasia marked a new stage in aphasia studies) as well as to Darwin, whose work, in turn, was powerfully influential on aphasia theory. Thus she shows early interconnections that some scholars have denied existed. About Freud's aphasia study she writes that it "raises questions about methodology for studying psychophysical processes that merge into twentieth century language studies" (312). As Heynick also did, she points out the limitations of Freud's assumption that the word was the most important unit of speech, and she maintains that his discussion of psychological processes is directed by the "spatialization bias inherent to all Standard Average European languages" (314). She believes that the "spatialization bias" lent itself to being assimilated into anatomic modes, thus partly determining aphasia theory (346). The second bias with which she is concerned is one toward literacy, which favors "language" over "speech," leading to a preference for certain cognitive models over others: "Early descriptions of aphasia had to do with human speech. Subsequently, our observations have been conditioned by literacy, as much as they have been conditioned by our amorphous objects of study and by the languages of our research" (348).

30. Riccardo Steiner's review of Forrester's book shares my agenda of considering Freud's readings of his sources to an extent not done before; see *International Review of Psycho-Analysis* 8 (1981): 480–484.
31. Rachelle Smith Doody, "A Reappraisal of Localization Theory with Reference to Aphasia," *Brain and Language* 44 (1993): 296–326 and 327–348, here 296.

There is much to be said for taking the inherent biases into consideration, but there is at least one contradiction in this view when applied to Freud. Doody believes that the localizationist view of language function was driven by the inherent tendency of Standard Average Europeans to "spatialize abstract ideas" (345). If this is so, however, how could Freud's critical dismantling of the prevailing localizationist theories be explained? The article contains several factual errors about Freud's work, such as that his theory of the unconscious is "a departure from his monograph on aphasia and uses little linguistic evidence" and that "he did not even mention paraphasias when he discussed slips of the tongue . . . indicating how widely he had diverged from linguistic concerns" (339). James Strachey and others have examined the dependence of "The Unconscious" on ideas developed in the aphasia book. Chapter 5 of *The Psychopathology of Everyday Life* opens its discussion of "slips of the tongue" by mentioning "the paraphasias." Both of these works are steeped in linguistic concerns.

It is clear that the figure of Freud, in his association with aphasia studies, is chameleon-like: its location and standpoint take on a different hues according to the disciplinary perspectives and times from which they are viewed.

Freud's letters show that he had made a special emotional investment in the aphasia book. That investment, I believe, had much to do with its composition and the hopes he attached to it. Beyond its merit as scholarship of the first rank, the book also stands as evidence of Sigmund Freud at a particular moment and a particular place in his life and career. The aphasia monograph is a performance that postulated and presented, as if on a stage, the persona of the researcher.

There are, I believe, three main elements that enter into the rhetorical performance of the aphasia piece: Freud's defiant attitude toward certain scientific authorities, his concern about his own position, and his positive feelings toward England. All three are intimately bound up with one another, and the first lends itself in retrospect to a psychoanalytic perspective. In an early letter to Wilhelm Fliess (May 2, 1891) Freud wrote this about the aphasia book: "In a few weeks I shall afford myself the pleasure of sending you a small book on aphasia for which I myself have a great deal of warm feeling. In it I am very impudent, cross swords with your friend Wernicke, with Lichtheim and Grashey, and even scratch the high and mighty idol Meynert" (*FL* 28; *FB* 14). Though the flavor of his remarks is nicely captured in the English translation, one phrase loses a psychoanalytic meaning that is not to be found in the English idiom "cross swords" but does become apparent in Freud's German phrase, which is actually "measure my blade." The next paragraph announces the birth of Freud's second son. If we take the perspective that Freud later taught us to take, we must conclude that in the challenge by the youthful academic outsider to the well-known, securely established authorities (especially his former teacher Theodor Meynert) the weapon of choice is a book that stands in for the male organ, whose reproductive performance has passed muster but whose symbolic success in an academic contest has yet to be achieved. In the aphasia text we can see examples of Freud's competetive posture toward his intellectual opponents' theories and, as subtext, toward the opponents themselves.[32]

Freud's sense of his own position on aphasia theory is expressed in the rhetorical stance of the lonely hero: "Since I know that I am quite isolated in claiming that the special psychic status attributed to the speech centers ought to reveal itself in some way in the clinical symptoms of speech disorders, I do not want to fail to mention that Wattville expressed a very similar line of thought in a short but substantial paper" (*AA* 18). The rhetorical layers include a tone of light sarcasm, which we meet here and there in the first half or so of the aphasia text. It is not possible to determine to what extent the tone reflects a real feeling of isolation and a genuine need to draw on the support of intellectual allies. We have learned from psychology that brashness may cover insecurity. Three years later, on May 21, 1894, Freud writes to Fliess with much the same complaint but without the sarcasm:

> I am pretty much alone here in the elucidation of the neuroses. They look upon me as pretty much of a monomaniac, while I have the distinct feeling that I have touched upon one of the great secrets of nature. There is something odd about the incongruity between one's own and other people's estimation of one's intellectual work. Look at this book on the diplegias, which I threw together with a minimum of interest and effort, almost in a frivolous mood. It has been tremendously successful. The reviewers say the nicest things about it; ... And of the really good things, such as the *Aphasia*, the "Obsessional Ideas" which now threaten to appear in print, and the forthcoming "Etiology and Theory of the Neuroses," I can expect nothing better than a respectable failure. It confounds one and makes one somewhat bitter. (*FL* 74; *FB* 67)

32. His well-known self-presentation as a "conquistador" occurs in a February 1, 1900, letter to Fliess (*FL* 398; *FB* 437).

Freud's commitment to his aphasia study never flags, reinforcing the idea that this work had deeply absorbed him. He writes to Fliess about it again on December 6, 1896, in the context of discussing his thinking on the subject of the overdetermination of memory: "Thus what is essentially new about my theory is the thesis that memory is present not once but several times over, that it is laid down in various kinds of indications. I postulated a similar kind of rearrangement some time ago *(Aphasia)* for the paths leading from the periphery [of the body to the cortex]" (*FL* 207; *FB* 217). We find the topic of aphasia recurring in several later works. Freud carefully summarized the aphasia book for the abstracts he submitted (unsuccessfully) in 1897 for appointment to the next academic rank ("Professor Extraordinarius"), and he mentions it again in his "Autobiographical Study" of 1925.

Although we might well take with a grain of salt Freud's expressions of feeling alone and isolated, particularly in the youthful letters to his friend Eduard Silberstein, nevertheless, feeling marginalized if not isolated was inevitable for a Jew in the profoundly anti-Semitic environment of Vienna. Freud could always feel under overt or covert onslaught, whether that took the shape of open insults to Jews or of the more secretive discrimination that interfered with his academic promotion. Sander Gilman draws a dark, powerful portrait of the racism that pervaded the sciences and intellectual endeavor generally and what it was like to be a medical scientist under explicit intellectual siege as a Jew.[33]

When, as a nineteen-year-old, Freud took his first trip to England, his anglophilia was confirmed. Two years before, he had written Silberstein in a tone of bemused infatuation: "I read English history, write English letters, declaim English verse, listen to English descriptions, and thirst for English glances."[34] On his return he wrote to Silberstein on September 9, 1875, that he would rather live in England, despite "fog and rain, drunkenness and conservatism" (127; 144), and he speculates in concrete terms how he might fare there as a physician and what great accomplishments might be possible. He was so impressed with the scientific writers he read in England that he intended to remain a supporter of the English: "The acquaintance with English scientific books I made over there will always

33. Sander Gilman, *Freud, Race, and Gender* (Princeton: Princeton University Press, 1993), and *The Case of Sigmund Freud: Medicine and Identity at the Fin de Siècle* (Baltimore: Johns Hopkins University Press, 1993).
34. Letter of August 6, 1873, in *The Letters of Sigmund Freud to Eduard Silberstein, 1871–1881*, ed. Walter Boehlich, trans. Arnold J. Pomerans (Cambridge: Belknap Press of Harvard University Press, 1990), 32; and *Sigmund Freud: Jugendbriefe an Eduard Silberstein, 1871–1881*, ed. Walter Boehlich (Frankfurt am Main: S. Fischer, 1989), 40.

ensure that in my own studies I shall always be on the side of the Englishmen in whose favor I am now highly prejudiced: Tyndall, Huxley, Lyell, Darwin, Thomson, Lockyer, et al." (128; 144).

Ernest Jones (178–179) quotes Freud's letter of August 16, 1882, to his fiancée, Martha Bernays, in which he calls the trip to England "one that had a decisive influence on my whole life" and reports that he is rereading "the works of the men who were my real teachers—all of them English or Scotch." He also wrote in his report to Martha in October 1882 of his stressful job interview with Hermann Nothnagel, the prominent professor of medicine, in which the supplicant expressed the need to establish his (financial) independence as soon as possible, "probably in England where I have relatives."[35]

Thus, in psychological terms, the ground is prepared—both in a negative and in a positive sense—for a special effort some years later to make use of those English neurologists whose writing would be congenial and whose theories or clinical reports would be relevant and important in the field of aphasiology. The anglophilia of the nineteen-year-old did not fade in the older Freud. John Stuart Mill, whom the young man read even before his trip to England, makes an appearance as the only philosopher cited as evidentiary for a theory of perception in the aphasia book. The anglophilia is in evidence, I would argue, in his heavy reliance on the work of Hughlings Jackson and Bastian as well as on the contributions of Frederic Bateman, William Henry Broadbent, James Ross, Allen Starr, and others from the English-speaking world; and it is reinforced by the fact that the main targets of criticism belong to the German-speaking world.[36] To Theodor Meynert, Freud devotes the most extensive critique

---

35. *Sigmund Freud: Brautbriefe*, ed. Ernst L. Freud (Frankfurt am Main: S. Fischer, 1988), 33.
36. Despite extensive communication among aphasiologists across national borders, the field can be and has been divided along national boundaries. Günther Opp connects Carl Wernicke's pathbreaking study *The Aphasia Symptom-Complex* (1874) to a shift in "the center of medical research" from France to Germany after the German victory in the Franco-Prussian War of 1870–1871; see Opp, "Historical Roots of the Field of Learning Disabilities: Some Nineteenth-Century German Contributions," *Journal of Learning Disabilities* 27 (January 1994): 10–19, here 11. In her commentary in *Wernicke's Works on Aphasia: A Sourcebook and Review*, ed and trans. Gertrude H. Eggert (The Hague: Mouton, 1977), Eggert contends that by the last decade of the nineteenth century, "the aphasia scene was unmistakably centered in Germany" (43) and "workers in Britain, France, Italy, and America largely followed the path broken by the Breslau-Halle school of aphasia" (44). Anne Harrington mentions the possibility that there may have been "differences in 'national styles' of physiology and psychology," which were accentuated after the German victory; see her *Medicine, Mind, and the Double Brain* (Princeton: Princeton University Press, 1987), 103. Nationalism in one form or another is a common undercurrent. For an English version, see the example of James Ross in Chapter 3.

of all. Clearly, an element of private antipathy is involved. Freud, who shows himself in the aphasia book to be a brilliant rhetorician, sometimes cannot help, because of the nature of language and metaphor, suggesting more than he might consciously have had in mind. One example is his treatment of Meynert's idea that there are cerebral language areas without function—empty, so to speak—which fill when new linguistic knowledge is acquired. In presenting this theory (before exposing it as without foundation), Freud uses the revealing metaphor that, following Meynert, the addition of new knowledge would depend on the occupation of previously unoccupied cerebral territory, "something like the manner in which a city expands by settlements in areas outside of its walls [*Ringmauern*]."[37] This peculiar metaphor, which is strikingly out of place in its neuroanatomic context, could have been derived from the impression made by Vienna's dramatic expansion in the 1860s and 1870s beyond its former fortified walls and eventually beyond the *Ringstraße* constructed where the walls had been. The metaphor conjures up the idea of breaking forth, out of a confined space. It invites us to speculate whether Freud's feelings about his position in Vienna may have been connected to memories of the sober pragmatism and "feeling for justice" he had experienced as a young man in England, "where human worth is more respected" (Jones 178–179) (implying that in England he had been spared the experience of overt anti-Semitism). These thoughts may have extended to his admiration for the English scientific writers, leading, finally, to an inclination toward aphasia theory as developed in this admired culture.

37. *AA* 61. The word *Ringmauer* gives the sense of a circular enclosure with a high, thick, fortified stone wall that both protects and confines. The grand boulevard built in Vienna in the place of the *Ringmauer* was given almost the same name—*Ringstraße*—thus conjuring up the memory of the wall and fortifications that once stood there.

2

BUILDING HIS CASE

"If, without having new observations of my own, I attempt to treat a topic to which the best minds in German and foreign neuropathology—such as Wernicke, Kussmaul, Lichtheim and Grashey, Hughlings Jackson, Bastian and Ross, Charcot, and others—have devoted their efforts, I had best immediately indicate the few aspects of the problem which I hope to advance through my discussion" (*AA* 1). The rhetoric of modesty commonly serves as the opening figure in scientific articles of the time, but here Freud combines it with the self-confidence of one who does not mind taking on the world, who believes that he can not only enter the lists with the "best minds" but improve on their accomplishments. The status of such a contender is enhanced by the prestige of both his opponents and his allies. He must develop a strategy for utilizing the named parties (and others) on behalf of his own cause. That strategy will involve readings that are revealingly idiosyncratic. To succeed it has to take advantage of the potential for enhancement while also constructing a tight and persuasive argument. At the same time, the strategy may be driven by an unacknowledged private agenda.

The order of Freud's list of names suggests the respective roles of these researchers in his book. Carl Wernicke (1848–1905) had been a dominant figure in aphasiology since the publication in 1874 of his pathbreaking

The Aphasia Symptom Complex, which identified and localized "sensory aphasia" (loss of comprehension) in the posterior portion of the first left temporal convolution, a site that is still today called "Wernicke's area." (It is posterior to "Broca's area," the site of "motor aphasia," or loss of ability to produce speech.) In so far as he was grappling with Wernicke, Freud was grappling with a giant in the field of aphasia theory.[1] Initially, Wernicke and his theory are Freud's main targets, although Freud's treatment of Wernicke's views evolves in the course of the book toward crediting Wernicke for certain insights and agreeing with his judgments of several other researchers. The ambivalent relationship can be traced in the subtitle of Wernicke's 1874 book—*A Psychological Study on an Anatomical Basis*—which lays out Freud's own goal. It is as if this "classic" work posed a direct challenge to Freud, who responded with his own version of the same agenda. One name conspicuously missing from Freud's opening list is that of Theodor Meynert, who had taught Freud and Wernicke and to whom Wernicke in the opening passages of *The Aphasia Symptom Complex* gives full credit for anything of value in his book. As with many of Freud's sources, there is a complex intertextual give and take with Wernicke.[2]

Freud refers with approval at several points in his book to Adolf Kussmaul's influential *Disturbances of Speech* (1877). Wernicke had accused Kussmaul of taking over Wernicke's concept of sensory aphasia without acknowledging its author and of giving it a new name that distorted Wernicke's original concept. Bitterly, he also accused Kussmaul of suppressing

1. Norman Geschwind wrote of Wernicke's "epoch-making work . . . that was to set the tone of research in aphasia over the next forty years. . . . [and make] possible the development of a scientific approach to aphasia." "Carl Wernicke, the Breslau School, and the History of Aphasia," in *Brain Function*, vol. 3, Proceedings of the Third Conference, November 1963, "Speech, Language, and Communication" (Berkeley: University of California Press, 1966): 1–16, here 4. Gertrude H. Eggert wrote that "the thirty-five year period extending from the mid 1870's through the first decade of this century might rightly be called the 'Wernicke era' in the history of aphasia." *Wernicke's Works on Aphasia*, 20.
2. A letter Freud wrote to Ludwig Binswanger twenty years later shows the psychological intensity of Freud's internal competition with Wernicke. He writes with bitter irony that Wernicke had a "far better claim to recognition," being already dead, whereas Freud's "fate" is to "disturb the peace of this world." Freud found Wernicke to be an "interesting example of the poverty of scientific thought. . . . He was a neuroanatomist and could not help dissecting the mind [*die Seele*] into sections like the brain. His great aphasia discovery imposed on all his work the scheme a-, hypo-, and hyper-or cortical, sub-, and transcortical, which he then felt compelled to apply to the least suitable objects. But when I judge him thus, I am measuring him by a high standard; I know well that in the case of others whose names inspire the world, scientific thought is completely out of the question." Letter 59 F, September 10, 1911, in *Sigmund Freud, Ludwig Binswanger: Briefwechsel, 1908–1938*, ed. Gerhard Fichtner (Frankfurt am Main: S. Fischer, 1992), 86–87.

"the facts" of his (Wernicke's) theory of localization.[3] Ludwig Lichtheim (1845–1915) was a follower and an influential expounder of Wernicke's views (which he also elaborated) but was a less important figure, whose schematic diagrams of language functions in the brain were shown to be incorrect by Freud and by a whole series of researchers since Freud's time.[4] By contrast, Freud shares Wernicke's critique of Hubert Grashey and uses Grashey as a foil to build a case for the validity of localization in certain instances of aphasia. The three British physicians—Hughlings Jackson, Charlton Bastian, and James Ross—Freud supports without qualification. Finally, Freud distances himself from his former mentor, Jean-Martin Charcot, whom Eggert credits with having "contributed substantially to the adoption of . . . [Wernicke's] . . . views in France and supported them with case studies" (43). In summary, the intricacy of Freud's enterprise in the context of aphasia studies is conveyed in the very first sentence of his book. He is attempting to contribute to aphasia studies at a time when they are beset by what may be called a mania for classification. Each of the authors he names, and dozens of others, had supplied their own descriptive versions—and more importantly, their own names —of categories and subcategories of aphasic disturbances. Many researchers had lost sight, in the end, of the overriding theoretical and disciplinary issues.

The analytic method Freud is proposing—"without having new observations of my own"—consists of the review, assessment, and combination of many authors' results, with a view toward conclusions that will have greater accuracy than any one study. Freud explains that he will attempt

3. Carl Wernicke and Carl Friedländer, "A Case of Deafness as a Result of Bilateral Lesions of the Temporal Lobe," 1883, in *Wernicke's Works on Aphasia*, 164–172, here 171. The seriousness of Wernicke's quarrel with Kussmaul is made evident by a further critical reference to Kussmaul in Wernicke's "Recent Works on Aphasia," 1885–1886, in ibid., 174–205. Both articles are also reprinted in *Carl Wernicke: Gesammelte Aufsätze und kritische Referate zur Pathologie des Nervensystems* (Berlin: Fischer, 1893).
4. Ann Stuart Laubstein, "Inconsistency and Ambiguity in Lichtheim's Model," *Brain and Language* 45 (1993): 588–603, shows that Lichtheim's model is internally inconsistent and "fails even *within* its 19th century limitations" (588). Lichtheim's most important work on the subject is the monograph *Über Aphasie*, in *Deutsches Archiv für klinische Medicin*, vol. 36 (Leipzig: F. C. W. Vogel, 1885), 205–268. A condensed version was published in an English translation by Armand de Watteville as *On Aphasia*, in *Brain* 7 (1885): 433–484. Lichtheim's most often reprinted diagram has the shape of a little house with a pointed roof, and his introductory remarks refer to the "building the edifice" that will lead to an exact correlation between the interruption of any nerve path and aphasic symptoms. He also writes of "building" on the already established "foundations" (*Über Aphasie*, 204–205), while showing (in contrast, for example, to Freud and Jackson) no awareness of the role of metaphor in theory formation.

to show that aphasia theory, as it has been developed by the efforts of the above-named researchers, contains two unwarranted assumptions. The first, shared by *almost* all the authors, is the "distinction between aphasia caused by destruction of centers and aphasia caused by destruction of pathways," and the second, shared primarily by Wernicke and those associated with his views, has to do with "the relationship among the individual presumptive language centers" (*AA* 1). As both hypotheses are at the heart of Wernicke's theory, Freud intends to couch his main objections in the form of a critique of that theory. In addition, because the hypotheses are intimately related to the idea "that pervades all of modern neuropathology," that is, "the restriction of the functions of the nervous system to anatomically definable areas of the nervous system," or "localization," Freud intends to take into consideration the general significance of this "topographic factor" for understanding aphasia (*AA* 2).

Section 1 of Freud's book, the first ten pages, is devoted to a recapitulation of the history of the theory of localization, beginning with Broca's determination in 1861 that a lesion in one particular site of the brain caused the loss of the ability to articulate speech; going on to a review of Wernicke's views on localization of separate language functions at specific sites, and finally to Lichtheim's more complex schematic image of the brain.[5] Freud is able to draw on evidence to show the inadequacy of these hypotheses, for example, in the case of Lichtheim, that his schema could not account for one of the common types of aphasia. Freud quotes from a reported case, and the opinion of "one of the most prudent German neurologists," Carl Eisenlohr,[6] who finds Lichtheim's theory inadequate, terming it "only of primarily didactic value" (*AA* 10).

In Section 2, Freud turns to a more detailed examination and refutation of the theory that speech disorders, "if they have an anatomic basis at all,"[7] are caused either by disruption of the speech centers or destruction of speech association pathways, thereby justifying differentiation between

---

5. Harrington, *Medicine, Mind, and the Double Brain,* esp. 38–40, details the mid-nineteenth-century French debate on the political and social implications of localization versus the unitary brain theory, in which the church and conservative social forces were arrayed against Broca and others who were proponents of the theory that specific functions were located at specific sites in the brain. In some ways, the situation was reversed in Freud's time, and his struggle was against a kind of intellectual rigidity associated with localization.
6. Carl Eisenlohr, "Beiträge zur Lehre von der Aphasie," *Deutsche medicinische Wochenschrift* 15 (September 5, 1889): 737–741. Eisenlohr was director of a hospital in Hamburg; he treated Freud well when Freud visited there for six weeks in 1885.
7. *AA* 10. Freud reveals with this remark his engagement with independent psychic phenomena such as hysteria.

center aphasia and conduction aphasia. He examines inconsistencies in Wernicke's theory. The argument turns on Wernicke's conduction aphasia, which would require that a patient's ability to repeat would be lost while the ability for spontaneous speech would be retained. Freud maintains that this does not occur in the sense in which Wernicke's theory requires. He knows, Freud writes, of only one instance where spontaneous speech is not accompanied by the ability to repeat. That instance is taken from an example described by Hughlings Jackson, in which patients unable to produce speech ("motor aphasia") nevertheless occasionally bring forth a curse or a "complicated word" (*AA* 12) that is otherwise not part of the "speech remnants" they have retained.[8] These patients cannot, however, repeat that fragment when asked to do so. Freud thus concludes that "Wernicke's conduction aphasia does not exist because a form of speech disturbance with its characteristics cannot be found" (*AA* 12). From the fact that Wernicke believed this disturbance was to be found in the insula, it follows that damage to this region of the brain must produce another kind of disturbance. For supporting evidence Freud turns to Charlton Bastian's "excellent presentation of aphasia" (*AA* 12),[9] which definitively states that damage to the insula causes a typical motor aphasia. Freud points out that the question of insular aphasia remains, however, unresolved, with disagreements between Meynert, Henry C. de Boyer, Wernicke, and others, on the one hand, who believe that the insula belongs to the speech area, and Charcot's pupils, such as Désiré Bernard, on the other hand, who deny this connection of the insula. Freud here adds, in a footnote to Bastian, that Bastian "is inclined to explain" one syndrome "as the result of the anatomic contiguity of the connections between Broca's and Wernicke's areas passing through the insula" (*AA* 13).

Bastian can be considered to belong, at least partly, in the camp of the theories Freud is trying to refute. Nevertheless, Freud drew on his work more frequently than any other. Henry Charlton Bastian (1837–1915), a British neurologist and bacteriologist, was a rather quirky scientist who,

8. The reference is to John Hughlings Jackson, "On Affections of Speech from Disease of the Brain," in three parts, *Brain* 1 (1878–1879): 304–330 and 2 (1879–1880): 203–222; and 323–356; all reprinted in *Brain* 38 (1915). These articles are included in the collection *Selected Writings of John Hughlings Jackson*, ed. James Taylor, 2 vols. (New York: Basic Books, 1958) 2:155–204. Citations from the articles Freud referenced are from the Taylor collection.
9. H. Charlton Bastian, "On Different Kinds of Aphasia, with Special Reference to Their Classification and Ultimate Pathology," *The British Medical Journal* 2 (July-December 1887): 931–936 and 985–990.

beyond his interest in clinical neurology, was "the last scientific believer in spontaneous generation,"[10] to the study of which he devoted his later years.[11] Bastian's position in aphasia studies can be described as follows:

> At a time when it was thought that speech was controlled by independent brain centers, Bastian was the most important of those who represented this view by means of diagrams almost akin to electrical circuits. . . . His views on aphasia, which were founded on an assumption that there is a direct relationship between psychological functions and localized areas of brain, were an oversimplification and are no longer accepted. (*DSB* 496)

Nonetheless, Bastian can also be described, as in one obituary, as "one among the four or five whose work laid the foundation of scientific neurology in England, and whose contagious enthusiasm attracted others to follow along the same lines." He had also anticipated by five years the description by Wernicke of what has become known as "Wernicke's aphasia."[12]

In "On Different Kinds of Aphasia," Bastian associates himself with the camp of Meynert and opposes the views of Hughlings Jackson. How, then, can we explain Freud's postive reception (Bastian's "excellent presentation") and the role Bastian's work plays throughout the aphasia book? In Bastian's article we encounter the tapestry of international connections we

10. *Dictionary of Scientific Biography*, ed. in chief, Charles Coulston Gillispie, vol. 1 (New York: Scribner's, 1970), 497, referred to hereafter as *DSB*.
11. Jones, *Life and Work of Sigmund Freud*, 214, sheds a somewhat different light on Bastian's later years, with an anecdote that Jones sees as "striking confirm[ation]" of Freud's doubts about explaining aphasia by the so-called subcortical lesions in the associative paths. Jones writes about "Bastian, the great English authority on aphasia." In 1892 "in a subtle case of aphasia Bastian postulated a minute lesion between the supposed associative fibers below the cortex, but when the autopsy revealed a huge cyst that had destroyed the left hemisphere of the brain, he was so stunned that he resigned from the hospital." This anecdote is reported in even more poignant detail by Henry Head, whose account begins: "For eighteen years at University College Hospital, Bastian had demonstrated to generations of students a man who had been seized with loss of speech in December, 1877" and concludes: "He did not recognize that what he called the 'clinical condition' was nothing more than a translation of the phenomena into a priori conceptions, which had no existence in reality." *Aphasia and Kindred Disorders*, 1:57.
12. Unsigned obituary, *Lancet*, November 27, 1915, cols. 1221–1224, here 1222–1223. In a discussion with Roman Jakobson, Norman Geschwind remarked that "Bastian was probably the first to point out on the basis of clinical observation that there were aphasias in which comprehension was impaired. . . . It is interesting that despite his brilliant contributions Bastian was severely criticized by Head, in my opinion quite unfairly." From a discussion of Roman Jakobson, "Linguistic Types of Aphasia," in *Brain Function* 3:78–79 (see n.1 above).

find in Freud's book and his other sources. Many of the same names, in different arrangements according to emphasis, recur in all these works. There was an informed "aphasia" community of scholars who read and responded to each other's work, whether in French, German, or English. Bastian, however, like Hughlings Jackson, relies heavily on British philosophers, the very same ones who appealed to Freud.

Bastian begins with a quotation from Sir William Hamilton which makes a distinction between memory, "the power of retaining knowledge in the mind, but out of consciousness," and recollection, the power of bringing it into consciousness, or reproducing it. "This reproductive power is governed by the laws which regulate the succession of our thoughts—the laws, as they are called, of mental association" (Hamilton in Bastian 931). Bastian reviews the terminology in an effort to achieve a certain precision or general agreement. Concern with establishing a standard set of terms is characteristic of the early stages of a field, in this case neurology (although it also persists to the present time in aphasia studies). Bastian also wants to establish a discourse on "mind" which includes unconscious states, or "nerve actions," and in order to do this he draws for support on John Stuart Mill. Freud in the aphasia study draws on only one philosopher—Mill—and, in particular, on Mill's *An Examination of Sir William Hamilton's Philosophy* and his *A System of Logic* (*AA* 80). We will find Mill used also by Hughlings Jackson, who in turn also attributes one of his main ideas on aphasia—dissolution—to Herbert Spencer, a close friend of Bastian's. Thus we find Freud immersed in a tightly knit web of British associationist philosophy.

Bastian's further discussion of Hamilton, of memory as a process of association accompanied by molecular activity, and its relation to conscious versus unconscious states sketches with a broad brush the problems Freud will address in detail in his "Project" of 1895. Bastian's scheme of four different kinds of "word-memory" resembles Freud's analysis of the four components of a word, but Bastian assigns each of these forms of "memory" an "organic seat" in a "word-center," which puts him in the opposing camp. Bastian offers a diagram, in the shape of a rectangle, with a "word-center" at each corner and straight-line connections drawn from center to center. (For a reproduction of this diagram, see Figure 2 in Chapter 4.) The simplistic diagram reflects the fact that Bastian has developed no theory of language. He thinks no further than the notion of "words": "Looking to the extremely important part which 'words,' either spoken or printed, play in our intellectual life, and to the manner in which they are interwoven with all our thought-processes, it becomes highly probable that most important sections of the auditory and visual perceptive centres are devoted to the reception, and consequently to the revival in thought, of impressions of words" (Bastian 933). This perception that "words" are the key language phenomena, and thus the focus of analysis, diagnosis, and theory formation, is common among the neurologists who studied aphasia; few felt the need to think about more than the word.

Bastian's traversal of the aphasia scene touches on someone important in Freud's professional life: his former mentor in Brücke's laboratory, Sigmund Exner. Bastian refers to Exner's localization of a word center at a specific site in the brain. Freud, however, does not include Exner, along with Wernicke, Lichtheim, Meynert, and others, among those whose theories he deconstructs. His one footnote to Exner gives credit for the impetus for the aphasia book to a report by Exner and Josef Paneth. Not only Exner, but Wernicke, Kussmaul, Charcot, Ross, Lichtheim, Jackson, and Broadbent—most of the prominent members of the aphasia scene— appear either as allies or opponents in Bastian's article. Bastian cites Ross on a point—the dissolution of language functions—that originates with Jackson. On the last page of this article Bastian mentions and dismisses the idea that aphasic disturbances could be hysterical in nature (although he acknowledges the idea of an organically based hysteria) and refers to paraphasia as a topic of great interest.

These mentions remind us to what extent Freud's interests had been anticipated in other quarters. Freud's selection of points from Bastian's article is accurate, though seemingly somewhat arbitrary. The Grasset footnote picks up on what was for Bastian merely a minor point in passing, although it is found in the midst of a discussion (quoted from a previously published book of Bastian's) that is critical of Broca's limitation on the site of aphasia. It also makes a statement that might appeal to Freud's way of thinking and to the ideas already in his mind: "We must now be prepared to admit the existence of many closely allied forms of aphasia and a comparatively wide area in which lesions may give rise to this or that variety" (Bastian 986).

We are left with the question Why did Freud refer so frequently to Bastian and refrain from criticizing him as he criticized Bastian's compatriots in diagram making and localizing? In addition to the fact of Bastian's nationality and the moments when he seems to bypass his own views on narrow localization, there are other aspects of his article with which Freud is in sympathy. Coinciding with Freud's thinking about the broader context of aphasic disturbances are, for example, Bastian's ideas on memory and the unconscious and his adherence to associationist philosophy. (I consider in detail in subsequent chapters Bastian's further role in the aphasia book.)

Freud continues his argument in Section 2 by promising to elaborate at some later point on the significance of paraphasia (and how Wernicke used it to support the notion of the interruption of a specific pathway) and yet goes on to insert a brief statement many commentators on the aphasia book have called a forecast of *The Psychopathology of Everyday Life*: "The paraphasia observed in patients does not differ in any respect from that mixing up and garbling of words which the healthy person can observe in himself when tired or distracted, or under the influence of disturbing affects." For this reason, Freud concludes, "paraphasia might well be regarded as a purely functional symptom, a sign of reduced efficiency of the apparatus of speech association" (*AA* 13). By inserting an observation at the level of psychology, he has been able to expand the concept of a phenomenon otherwise limited in the neurological perspective and to fit the expanded concept like a supportive brick into the theoretical construct he is building, which argues for functional rather than purely anatomic and site-specific definitions. Yet—and here we see the rhetorician in a characteristic maneuver—"this does not exclude its appearing in the most consumate form as an organic focal symptom," a phenomenon investigated by Allen Starr, to whose article Freud inserts a footnote.[13] Just as in his reading of Bastian, Freud draws attention to options that do not obviously bolster his standpoint, only to show, by reporting Starr's research, that those options are not supported by the evidence: "However, one meritorious author, Allen Starr, took the trouble of investigating the anatomic foundations of paraphasia. He came to the conclusion that paraphasia can be produced by lesions in very different regions. He found it impossible to discover a consistent difference in the pathology of cases of sensory aphasia with or without paraphasia." (*AA* 14). This conclusion is part of Freud's refutation of Wernicke's theories, which Starr also mentions as contradicted by this finding. The fact that Freud refers once

---

13. Allen Starr, "The Pathology of Sensory Aphasia, with an Analysis of Fifty Cases in Which Broca's Centre Was Not Diseased," *Brain* 12 (1889): 82–99 (reprint, New York: Johnson Reprint, 1955). Starr, who was a professor of diseases of the mind and nervous system at the College of Physicians and Surgeons in New York, is the subject of an anecdote reported by Ernest Jones (202): "Two distinguished American neurologists afterwards asserted that they worked with Freud in Meynert's laboratory, but their statements are not easy to substantiate. . . . Allen Starr, worked in Meynert's laboratory from October 1881 to March 1882, when Freud was still in Brücke's Institute." Jones adds a quotation from a 1912 letter from Freud reporting on an attack on himself that had appeared in the *New York Times*, written by Starr, who claimed to have worked with Freud, although Freud denies ever knowing him.

again, at the end of his third section, to Starr's finding demonstrates the importance to Freud's case of evidence provided by pathology.

Starr's article has several additional points of interest. First of all, in contrast to Bastian, he presents himself as primarily a pathologist, and on pathology, he believes, rests the "final appeal" "in questions regarding the localisation of cerebral functions" (82). He points out, however, that "in the study of aphasia and in the localisation of the various functions which take part in the use of language, clinical observation has always outrun pathological data," and in this connection we encounter a concern of Freud's: priority of discovery. Starr asserts that "English physicians had described and accurately differentiated the two great varieties of aphasia —ataxic and amnesic, or as they are now generally known, motor and sensory aphasia—some years before Wernicke recorded the first cases with autopsies" (83). Bastian (934) had asserted his claim to five years' priority in recognizing sensory aphasia before Wernicke. Freud himself is at pains to let his readers know that his ideas are his own: A long historical footnote to Section 5 explains that he had presented the basic content in a lecture of 1886 before the "Vienna Physiological Club," whose proceedings, however, were not permitted to be used in claims of priority. In 1887, Hermann Nothnagel and Bernhard Naunyn presented a report—"On the Localization of Brain Diseases"—that coincides, Freud states, with his study on several important points.[14] With regard to two of their points, he believes that "any reader" (*AA* 68) will think that he was influenced by their lecture. He writes that this is not correct; the actual motivation for his aphasia study originated with work published jointly by Exner and Paneth. That Freud's concerns are not without foundation is illustrated in Starr's article (98) where he refers to evidence on the location of the visual area as a "conclusion, now accepted in Germany, France, and America" and uses the 1887 Nothnagel and Naunyn lecture to support his claim. That is, the lecture was being internationally cited two years before Freud published his aphasia study.

For now, these concerns provide some insight into the prevailing sociology of science. Starr cites many of the usual experts, including, approvingly, Meynert, and he agrees with Bastian that Kussmaul and Broadbent are wrong when they postulate a center for ideas in the brain. It is also significant that Starr, too, has no theory of language at the base of his

---

14. Hermann Nothnagel and Bernhard Naunyn, "Ueber die Localisation der Gehirnkrankheiten," in *Verhandlungen des Congresses für innere Medicin* (Wiesbaden: Bergmann, 1887), 109–162. The significance of their work for the aphasia book is discussed in Chapter 4.

deliberations: all theory revolves around the notion of the word. Starr's diagram, more complex than Bastian's, shows places for "word hearing memory," "word seeing memory," "word uttering memory," and "word writing memory" in criss-cross relations with more general seats of memory. Starr is a strict physicalist with regard to the explanation of aphasic symptoms, but he does not extrapolate sites for complex brain functions, such as concepts: "Thought being regarded as the play of consciousness along lines of association between memory pictures cannot be located" (97). Although there is a spectrum of positions among the researchers Freud cites approvingly, none represent the wrong-headedness he finds among Wernicke and, above all, Lichtheim and Meynert; but neither do any part company from the prevailing views with as significant theoretical elaboration as Hughlings Jackson did.

In his second section Freud exposes contradictions and faulty logic in Wernicke's theory of conduction aphasia (the postulation of centers versus pathways). He does so by taking hypotheses of Wernicke's and showing that they do not coincide with clinical observations. He maintains, in the case of one particular syndrome ("word deafness"), that the theory of aphasia would have taken a different course if Wernicke's first cases of sensory aphasia had been of that type. An implication of this suggestion is that Freud's method of critically surveying the literature will bring a researcher closer to the truth than will the hit-or-miss method of examining a few cases in a hospital or in one's own practice. With his usual rhetorical panache, Freud even enlists Wernicke's follower Lichtheim as an ally: "Lichtheim must have sensed the flaw in Wernicke's explanatory effort, because he defined much more concisely the conditions under which paraphasia did not occur" (*AA* 16). "Only one step more," Freud writes, and Lichtheim would have arrived at the proper insight. Freud's own conclusion at this stage is that "the destruction of a so-called center is characterized only by simultaneous interruption of several fiber tracts [pathways]" (*AA* 17), That is to say, there is no anatomic evidence for the presumption of the distinction between centers and pathways based on aphasic symptoms. At this point Freud turns to a long quotation from Armand de Watteville for support, in view of his feeling of "isolation" in demanding that theory be supported by clinical observations.[15] He translates a passage whose central proposition for Freud's purposes is that lesions that do not produce recognizably different symptomology nonetheless produce very

---

15. Armand de Watteville, "Note sur la cécité verbale," *Le Progrès Medical*, ser. 2, vol. 1 (1885): 226–228.

different psychic consequences. Although Freud agrees with this premise because it produces more grist for the mill of a functional theory, he rejects Watteville's conclusion that greater "intellectual damage" will necessarily be associated with a "central" lesion than with a lesion in pathways.

Freud's third section brings the next step in the construction of his case for a functional interpretation of aphasia. He couches his move in terms of an explorer who stumbles upon a surprising new find: "While we were trying to find out which circumstances in the clinical presentation of language disorders confirm the alleged psychic significance of the language centers, and for this purpose subjected Wernicke's conduction aphasia to a critical review, we came across facts that must stimulate doubts about the correctness of a scheme based mainly on localization" (*AA* 19). Though he calls the "Wernicke-Lichtheim schema" one based on localization, Freud also gives them credit for taking functional factors into consideration in the explanation of speech disorders. Freud draws not only allies, but even his opponents, into the service of his argument. Also in this section we find the only instance of Freud's drawing directly on the work of a linguist (philologist); thus by implication, language from other than a neurological perspective becomes a factor in the case Freud is building.

Freud's critique of Lichtheim also translates into a critique of scientific method: he points out that the results of testing by recognizing the number of syllables in a word, which Lichtheim uses to demonstrate whether or not patients with motor aphasia have retained "inner language," would depend on the intactness of the very pathway that is considered to have been destroyed in motor aphasia. This mode of testing thus rests on a logical error.[16] Freud adds a footnote reference to a supportive comment in an article by J. W. H. Wysman.[17] Indeed, Wysman (48) does suggest that syllable testing is misleading. He uses the example of the ability of the beginning learner of ancient languages to scan lines of verse—in other words, to recognize syllables—without knowing what the words stand for. Wysman (46) also points out on the basis of his own experience with Greek that Lichtheim is incorrect when he presumes that comprehension of the words is a necessary condition of fluent reading. Wysman's article is also noteworthy for several other reasons. His affiliation is with a hospital in Java—which indicates how broad the geographic reach of the aphasia

16. For Freud's additional critique of experimental method and logic, see Chapter 5.
17. J. W. H. Wysman, "Aphasie und verwandte Zustände," *Deutsches Archiv für klinische Medicin* 47 (1891): 27–52.

community could be. Wysman includes striking diagrams (discussed in Chapter 5) that reflect technology of the day, and he compares the cortex to the "cylinder of a phonograph" (28) in so far as it can reproduce only what has been recorded. This and other technological metaphors (see the discussions of Kussmaul and Grashey below) give evidence for the long history of trying to envision the brain along the lines of whatever newly constructed machinery has captivated the imagination of scientists. By contrast, Freud's relation to neuro-imaging in the aphasia book is a product of the higher degree of abstraction that prevails in theoretical physics (discussed in Chapter 5).

The third section contains Freud's first mention of Adolf Kussmaul author of *Disturbances of Speech. An Attempt in the Pathology of Speech*, whom he cites as one, among "almost all earlier authors," who maintained that spontaneous speech takes place via the same pathway as repetition.[18] The second mention also occurs in Section 3, this time in the form of a footnote reference to a another researcher's case as reported by Kussmaul. The last reference to Kussmaul occurs in the last section of the book in the context of a list of examples of Hughlings Jackson's theory of "disinvolution" of language capacity as a consequence of aphasia. Freud brings in Kussmaul—who had discussed association as a clinical symptom and as brain physiology—as one of his sources of clinical examples for the phenomenon that the words best retained are those that are members of a series or embedded in a broad range of associations.[19] Altogether then, Freud draws on Kussmaul's work in an arc that reaches from the beginning of his book to the end, supporting his opening case in neurological terms and then his closing synthesis of the associationist, evolutionary, and linguistic strands of his argument.

Kussmaul, as Marx and others have pointed out, was a key figure in early aphasia studies and perhaps the only researcher who truly bridged the medicine/linguistics gap. Thus it makes sense that the first mention of him should immediately precede reference to one of the leading philologists of the day. Kussmaul saw language as a more complex phenomenon

18. *AA* 22. Kussmaul, whose last position was at the University of Strassburg, had a distinguished academic medical career with publications on a great variety of clinical topics. His book on aphasia, *Die Störungen der Sprache: Versuch einer Pathologie der Sprache* (Leipzig: F. C. W. Vogel, 1877), is cited by most of the contemporary writers on the subject. A translation —*Disturbances of Speech: An Attempt in the Pathology of Speech*—appeared in the English version of Hugo von Ziemssen's *Cyclopaedia of the Practice of Medicine*, vol. 14 (New York: William Wood, 1877). Because the translation of Kussmaul is out of date, I have made my own translations.

19. Freud writes "Kussmaul and others" (*AA* 90), which can be understood as including the linguist Berthold Delbrück, whose article includes a detailed discussion of this topic.

and was aware of the limits the current state of knowledge imposed on understanding it in terms of brain physiology. Marx writes of Kussmaul that his "work is remarkable for its psychological insight and its lucid elaborations on the nature of language and the problems it poses."[20] But Kussmaul's book mixes perceptive analysis with ill-founded hypotheses and metaphysical assumptions. The eclectic reader Freud selected what he found of interest, following his preference for making selections from writings by authors who peer, convincingly or not, into a larger world of thought.

Kussmaul, who draws on the work of Jackson, Bastian, William A. Hammond, and others who play a role for Freud, depended equally on Heymann Steinthal, a student of Wilhelm von Humboldt. Steinthal was dedicated to providing language studies with a scientific foundation which, in the context of the time, meant shifting them from a philosophic discipline to one for which psychology was central. His interest in aphasia from the linguistic perspective makes Steinthal a lynchpin in the connections that tie Freud's study to language theory; for the family tree of "neo-grammarians" originating with Steinthal passes via Hermann Paul to Berthold Delbrück, who is the only linguist-philologist Freud cites. Katherine Arens makes the point that a major emphasis of the redefinition of philology by Steinthal and his followers and successors was "on semantics as based on psychological rules of association",[21] thus touching Freud's emphasis on association in his aphasia theory and his reliance on Mill and, via Hughlings Jackson, on Spencer. Steinthal wrote critically of the aphasiologists: "Over exertions to find its location (the center of articulated speech), observation of the psychological manifestations of the disease has been neglected. The clinical descriptions are much too incomplete and are inaccurately recorded. Our physicians have as yet no clear concept of what the function of language is."[22] This might be a mandate that Freud took up when he began to write his study. Whether he responded fully to the last item is open to question.

Kussmaul recounts a case history of Steinthal's and deals with several of

20. Marx, "Aphesia Studies," 344.
21. I am indebted for much of the discussion of Steinthal to Katherine Arens, *Functionalism and Fin de Siècle: Fritz Mauthner's Critique of Language*, Stanford German Studies, vol. 23 (New York: Peter Lang, 1984), 117. John C. Marshall called Freud "the first neo-grammarian neurolinguist," which states the case more strongly than I would; see his "Freud's Psychology of Language," in *Freud: A Collection of Critical Essays*, ed. Richard Wollheim (New York: Doubleday, Anchor Books, 1974), 349–365, here 359.
22. I quote Marx's translation (334). Marx is quoting from Heymann Steinthal, *Einleitung in die Psychologie und Sprachwissenschaft* (Berlin: Duemmler, 1871), 454–463.

the classifications Steinthal set up for types of aphasia. More important, Kussmaul's conception of language is derived from Steinthal. As part of building a case for the nature of language and thus the nature of language disturbances, Kussmaul, although a physician, delves deeply into Steinthal's story of language evolution. Variations on this narrative will return in Freud's future writings and serve as the basis of some of his most well-known cultural-historical commentaries. Later, under the influence also of other writers such as Rudolf Kleinpaul, whose work is recognized today as important in the development of psycholinguistics, Freud presumed that there were traceable original, or "ur," forms of language and of individual words. One cannot fully appreciate Freud's thought without considering the historicism, and in particular the evolutionary historicism, that pervaded the thinking of those authors whose writings on language he studied. Steinthal's tale as retold by Kussmaul is aesthetically satisfying, emotionally comforting, easily understood, consistent with evolutionary ideas, and supportive of common notions about the history of tribes and peoples. It is a folk myth that was provided intellectual legitimacy by finds of archaeologists and the deciphering of ancient documents. Kussmaul writes:

> In so far as comparative linguistics [*vergleichende Sprachkunde*], by comparing the oldest literary monuments of humanity, has succeeded in tracing the languages of peoples to their deepest etymological roots, we everywhere come upon stable nuclei of language whose original onomatopoeic character is only partially recognizable. These "word roots" in the sense of comparative linguistics are far beyond simple sounds for feelings or imitation; they are the nuclei of thoughts serving as centers of knowledge [*Bildung*] around which gradually the entire world of ideas, whose possession delights humanity today, arose as word creations. (11–12)

Here Kussmaul interrupts with an etymological note on the "ayrian root MAR," tracing it in the fashion of the time through variations in languages, such as Latin, Greek, Irish, Bohemian, Lithuanian, Sanskrit, and others, to modern German. Freud read footnotes, so we might presume that he saw this one, with Kussmaul's concluding sentence about the satiric novelist and social critic Jean Paul (Johann Paul Friedrich Richter, 1763–1825), that Jean Paul was not amiss in comparing language to a lexicon of faded metaphors. Jean Paul, who might be compared with Laurence Sterne, has been discovered by late-twentieth-century literary theorists for the postmodern qualities of his texts. Freud himself read Jean Paul closely, quoting his books in *Jokes and Their Relation to the Unconscious* and listing them in his bibliography for *The Interpretation of Dreams*. Kussmaul's comment on Jean Paul suggests a "poststructuralist" connection for the ideas on language that Kussmaul presents. From the stage of roots, language developed the second stage of words. This stage is characterized by ideas that find their concrete, corporeal realization in words. Like Nietzsche, Kussmaul builds the contrast between an originary, colorful, sensual world and a man-made world of colorless, abstract concepts in which, however, the sensual pictures continue to live in paler form behind the concepts, where they can always be renewed through a fresh perception. Freud accepted this distinction and assumed it in *The Interpretation of Dreams*, where he adheres to the view that concrete words are superior to abstractions.

Kussmaul develops the idea of an "intellectual work field" between the picture produced by the senses, on the one hand, and the word, on the other. Before a word is spoken, this area must be activated. The word is the "expression and conclusion of a movement of thought," (14) which thought, however, may just as well be produced by another thought as by a sensual impression. Two ideas of Freud's are expressed in approximation here: that of a language "field" in the brain and that of thought occurring by a process of association. This does not mean that Freud took these ideas from Kussmaul; rather, it means that both men belonged to the same context of inquiry, that Freud may have found in Kussmaul stimulation of or reinforcement for his own views. It also means that Freud found in Kussmaul a predecessor who breached the intellectual gap between the disciplines. Kussmaul's text treats the entire complex of ideas Freud's treats; possibly, it is the source of some of Freud's ideas, although, on another level, the two part company drastically.

There are, however, two additional points of language theory that bring Kussmaul and the later Freud together. Kussmaul looks at human behavior "from the psychological standpoint, aside from all neurology,"[23] and concludes that it is never determined merely by ideas, but always by the feelings attached to them, "feelings of duty, righteousness, mercy, etc. . . . Thus we see that when an idea is expressed through speech, the emotions are the prime movers of the spoken word" (15). Kussmaul also believes that language is a product of the unconscious and that all conscious activity is prepared in the unconscious. The territory blocked out by Kussmaul

23. Kussmaul's term for neurology is *Nervenphysik*, or "physics of the nerves."

here is not foreign to the territory in which Freud operates in *Studies on Hysteria*. Freud and Breuer did not claim a beachhead in an unpopulated landscape. Kussmaul, for one, had set up camp before them, tracing the paths from the unconscious to consciousness, from emotions to the spoken word.

Kussmaul distinguishes between this psychological perspective and a physiological one, and here we have the heart of his view of aphasia, and a point at which he parts company from Freud and Hughlings Jackson on the mind/matter, or psychology/physiology, relation. Emotions and ideas, writes Kussmaul, are to the physiologist "only the mental [*seelisch*] expression of material processes in the organic ground of the nervous system." He sees the two—"mechanical" and "mental"—as functioning in concert. The task is to "uncover the organic conditions in the nervous system from which both spring like twins. The physiology of language must ascertain where and how nerve matter is enabled to create speech by ideas and emotions via word pictures" (15). This narrative differs from the interpretation Freud accepted from Hughlings Jackson: that the physiological and the psychological processes, though parallel to each other, do not meet. The physical cannot be determined to cause the psychic; ideas, for example, cannot be traced to a specific neural impulse. Altogether, there is a pattern of assent and dissent in Freud's reading of Kussmaul, leaving unanswered the larger questions Kussmaul raised about language.

Kussmaul raised the fundamental medical question about aphasia which Freud sets out to answer. Kussmaul writes that it had already been apparent to Broca that the extent of a lesion in the gyrus bears no specific relation to the size of the aphasic disturbance it has set up. "Also we see from time to time that less extensive destruction of a specific area will one time permanently, another time only temporarily, damage the same function" (132). Kussmaul's description of indeterminacy is related to Freud's case for a functional interpretation of damage to the language areas in cases of aphasia; his case against the argument for a one-to-one equivalent of physical damage (lesions) to consequences for language; and his case against the hypothesis that certain distinguishable symptoms result from damage to pathways, others from damage to centers. Freud credits the work of Sigmund Exner and Josef Paneth with inspiring his aphasia book, perhaps partly out of respect for Exner and because of his conflicted relationship with Paneth, who died prematurely.[24] Kussmaul's

24. Josef Paneth (1857–1890) is a key figure and focus of guilt feelings in one of Freud's dreams as he reports it in *The Interpretation of Dreams* (SE 5:482; GW 2/3:486).

book, with all its contradictions, might equally have been Freud's source of inspiration. Kussmaul continues, "The reason [for the above-mentioned discrepancy] is still completely obscure. Perhaps in every area [of the brain] there are especially important nodal points in the pathways of the cortex which are more difficult to replace than others" (132). Although Kussmaul speculated no further, Freud took up the challenge of shedding light on the obscurity of the discrepancy between the coincidence aphasiologists expected to find between injury and symptom, and the actuality of their sometime disjunction.

In some ways Freud's and Kussmaul's minds seem kindred. Their recurring themes are the limitations of present knowledge and the overwhelming complexity of brain networks. Kussmaul (61) uses, as Freud did at another time, Darwin's *The Expression of the Emotions in Man and Animals* (1872) as well as the essays of Herbert Spencer, the philosopher of evolution. He relies extensively on Hughlings Jackson's case reports and analyses, calling him an "excellent observer," without, however, deeply absorbing Jackson's theories as Freud did. Jackson once even felt constrained to reply to a statement by Kussmaul which sheds an incorrect light on his procedures with a patient (discussed in Chapter 5). Kussmaul's sources also include Bastian, Broadbent, Charcot, Ferdinand Carl Maria Finkelnburg, Hammond, Meynert, Carl Spamer, Wernicke, and others who appear in Freud's book as well as a broad range of earlier authors on aphasia, philosophers, and representatives of related disciplines. Kussmaul engages in a lengthy discussion of paraphasia, using several of the same examples of errors Freud uses, without, however, suggesting that errors may be prompted by unconscious motives. Among "healthy people," he sees misspeaking as primarily a result of inattentiveness, and in the aphasia book Freud also focuses on the role of attentiveness in speaking and reading. Kussmaul acknowledges, however, the temporary loss of speech which occurs as a result of the "violent emotions" of hysteria and "other neuroses" (200). His account of a case history of hysteria sounds as if it came from Freud's or Breuer's practice: "A lady of thirty-plus years suffered from hysteria with paralysis of the legs and the left arm. Now and then she would lose speech for hours or for days. Pressure applied to any arbitrary point on the side of her throat would always immediately eliminate this 'aphasia.' When she was removed from my presence she lost speech entirely" (201). He treated her successfully with a placebo, a comfortable room, and pleasant conditions. Freud's "laying on of hands," that is, applying pressure, usually to the forehead of patients, as he recounts in

Studies on Hysteria, also proved an effective device, although not for purposes of a remedy as it had been for Kussmaul. Characteristic also is the patient's emotional dependence on the therapist. Lacking in Kussmaul's account, however, is any suggestion that unconscious motives or repressed traumatic memories could play a role. What lurks beyond the surface impression, he indirectly acknowledged but did not explore. Kussmaul's full acknowledgment of the unconscious and its role in language formation does not appear to have led him to a strategy for clinical, therapeutic applications on behalf of patients whose aphasia was of hysterical origin.

Kussmaul offers a theory of conflict between inner drives and social and moral controls. When propriety is breached by powerful drives, language reflects the emotional turmoil:

> All human education is for the purpose of controlling inborn and acquired reflexes by means of reasonable and rational motives. The inner driving and inhibiting processes are not accessible to our observation. External measures are discipline by warning, example, and punishment, by reasons of prudence, appropriateness, morality, and many others. School, state, and church compete with each other to spoil our pleasure in the natural reflexes.[25] . . . Affects and drives are continually threatening to break out of the cage like wild animals. . . . When abnormal excitement causes emotions and drives to become overly powerful and delusion rules, then all volitional barriers are breached, and unbridled language becomes a plaything of emotional storms. (42)

In view of such consonances, why do we not read of Adolf Kussmaul as the founder of psychoanalysis? For one reason, I have already mentioned that Kussmaul seems not to have followed through on his insights in the clinical setting. In another respect, his writing stands for entire fields of inquiry mired at that time in a metaphysical discourse that was no longer tenable. Kussmaul's insights struggle against the terminology—(*Empfindungen* and *Vorstellungen, Gedanken, Gefühl, seelisch, geistig*, plus their many compounds such as *Vorstellungsgruppen, Gedankenfluth*, and *Gefühlsmacht*) of a philosophic tradition in the process of becoming obsolete as a discourse of the sciences because it no longer served the purposes of clear

---

25. The version published in the English translation of 1877 is a distortion of Kussmaul's text in the direction of a puritanical affirmation of social controls. Kussmaul's critical distance from the institutions that control behavior was elided in that translation, which is one of the reasons it is not usable.

and logical argument. At such a stage in disciplinary development, skilled rhetoricians are required to provide a new master discourse pruned of the discursive thicket that hampers clinical progress. Tapping many sources (for instance other scientific models, literary models, and probably other languages such as English and French), Freud selectively joined his choice of language to the discursive environment in which he found himself, yet at the same time reshaped that environment.

On the question of localization in aphasia, Kussmaul is difficult to pin down because his views shift within his book and do not lend themselves to an either/or categorization. His pièce de résistance is a graceful schematic diagram showing dotted-line connections between pathways and centers, the main center being the one for ideas or concepts, for which he was criticized by Bastian and Starr.[26] Kussmaul's diagram shows a pathway for each separate function, for example, one for repeating and one for copying words. He also believes there is a pathway between thoughts and words. Pathways are not, however, bound to actual brain anatomy, according to Kussmaul, who criticizes Wernicke for the "error" of attributing the centers to specific sites in the brain: "For that purpose, the localization of elementary language functions is not yet sufficiently mature" (183). He writes that we can only smile at naïve attempts to find a "seat of language" in this or that convolution of the brain. Kussmaul believes that language covers an "enormous associational area" in the brain with widespread "functional connections." Yet when it comes to specific manifestations of cerebral damage—motor or sensory aphasia, for example—he insists that "for anyone who does not imagine words and thoughts as floating [schweben] over the nervous system, logic necessarily requires the localization of language functions in the sections of the cortex. The motor word formations have to come about in different pathways from the auditory or visual word pictures, and these in different ones from the ideas [Vorstellungen]" (127).

Kussmaul, like Freud and other researchers who focused on the word as such, interprets "the word" as made up of four parts: sensory, motor, auditory, and visual. Under this model, speech follows as these areas are stimulated and enter into association with one another. But Kussmaul sees the word "as an auditory or visual picture transferred in its sensory sound parts to the sound keyboard where the word text, previously transposed to the [musical] notation of the remembered motion pictures, is played out"

26. Kussmaul's diagram is reproduced in Chapter 5.

(126). Feeling his way on the uncertain ground of hypothesis, he resorts to the musical metaphor to convey his intuitive sense of how things work.

The crossings and partings that characterize the relationship of Freud's book to Kussmaul's stand out in relief when we examine the latter's ninth chapter. It begins with a philosophic statement about how we conceive of objects and a review of the nature of the ego, which touches in more ways than one on the future development of psychoanalytic theory. More specific to aphasia theory is Kussmaul's description of the move from acquiring knowledge per se to formulating and expressing it. Knowledge acquired through a process of apperception must be "sharply distinguished from the logical, metaphysical, and grammatical form, into which it is pressed by our mental organization." Everything we think and perceive must enter the ego via the capacity for judgment and there adapt to categories such as cause and effect, thing and quality, space and time, and "in the grammatical configuration [*Gestalt*] of noun, verb, adjective, etc., find its expression as subject, predicate, etc. Through apperception the human being, as he is constituted as psychological entity, acquires the material of thought, while logic, metaphysics, and grammar give form to the material—logic as it is received into the ego [*Ich*], metaphysics as it is arranged in the ego, and finally grammar as it is expressed through the ego" (30). "[A] thought is true if it has survived the triple test by fire of logical dissection, metaphysical classification, and grammatical expression. . . . The consequence for language is that, as the expression of thought, it must be capable of representing on the one hand the material of thought, on the other hand its logical and metaphysical formation" (31).

The et ceteras that conclude Kussmaul's short lists of parts of speech and parts of the sentence indicate that he is not inclined to enter more deeply into linguistic analysis. Nonetheless, we must note that he has developed a concept of language significantly more complex than most of the other aphasiologists. Under the influence of Steinthal's theories, his concept has a historical dimension and is inseparable from the culture of a particular time and place. Logic, metaphysics, and grammar are presumed to be universal categories extant in the mind. Metaphysics in *this* context seems to be the principle that imparts meaning (whereas elsewhere in his book Kussmaul draws on metaphysics as the principle that one must turn to when scientific explanation or knowledge fails). Freud's examination of aphasia theory dispenses entirely with the notion of metaphysics. Freud does not treat grammar and logic as properties of the mind but as formal or convenient categories. Kussmaul presents logic as something having to do with processing what enters the mind; grammar has to do with processing what exits, yet there is no mention of a receiver of the grammatically formed material. It seems, by implication, to be expressed in a vacuum. Yet diagnosis of patients with speech disturbances is a function of whatever processes are responsible for the *reception* of more or less grammatically formed material. Absent from Freud's narrative is Kussmaul's untenable distinction of the tripartite duties of language to represent content and, separately, form, as if language—before it became language—were capable of expression. But by granting grammar equal standing with logic and metaphysics, Kussmaul is acknowledging language as a phenomenon to whose complexity and historical evolution one must attend when striving to find explanations for its pathological forms in the course of illness. In a text that Freud read with care, language theory is developed beyond reductive assumptions about words.

How does Kussmaul get from this point to language pathology? He does so via a great intellectual leap from the idea of the root, or "*Urform,*" in the language of children and the earliest stages of historical development of peoples. These "protoplasms" of language evolve into the advanced forms that are organized grammatically to meet the requirements of logic and metaphysics. "If language is the faithful mirror of the human mind [*Geist*] as it has formed itself during the endlessly varied internal and external conditions of its diverse development in peoples and individuals, *then it also faithfully reflects the pathological disturbances of that mind*" (my emphasis)(31). This kernel of early psychoanalytic theory thus dates back to Steinthal and reaches us in Kussmaul's narrative filtered through the predilections and theoretical inclinations of a physician/aphasiologist. It reaches us also as evidence of the immersion of theory in the culture of late-nineteenth-century central Europe. Historicism, philology, evolutionary theory, archaeology, technology, and imperialism can all be found in Kussmaul's text. In another chapter, Kussmaul uses an example from technology—composition in photography—as a metaphor to explain and clarify the distinction between observation and critical judgment. In his discussion of apperception in Chapter 9 he compares the mind's acceptance of ideas with chemical processes driven by affinity. If there is no such affinity, ideas will not be accepted, his example being the "savages" (30) who, until they have learned the alphabet and counting, can have no use for the microscope or the telescope, for Aristotle or Euclid. It is as if these latter devices and names represented the highest attainable goals for the human species. Cultural assumptions of this kind are not reproduced in Freud's aphasia text.

In closing chapter 9, Kussmaul turns to questions of language and brain. In doing so he attributes to language a large, complex "apparatus" (32) of nerve pathways and ganglionic centers. Here is a forerunner of Freud's central concept of the "language apparatus." Kussmaul's description of this hypothetical arrangement resembles Freud's and, via Freud's reinterpretation, is not too distant from some current views on language and brain. It has been written of Kussmaul that he "deserves recognition as a pioneer of cognitive neuropsychology on the basis of his model of language function because he understood that a functional model . . . [could] . . . be developed without being constrained by considerations of localization, as long as the neurological foundations of language remain underspecified."[27] We will see that the same description can be used for Freud's model.

Kussmaul begins by denying the existence of anything like a "language (or speech) center" or a "seat of language . . . ; rather, the central organ of language is composed of a large number of separate ganglionic apparatus, joined to each other by countless pathways and carrying out mental, sensory, and motor functions" (33). Next he introduces the notion that practice, or usage, creates connections in the brain that make language and other means of expression possible—an idea that also reaches into our time. From this notion he extrapolates that "a central language organ" is gradually created in the brain by language itself, implying, he believes, that "central organs for the plastic arts, painting, music, dance, and for those forms of thought that do not rely on words, but on numerical symbols and other pictorial forms" are also created by these activities respectively. Although Kussmaul's descriptive terms would not be accepted today, nevertheless, the debate continues over the question to what extent language functions are preexisting in the brain and to what extent language use shapes those functions; so does the interest in gesture and other forms of language without words. In other words, to what extent is the brain a product of culture? In many ways Kussmaul, minus his metaphysical discourse, can still be read as a relevant thinker on the subject of language.

In immediate proximity to his first reference to Kussmaul, Freud introduces a discussion on paraphasia taken from a published lecture by Berthold Delbrück (1842–1922), the only linguist/philologist whose work

---

27. Gonia Jarema, "*In Sensu Non in Situ:* The Prodromic Cognitivism of Kussmaul," in *Brain and Language* 45 (1993): 495–510, here 495. Jarema also gives credit to Kussmaul for "his unique capacity to integrate insights drawn from philosophy, philology, psychology, and medicine in order to capture the nature of language and of its disturbances in a unified way" (496).

makes an appearance in the aphasia monograph.[28] Freud had referred to Kussmaul as one of the "earlier authors"; to Delbrück he refers simply as "a philologist" (*AA* 22), a distinction that emphasizes that Kussmaul belongs to a different and earlier era. Delbrück, whose texts are a model of cogent writing and clear thinking, was professor for Indic and Indo-Germanic linguistics in Jena and one of the most prominent historical linguists of his time.[29] Freud's choice of Delbrück may have rested as much on the persuasive logic, clarity, and coherence of Delbrück's presentation as on interest in the linguistic perspective per se. A student of Steinthal's, and of several of the other leading philologists of the day, Delbrück developed a specialty in comparative syntax, particularly of Sanskrit and other ancient Indian languages. He belonged to the group called neogrammarians who, working in the psychological tradition of Steinthal, saw a need for innovation in a field whose traditional precepts and methods they found flawed and outmoded. By style of thought, personality, and achievements, Delbrück would seem to be a thinker congenial to Freud. A brilliant public speaker, Delbrück was able to sway listeners with his rhetorical prowess and was nominated as a national liberal candidate for parliament in 1887. He had the intellectual breadth to make significant scholarly contributions to historical jurisprudence and to write essays on mythology for the journal edited by Steinthal and Moritz Lazarus.[30]

Why does Freud turn to Delbrück at this juncture in his text and not to his standard sources, all of whom also mention or discuss paraphasia (whereas Delbrück does not mention the term)? Why does he insert a consideration of the views of a linguist instead of the neurologist/aphasiologists with whom he is otherwise almost exclusively concerned? Responding to these questions entails looking at them from several perspectives: (1) how Delbrück's comments on aphasia can be distinguished from those of an older model, for example, that of Kussmaul, who is the reference immediately preceding in Freud's text; (2) how Delbrück

28. Berthold Delbrück, "Amnestische Aphasie," in *Sitzungsberichte der Jenaischen Gesellschaft für Medicin und Naturwissenschaft für das Jahr 1886*, supplement of *Zeitschrift für Naturwissenschaft*, vol. 20 (Jena: Gustav Fischer, 1887), 91–98.

29. Delbrück's prominence is indicated by an honorary doctorate of laws degrees awarded him by the University of Chicago and by his own University of Jena in recognition of the contribution to jurisprudence of his work in historical linguistics. He was elected rector of the University of Jena in 1908. Biographical material on Delbrück is from Eduard Hermann, obituary essay, *Indogermanisches Jahrbuch* 8 (1922): 259–266. It was published in English translation (with several omissions) in *Portraits of Linguists: A Biographical Source Book for the History of Western Linguistics, 1746–1963*, ed. Thomas A. Sebeok, 2 vols. (Bloomington: Indiana University Press, 1966), 1:489–496. Marshall (358–359) mentions Delbrück but does not undertake a critical analysis of Freud's relation to the Delbrück text.

30. *Zeitschrift für Völkerpsychologie und Sprachwissenschaft*.

presents his theories in the lecture to which Freud refers and what the linguistic perspective brings to Freud; (3) how Delbrück's views, as expressed in his widely known *Introduction to the Study of Language*,[31] can be related to Freud; (4) more broadly, how developments in the discipline of linguistics at this time reflect a cultural matrix of which Freud's work was a part; and (5) why Freud might have included a linguist at this stage in the construction of his argument on aphasia.

First it is necessary to return to Kussmaul's definition of paraphasia:

> We understand paraphasia to be the language disturbance whereby the connection between ideas [*Vorstellungen*] and their word pictures [*Wortbilder*] has gotten so disordered that instead of the corresponding meanings, other, incorrect meanings, or completely strange and incomprehensible word formations [*Wortgebilde*] are expressed. (Kussmaul 186)

We remain within the framework of an earlier era, with its terms of broad, philosophic scope which erect layers of spatial and visual metaphors between the phenomena to be investigated and the interpreter. This was a discourse against which the neogrammarians were protesting in their own field of philology. In terms of who falls prey to paraphasia, Kussmaul sees it as a problem of lack of attention, attention interpreted physiologically as activity of the "central language apparatus." For Kussmaul, key to avoiding such errors is concentration, as is personality type (self-confident as opposed to anxious) and appropriate attention while speaking not only to words but equally to thought and syntax.

Freud's definition reads:

> We must understand paraphasia to be a language disturbance whereby the appropriate word is replaced by a less appropriate one that always maintains a certain relationship, however, to the correct word. (*AA* 22)

The discourse has changed, and an element has been added: a contextual relationship. Kussmaul, too, had seen a contextual relationship in these errors, so the change from his definition to Freud's is above all a change to to a leaner discourse. Kussmaul always interprets the contextual relationship in terms of *Vorstellungen* and the words that represent them: the

---

31. Berthold Delbrück, *Introduction to the Study of Language: A Critical Survey of the History and Methods of Comparative Philology of the Indo-European Languages (1880)* was printed in six editions and translated into many languages. The excellent English translation is by E. Channing under the supervision of Delbrück (Leipzig: Breitkopf & Härtel, 1882).

Vorstellungen of daily life, such as walking stick and hat, salt and pepper, knife and fork; or *Vorstellungen* contained in proximity to each other within a thought; or finally, words associated with a particular *Vorstellung* by sound, such as *Mutter* instead of *Butter*, or *Campher* for *Pamphlet* (Kussmaul 188). These last two examples are used by Freud, Hughlings Jackson, and others writing on paraphasia. (Aphasiologists passed around examples in their publications as if no one wanted to make the effort to report new ones. Their sharing also has the larger significance of showing the interconnectedness, perhaps intellectual incestuousness, of the international fraternity of investigators. From where might provocative new questions arise?) Delbrück, however, uses the more telling example for Freud's interests, and Freud utilizes it in his text as well: *Vutter* instead of *Vater* [father]. Freud's rendition, though, drops (in a Freudian slip?) Delbrück's explanation, which skirts so closely the future concerns of psychoanalysis. This slippage is meaningful because it indicates how Freud's readings might sometimes have worked in his mind: his acknowledgments are often not equivalent to actual influence; they may in fact be inversely related.

Delbrück's interpretation reads:

> It stands to reason that what eventually presents itself as confusion of sounds may also be caused by other processes. Someone may say, for example, *"Vutter"* instead of *"Vater"* because at the same time he has in mind *"Mutter."* Externally, of course, a confusion of sounds is apparent; in truth, however, there exists a mingling of ideas in the mind [*Vorstellungsbilder*]. ("Amnestische Aphasie" 93)

Freud's version, which he had introduced at the beginning of Section 3 as being "on the basis of the observations of a philologist, Delbrück," consists only of the following brief statement: "It is also called paraphasic if two word intentions are merged to a miscreation, 'Vutter' for 'Mutter' or 'Vater' " (*AA* 24). Freud has chosen not to mention the key implication of Delbrück's text: that there is a class of errors with unconscious motivations. Nor does he pursue the implications of Delbrück's example. Could this example have worked in his mind over the years to contribute to the oedipal theory? If we look back at Freud's first comment on paraphasia (*AA* 13) in the discussion of Section 2, we see that it is not materially different from Kussmaul's views. If we add that to Freud's subtly altered version of Delbrück's remarks, we may be inclined to conclude that the linguist was a step ahead of the future psychoanalyst on this point. In more than one area, Delbrück's lecture may well have planted in Freud's mind suggestions that developed only later, when the ground of theory had been prepared for them.

Kussmaul recounts several cases of the more profound paraphasia that results from brain lesions (Freud prefers calling this "sensory aphasia" and limiting the term *paraphasia* to the less serious cases of error). The reaction of the physician Kussmaul, and apparently of those various physicians who saw the patients, is to hear only gibberish in the patients' profoundly distorted speech. Freud too refers to the "inexhaustible series of senseless syllables" (*AA* 23) that some patients produce. Delbrück, who was not trained in medicine and therefore did not delve into questions of brain pathology, nevertheless did observe patients. What he hopes to achieve with his lecture is to alert examining physicians to certain kinds of questions. By bringing linguistics to bear on therapeutic technique, he is anticipating the mandate issued by Roman Jakobson's essay on aphasia as well as the progress toward integrating a linguistic perspective into the investigation of aphasia. Delbrück maintains that sentence models—not merely words, as is the conventional wisdom—can be traced through history and thus that word order itself is (to use the parlance of today) hard wired. Speakers are not capable of fundamental violations of normal German word order:

> I have not found that this word-order model is destroyed in patients to the point that they will jumble the words around at will. Positive evidence that the word-order models are still extant is supplied even in an advanced stage [of aphasia] by a style of expression that one could call sketchy. A patient will say, for example, *"Eine Auge immer Thränen"* [one eye always tears—the noun], with which he means to say *"das eine Auge ist immer voll Thränen"* [one of my eyes is always full of tears]. Only, so to speak, the most prominent peaks of speech are visible, but they are in the correct location. ("Amnestische Aphasie" 97–98)

Delbrück adds that it is a matter of course that the capacity to form short sentences lasts longer than the capacity to form long ones. The model for a longer sentence may be internally still intact, but the patient cannot express it fully. With Delbrück's thesis, based on the research of a specialist in syntax, we see a reading strategy that is potentially of therapeutic value, at least at a certain stage of aphasia. Kussmaul, who had figuratively thrown up his hands in the face of "utter confusion," lacking "any key that might unlock the meaning of this jumble of words or verbal delerium" (189), would naturally lack the theoretical framework of the

specialist in analytic history of language. Thus Delbrück would see structure that Kussmaul and Freud (at this point) might overlook.

Freud was later to believe that meaning could be found in even the
most disconnected testimony, for example, of a hysterical patient. He
became with his own patients the kind of reader that Delbrück had been
—finding the deep and historically evolved connections that a patient may
at a particular time be unable to articulate. Freud's "The Psychotherapy
of Hysteria" section in *Studies on Hysteria* is marked by the same certainty
of an inner logic that Delbrück demonstrated:

> The peculiarity of this case lay only in the emergence of isolated key-
> words which we had to work into sentences; for the appearance of discon-
> nectedness and irrelevance which characterized the words emitted in this
> oracular fashion applied equally to the complete ideas and scenes which
> are normally produced under my pressure. When these are followed up,
> it invariably turns out that the apparently disconnected reminiscences are
> closely linked in thought and that they lead quite straight to the patho-
> genic factor we are looking for. (*SE* 2:276; *GW* 1:277–278)

It may be justifiable to suspect that, in some respects at least, Freud
learned from Delbrück how to read his earliest patients.

Freud takes another example of paraphasia from Delbrück's text: "It can
be classified as paraphasia when the speaker replaces words with those
that have a similar meaning or are connected by frequent association,
for example, . . . 'Potsdam' instead of 'Berlin' " (*AA* 23). The section of
Delbrück's lecture from which Freud has borrowed this example treats the
conceptual grouping of words. Delbrück concludes that the majority of
errors are due to words being grouped together: "Thus it is only natural
that someone would replace 'Berlin' with 'Potsdam' but very improbable
that he would replace 'Berlin' with 'table.' Where such an error appears
to have occurred, the question is whether we have judged it wrongly
because we do not know the intermediate links" ("Amnestische Aphasie"
94). The idea of the hidden intermediate links between words as the key
to a lost interpretive trail recurs as a central theme in *The Interpretation of
Dreams;* already in *Studies on Hysteria* we find a version of it. Thus we see
in Delbrück's thesis, which Freud chose *not* to incorporate into the aphasia
book, an example of the convoluted paths Freud-as-reader took. In the
ensuing years the seed of this idea blossoms in the context of reading
dreams and of reading patients' occulted testimony.

The second stage of our examination of Freud's relationship to Delbrück's ideas entails looking closely at the lecture Freud read. Delbrück opens his lecture by giving credit for its impetus to a lecture he had heard which urged a closer examination of the problem of aphasia from a psychological standpoint. Reading the literature convinced him even more of this necessity. Delbrück proceeds to set up a framework that both legitimates and sets limits for his remarks: they are framed by the literature he has read, supplemented by his observation of patients, and filtered through the point of view of a linguist. For Delbrück, linguistics clearly entails the discipline of psychology and qualifies one to make judgments in a clinical setting. He proceeds by setting out, point by point, some fundamental weaknesses in the medical studies of aphasia. His critique echoes Steinthal's but brings to bear his own observations and his own research in historical syntax. He bridges the disciplinary gap as Kussmaul did, but with a deeper understanding of language and a discourse much closer to Freud's.

According to Delbrück, a prerequisite for judging disturbances of language is understanding how normal speech works, particularly the speech of the same age group as the patient. He faults physicians who use the language of children as the standard to judge the aphasic disturbances of adults. He requires that examples drawn on in clinical practice come from contemporary German. (This tenet is violated by most of the aphasiologists, who quote from each other's cases freely, irrespective of whether the patient involved was a speaker of German, French, or English.) He is skeptical of using examples from "hypothetical ages" of the German language, reasoning that it is unlikely that a contemporary

> could revert to what his ancestors spoke many thousands of years ago, and then too all of these findings about prehistoric language conditions, to say nothing of the origin of language, are so uncertain that one does better to avoid them in the case at hand. By contrast, what we can observe on a daily basis in ourselves and others may have the disadvantage of triviality, but it has the advantage of being able to be verifed by anyone. (92)

This last statement reflects the conviction that a discipline with pretensions to scientific credibility needs to produce verifiable findings.

Disregarding the strictures of the linguist, Freud freely used case histories that he rendered from the original English or French, without taking into consideration the question of linguistic reliability and accuracy. The point of view of the linguist is that language must be considered in its cultural and historic specificity. The grammar and syntax specific to contemporary German will bear a relationship to the distorted versions presented by aphasic patients. This point strikes to the heart of early psychoanalytic theory in *The Interpretation of Dreams*, for example, where much of Freud's analysis depends on the workings of the German language (even though, in a reference added in 1911, he acknowledged Sándor Ferenczi's view that dreams cannot be translated from one language to another; see *GW* 2/3:104; and *SE* 4:99). Nor was Delbrück's skepticism about etymological tracings of an "origin" of language shared by the later Freud, in whose writings such etymologies played a role—for example, in *Leonardo* and other writings that show the influence of the bogus theories of Karl Abel.[32] It is a remarkable departure from the conventions of his field that Delbrück should dismiss the concern with "origins" as an uncertain undertaking, and it signals to a certain extent the kind of thinker he was. For those of his listeners who wanted to learn the basics about modern linguistic research, he recommended Hermann Paul's *Principles of the History of Language* (1880) as the best source.

Next Delbrück lays out his basic ideas on aphasia under three main headings. The first is the hypothesis that we learn not sounds, but words, and that our muscles develop habitual actions to produce our mother tongue automatically and without deliberating individual sounds. Consequently it is possible, he suggests, that a patient mixes up certain sounds, *Lieber* instead of *Lieder*, for example, not because he has confused the idea of "b" with the idea of "d" (as we do not learn individual sounds) but because a process of atony occurs; that is, a sound located further back is replaced by one located further forward. (This is the point where he interjects that in certain cases—*Vutter* for *Vater* with *Mutter* in mind— that appear to be a confusion of sounds, it is actually the ideas that have been combined.) Freud's rendering of this point of Delbrück's is "errors of articulation . . . when individual letters are replaced by others." Freud also goes on to pick up the question of location in the organs of speech which Delbrück raises: "One is tempted to distinguish these different types of paraphasia by the location in the speech apparatus where the awkwardness was initiated" (*AA* 23). (This is the only time Freud uses the term *Sprechapparat* as opposed to *Sprachapparat*—a distinction significant

32. See Sigmund Freud, "The Antithetical Meaning of Primal Words" (1910), a review of Abel's "Über den Gegensinn der Urworte," in *GW* 8:214–221; *SE* 11:155–161.

because it supports translating *Sprachapparat*, the term that describes Freud's main theoretical proposal, as "language apparatus" in English.)

Delbrück's second basic idea, building on the first, explains why certain classes of words are lost sooner than others. The words lost first are those that are isolated, that do not belong to one of three groupings: etymologically related words, which groups only rarely include proper names and foreign words; conceptual groupings (called "categories" today), the members of which are more often confused with one another (see the "Amnestische Aphasie" 94 quotation above) than they are with words belonging to different groups; and finally, parts of speech, which are also often confused with one another. That is, there tends sooner to be confusion within groups than supragroup. Because, all told, isolated words are forgotten first, patients tend to lose proper names first. Words that sound similar tend to be confused if they are not bound to associational groups. At this point Delbrück brings in the *Berlin/Potsdam, Berlin/Tisch* example with its significant implications.

The third idea is that the most important grouping of all is into categories Delbrück calls "external words" and "internal words," the former referring to objects in the world to which we can point, the latter referring to "purely internal events, facts, and moods, for example, 'I know,' 'yes,' 'no,' etc. It is generally maintained that these [latter] words at one time had a so-called concrete meaning. I prefer not to examine whether that is true or not" (95). (Freud, however, in *Studies on Hysteria*, accepts this notion—which he attributes to Darwin—as a possible source for an explanation of the relation between hysterical patients' words and symptoms.) Delbrück maintains that verbs are more "internal and abstract" than nouns. Using the examples of "to cut" and "scissors," he explains that the verb describes processes that are carried out with many more things than that one particular object. This relationship means that aphasic patients will sooner lose external words than internal ones. Patients will lose a word like *scissors* in the very early stage of illness, even though they still have the idea in mind, whereas they will retain a sentence like "I don't know" even in an advanced stage of illness. It is common for patients to define external words they can no longer say, perhaps indicating "scissors" by saying, "You cut with it." "Thus they explain an idea [*Anschauung*] with many attributes by means of an idea with fewer attributes, . . . One can express this observation figuratively as: the words that lie on the periphery of our mental capacity are more easily subject to being forgotten than those that lie in the interior" (95). With this spatial metaphor Delbrück touches on the possiblity that his views can also be expressed in neurological discourse and that they anticipate the metaphor of periphery versus interior core which governs Freud's narrative in the "Psychotherapy" section of *Studies on Hysteria*.

Delbrück's interpretation of the order of loss of elements of speech reflects the same observations discussed by Hughlings Jackson, but from a linguist's perspective. Hughlings Jackson's explanation is based on evolutionary theory. He asserts that what is lost first is what is most recently acquired, least organized, and most loosely associated. For Jackson, this means also what is most highly abstract. Thus conceptual terms are lost before the often-used terms of everyday life, which is how he explains the loss of proper nouns and of languages acquired after the native language. He and Delbrück agree that "yes," "no," and "I don't know" are the kinds of elements retained longest as an aphasic disturbance worsens, and they agree that there is a regularity in the order of losses. But the neurologist turns to an explanation that accords with notions of evolution of brain structures; the linguist, to one that accords with notions of language structures. Because Freud gives enormous credit to Hughlings Jackson's influence on the aphasia study, it is worthwhile to examine how he really positions himself between the two interpretive options. I am suggesting that there is more Delbrück than has been recognized up to now.

As Freud continues his Delbrück section of the aphasia study, he moves away from applying Delbrück's lecture to the concept of paraphasia and on to the more serious disturbances of "sensory aphasia," in which patients may not be able to say even a single comprehensible word. Freud is striving for greater terminological clarity by jettisoning the common usage of the term *paraphasia* to encompass disturbances from the minor to the most serious. Delbrück did not use that term at all, but Freud chose to classify Delbrück's remarks under the term he himself was restricting to the less serious type of disturbance. Nevertheless—and here we come to the weakness of this move—Freud cites examples from Wernicke to show how much more serious sensory aphasia is than paraphasia, and those examples are of the very kinds of grammatical processes that lent themselves so profitably to the linguist's analytic strategy: "In other cases, such as that of Wernicke himself, at least the poverty of word formations with any more specific meaning, the overabundance of particles, interjections, and other linguistic embellishments, the frequent repetition of nouns and verbs is noteworthy" (*AA* 23).

Freud follows with the case of a woman patient he had seen (not one of his) in the Vienna General Hospital. Her speech was characterized by "impoverishment of all more specific parts of speech, nouns, adjectives, and verbs, an abundance of indifferent parts of speech, along with repetition of those words she had once managed to say" (*AA* 24). This report largely coincides with Delbrück's analysis, which could have provided it with a theoretical framework. Without such a framework it remains an unanalyzed report of observations and gives the impression of a certain helplessness on the part of the neurologist faced with linguistic phenomena. The report is marked by definite assumptions about a hierarchy of value in parts of speech but shows no inclination to ask what the presumed hierarchy might have to do with the formations presented by the patient. Freud suggests naming the phenomenon "word impoverishment with copious speech impulses" instead of Wernicke's name "conservation of vocabulary with paraphasia" (*AA* 24); that is, Freud is using terminology of quantity, despite having noted characteristic features of the speech. He proceeds no further on this matter but rather returns to questions of localizationist neurology as part of his continuing response to Lichtheim's diagram.

Further light is shed on the symptoms of the patient Freud saw by Delbrück's move to the next logical step in his lecture. Having begun by examining aphasic disturbances in terms of sounds and letters, and then of words, he turns to grammatical structures which he calls "schemata" or "models." Stored in our memory are not only a mass of individual words but also various models, such as conjugations and declensions, or sentence types. Delbrück stresses the fact that the models are followed irrespective of level of education; they exist whether or not the speaker is conscious of them. The implication is that grammatical patterns are internalized, part of the subconscious mind. When an aphasic patient whose natural language is a dialect tries to switch to standard German, it will become increasingly difficult to speak the latter correctly, "just as we manage the difficulties of a foreign language less well when we are exhausted" ("Amnestische Aphasie" 96). Here Delbrück intersects Hughlings Jackson's theory of disinvolution—what is learned last and used least is lost first in the aphasic patient. Whereas Hughlings Jackson and Freud believe that a later-acquired language would be lost before the native language, Delbrück's interpretation, by contrast, is couched in the more linguistically refined terms of grammar and syntax as opposed to whole language loss. He believes models of inflection are maintained in the early stages of illness. For example, the error of forming the past tense of a strong (irregular) verb along the pattern of a weak (regular) verb is one that may be made even by a healthy person just as well as by one who is suffering from aphasia. He goes on to discuss types of suffixes in German and to suggest that a patient might be observed for confusion of a certain type of suffix. In other words, Delbrück's reading of aphasic symptoms grows out of specific qualities of the German language. In combination with his notion of inherent linguistic types or models, this language specificity suggests that a cultural unconscious is at work.

It remains to be seen to what extent Freud took cultural differences into consideration; clearly, his priority was what he saw as universally human. Freud does, however, show awareness of comparative linguistics when he discusses the "visual element" in language comprehension: "The visual element is not directly connected to object associations (our characters are not, like those of other peoples, direct symbols of concepts, but rather of sounds)" (*AA* 94). This is a significant aside; for such a fundamental difference in the functioning of a language must indicate a corresponding difference in how aphasia manifests itself (although Freud did not raise this point). Thus we are brought back to Delbrück's insistence that aphasia theory be developed on a local linguistic basis.

After treating his theory of sentence models as imprinted on the mind, Delbrück concludes his lecture with a remark on the nature of a sentence: "Ow!" "No," and expletives must also be considered sentences, and these very sentences survive the longest, partly because they are the most simple, partly because they are expressed in a condition of excitement. Now this is the same point as made by Hughlings Jackson, who supplies several other examples used by Freud in the aphasia study. Perhaps Hughlings Jackson's articles were among those Delbrück had read. If so, we see another strand in that tightly knit web of the community that studied aphasia.

Freud, it would seem, made a rather narrow and superficial selection from Delbrück's lecture, merely to illustrate a point about paraphasia; but then he seems to have filed some of Delbrück's more congenial points in his mind, where they may have worked as an unacknowledged (or subconscious) influence on the construction of psychoanalytic theory. Considering that many of the authors Freud read discussed paraphasia by name—as Delbrück did not—the questions remain, What drew Freud to Delbrück? Why did he bring a linguistic text into his aphasia study? If this one, why not others? It is clear, in answer to the third question, that linguistics would not have served politically to support Freud's argument. As in the case, years later, of the psychoanalytic movement, Freud needed, above all, scientific legitimacy to support his controversial position. In medical-scientific circles, a linguistic argument might undermine, and certainly would not bolster, the legitimacy of a neurologically ambitious theory based on refutation of reigning authorities. The answer to the second question is a main thesis here: the linguistic point of view fed into Freud's own evolving language theory, which grew into psychoanalysis.

To respond to the first question, we must address our third point and consider Delbrück from a perspective somewhat larger than the one lecture. A good source, because it addresses itself to more general interests than do his historical studies of syntax, is Delbrück's well-known and widely translated *Introduction to the Study of Language*. This slender volume first appeared in 1880. In it Delbrück critically reviews major theories and theorists in his field, including Franz Bopp, Friedrich Schlegel and Wilhelm von Humboldt, August Schleicher, and many others. In relation to Freud, however, I have isolated four distinct but related topics that I believe reveal deep cultural affinities between the two researchers.

First of all, Delbrück situates his field in such a way that we can draw parallels to the historical state of the disciplinary setting in which Freud found himself. Because of the intellectual community of shared questions and forms of inquiry and the reach of scholarship that ignored what are today considered fast borders among disciplines, we are justified in generalizing from broad developments in a key field that in many ways stands for others because it impinges on them in so far as they use or study or are interested in language. In other words, Freud in 1891 faced a situation not unlike the historical juncture Delbrück described, and he responded in much the same tone as Delbrück. In his preface to the English translation of 1882, Delbrück draws the field in broad outline:

It is universally acknowledged by those who have traced the history of German development, that there is an immense gulf between the views of the Germans of today and those prevalent up to the fourth or fifth decennium of this century. This difference of view is almost as great in scientific fields as in the domain of politics. One side of this mighty revolution can be concisely expressed in the statement that we have passed from a philosophical epoch into a historical one. I attempted to show (as no one to my knowledge had done before) that the science founded by Bopp stands in evident connection with the philosophical endeavors of German scholars, and also how it has come about that in linguistic science a sort of metaphysics has arisen, which is at present undergoing a process of dissolution. But at the same time I wished at least to intimate that it is wrong to undervalue endeavors of this nature, since the occasion for such investigations is found in the linguistic material itself, and will probably continue in the future.[33]

Delbrück draws a broad sweep of change across the whole realm of ideas. Today, like Thomas Kuhn, we might call it a "paradigm shift" or, with Michel Foucault, a new episteme." When we read Freud's text in comparison with Kussmaul's, or Delbrück's in comparison with some of his predecessors, the departure from a discourse of metaphysics becomes apparent. With his last point Delbrück is equating the metaphysical with the hypothetical, with what remains as yet unexplained by the evidence, and he is obviously not rejecting it out of hand.

Second, Delbrück's entire text is permeated by confrontations with the discourses of the natural sciences and, like Freud's text, by awareness of his own positioning among competing discourses. He shows how Bopp used the terminology of the natural sciences—terms such as *language-anatomy, anatomical dissection, chemical composition*, the *physics* or *physiology of language* (*Introduction* 17)—as a veneer over traditional philological terminology, into which it can easily be translated. In the case of Schleicher the usage becomes problematic:

> Bopp had already applied the expression "organism" to language, but he had simply meant that language is not arbitrarily manufactured. Such a figure can be tolerated, but when the metaphor is taken literally, the contradiction becomes evident. Language is not a being, but the utterance of beings; accordingly, if we are to use the phraseology of natural science, it is not an organism, but a function. It will also be found extremely difficult to classify philology with the natural sciences. Since language is manifested in human society, the science of language cannot belong to the natural sciences, at least, if this name is used in the accepted technical sense. (*Introduction* 43)

A defining moment of this passage is his introduction of the term *function* to classify language. We may understand this classification as part of a larger interest in the idea of function, which Freud shared; for he made it the central term in his recasting of the relationship between brain damage

---

33. Delbrück, *Introduction*, viii. The notion that theory is contained "in the material itself" is a common rhetorical convention of scientists (Freud uses it in *Studies on Hysteria*). It is a variation on the often-repeated assumption that "nature itself teaches us."

and aphasic symptoms. Delbrück goes on to point out another fallacy in the attempt to translate a discipline into the idiom of natural science: it does not work because "natural science" is not a monolith; each individual natural science has its own characteristic vocabulary and methods. He deconstructs Schleicher's association of linguistic methods with the methods of comparative anatomy by showing (1) that Schleicher builds associations around ideas that are so general or commonsensical that they do not require origination in another field; (2) that Schleicher's comparison must have been an analogy after the fact; and (3) that Schleicher makes incorrect assumptions about the proceedings of anatomists. These remain the typical false moves of those who would enhance a field of study by remaking it into a natural science. With its dissociation of "human society" from the natural sciences, Delbrück's analysis brings into sharp focus the confrontation of competing discourses, of which Freud was painfully aware, as he showed, for example, in *Studies on Hysteria* and "The Project," and which he eventually resolved by forging his own amalgam from several disciplinary strains. These deliberations raise the question Why did Bopp, Schleicher, and the others make these borrowings? The answer can only be that they sought the legitimacy and the power of the new discourse that seemed to dispense so effectively with metaphysics and to provide so reliable an evidentiary basis for its theorems.

Third, Delbrück, aware of the metaphorical nature of all discourses, is not subject to such a temptation. He calls one concept "nothing but a formal expression for the changing views of scholars" (*Introduction* 53); referring to "grammatical operations," he says, "In these we can err, and opinions may change as to what is correct and what false; . . . The form attributed to the individual roots merely exhibits the opinion of scholars regarding the method of analyzing the transmitted words of the Indo-European languages" (85). Delbrück extended relativism to the language of science as well. This recognition of the historical contingency of disciplinary discourses is detectable in Freud's texts and is a topic in the articles of Hughlings Jackson; thus it is a strain compatible with a certain kind of critical thinker, irrespective of disciplinary category. It leads Delbrück also to expose "the phonetic laws which we postulate" as "nothing but uniformities which appear in a certain language and period, for which alone they are valid" and as being conceptually incompatible with the usage of the term *law* "as employed in natural science and statistics." He accepts the term as a convenience but rejects equating it with "natural laws," because "these historical uniformities can evidently bear no resemblance to chemical or physical laws. Language is a result of human action, and consequently phonetic laws are not based upon the regularity of natural processes, but upon that of apparently arbitrary human activities" (130). One can read these deliberations as articulating the core of a compatibility dilemma that psychoanalysis set out to resolve via language. Freud began with a set of laws he had brought with him from his background and training. He tried to impose them on the fragmentary testimony of patients. Eventually, he allowed himself to be led, instead, by rules that seemed to be inherent in the very gaps that defied scientific laws and the logic of consciousness.

Finally, Delbrück is always mindful of "psychological probability" (*Introduction* 79) in linguistic questions. He considers "the nature of the psychic processes" that play a role in word formations by analogy, which result from associations of ideas (108). As he was to indicate in his lecture, he believes in the "series and network of formations under which the word-forms are ranged in the mind of the speaker" (*Introduction* 113). In addition, "the sounds of language (or a part of them) are arranged in series in the mind of the speaker, and . . . the change of one sound must inevitably induce a corresponding change of the remaining members of its series"[34]—an idea (presented in the lecture too) with the implication, stated directly in this text, that "we must regard it as certain that all (or nearly all) these acts take place unconsciously" (121). I believe Delbrück faced a variation on the same intellectual challenges Freud faced, conceptualized them in a similar way, and proposed the same genre of response Freud proposed with psychoanalysis. Delbrück presumes the unconscious and then envisions the most important processes in language formation as taking place there in a relationship of association and mutual influence. He envisioned that explanation in 1880 and still held to it in 1886, when he wrote the lecture that Freud read. Whether an influence or simply a parallel, Delbrück is a remarkable intellectual kin to Freud. Their compatibility suggests a perhaps unconscious motive for Freud's inclusion of a reference to Delbrück in the aphasia study; more than that, it reveals the disciplinary culture to which Freud belonged. Advances in linguistic theory, as filtered through Delbrück's critical, self-reflexive mind that ranged

---

34. This idea is being explored by Harry Howard in neurophysiological terms, "using the well-established format of neurological representation known as spreading activation to model grammatical phenomena." He argues that the notion of backward masking accounts for the phenomena of "doubling," "regressive nasal assimilation," and "weak crossover." See his "The Grounding of Linguistic Rules in Neurology: Repeated Morpheme Constraints and Allied Phenomena" (lecture at Tulane University, New Orleans, March 8, 1996). Thus we have an example of the kind of explanation Delbrück might have attempted, had the modern neurological discursive environment been available to him.

deeply into many disciplinary territories, allowed linguistics to jettison "metaphysical"/"philosophic" baggage, become congenial to Freud's evolving thought, and play out its role as shaper of early psychoanalytic theory.

To place Delbrück in the context of developments in linguistics, I turn to Arens's summary of the positions of the neogrammarians:

> [They] all began with a critique of their individual disciplines. . . . They realized that languages, as we know them, acted as arbitrary and histori-cally relative fields of concepts whose underlying structures could reveal features of the speakers' minds. . . . Language was seen to function as a concept-net changing through time, yet remaining at all points a closed and self-sufficient system. . . . The Neogrammarians' model for the sci-entific study of language acted as the groundwork for a scientific psychol-ogy able to draw valid conclusions about the constitution of the mind of a speaking subject, as least within the confines of a particular historical frame. (255–257)

There are strong connections between this description of the conceptual-izing of the neogrammarians and the nature of Freud's proposed structure of the language apparatus in the brain. Freud, too, envisaged a field—"the association field of language" (*AA* 68)—whose structures revealed features of the mind. He saw the language apparatus as a complex network framed by the field (although not a closed system).

If the linguists indeed prepared the ground for scientific psychology, then we need to look at another relationship: that between Delbrück and Wilhelm Wundt, founder of experimental psychology and a thinker whom Freud felt the need to challenge in *The Interpretation of Dreams*. Delbrück also challenged Wundt's theories, in a small volume called *Fundamentals of Linguistics. With Special Consideration of W. Wundt's Psychology of Language*.[35] In the same year, Wundt published a volume in response to Delbrück.[36] Thus we have a full-fledged methodological debate, with one interpreta-tion of disciplinary development ranged against an opposing one. Al-though the debate was published ten years after Freud's aphasia book, it

35. Berthold Delbrück, *Grundfragen der Sprachforschung: Mit Rücksicht auf W. Wundts Sprach-psychologie erörtert* (Strassburg: Karl J. Trübner, 1901).
36. Wilhelm Wundt, *Sprachgeschichte und Sprachpsychologie: Mit Rücksicht auf B. Delbrücks "Grundfragen der Sprachforschung"* (Leipzig: Wilhelm Engelmann, 1901). Wundt's magnum opus was *Völkerpsychologie: Eine Untersuchung der Entwicklungsgesetze von Sprache, Mythus, und Sitte*, 10 vols., 1st ed., 1900 (reprint, Aalen: Scientia, 1975), vols. 1 and 2: "Die Sprache." Wundt cited Freud's aphasia book in a footnote (1:50), as support for his (Wundt's) argu-ments against theories of localization in aphasia.

revisits and crystallizes a clash of disciplines that took shape, albeit in a shadowy or anticipatory form, in Freud's book. The debate also provides further insight into some of the suggestive points alluded to but not fully explained in the Delbrück lecture Freud read. Wundt's impassioned defensive reponse to Delbrück indicates what the flash points were for Wundt and thus highlights the roughhewn surfaces where emergent disciplines grated most harshly against one another.

Of Delbrück's assertions, Wundt takes offense at three in particular. First and foremost he rejects Delbrück's designation of him a "philosopher" whose "system" therefore necessarily entails "metaphysics."[37] Wundt called his field "modern psychology." It represented for him the cutting edge of scientific research. Philosophy and metaphysics, in contrast, were outmoded, fuzzy, prescientific systems of thought that had lost their former status. He naturally takes umbrage at being classified, by implication, as belonging to that past era.

Second, Wundt deeply resents Delbrück's presenting the systems of Johann Friedrich Herbart and Wundt as two equally valid options from which linguists may chose the one they find most practical for their purposes. Wundt writes, "There can only be one truth, not different, variable systems of truth." Linguists, he believes, are still at a stage where they regard "scientific psychology" (17) not as an "independent empirical scientific field" but merely as an "external aid" to be applied where useful. He argues that the linguists treat the Herbartian "or any other psychology" as if the differences among systems were of as little consequence as the difference between a "Remington or a Hammond typewriter" (18). In addition to placing himself rhetorically in proximity to the latest technology, Wundt is identifying himself with dogmatic positivism. Although he may be defensively overstating his case, for he acknowledges in Delbrück a worthy and significant opponent, nevertheless, Wundt is also delineating a position that not only places him in opposition to Delbrück but also captures the heady faith and imperialist gesture that marks the pioneer in the sciences of the late nineteenth century. In the flux of disciplines in those fecund years, legitimacy and, ultimately, survival of a new discipline meant marking one's territory, defending its borders, and if possible, encompassing and subsuming the Other. Wundt's response to Delbrück is a story of a struggle for the power to define. For Wundt there is "only one

37. Delbrück, *Sprachforschung*, 9. Delbrück further writes, "Wundt is of course above all a philosopher, and only as a sideline a linguist" [*nur im Nebenamt Sprachforscher*] (5).

history of language," "only one historical truth," and "only one psychological truth":

> Of two diverging psychological interpretations of a phenomenon, both can possibly be false. But that both can be simultaneously true, or that they, as Delbrück formulates it, both can be equally useful, that appears to me impossible. A false interpretation is per se also not a usable one, in so far as one sees the purpose of interpretation, as it necessarily must be, not to place a finding of fact into some arbitrary, perhaps completely fictional context, but rather to explain [*deuten*] it correctly. (11)

Third, Wundt faults Delbrück for his "utilitarian" and "practical" approach that necessarily follows from his "neutrality" toward divergent psychologies and that necessarily results in superficial judgments (15). Wundt himself analyzes language on the basis of psychological criteria that have been developed "out of language itself"; he does not "impose a preformed system" on language (12). Many historians of language (philologists), by contrast, impose their language-derived system on scientific psychology. Wundt distinguishes between an "external" and an "internal" history of language, the latter being the method that applies psychology to determine causes. The rhetoric of "external" and "internal" reveals the metaphysics that Delbrück finds in Wundt's theories. Wundt is operating with the notion that there is a disciplinary truth accessible to investigators who remain within the framework of that discipline. Violating the boundaries of that frame (set up by Wundt himself in this case) leads to external, superficial utilitarianism. Wundt observes that he has been the target of much recent criticism from "psychological and philosophic colleagues" who attribute to his psychological theories a "mystical metaphysics of the will" (22) despite the "purely empirical character" (23–24) of his work. His elucidation of his method inadvertently measures his discipline against the older one of linguistics, which, he believes, needs to become aware of the "treasures that language puts at the disposal of psychology, . . . but only a psychology that behaves just like historical linguistics does in its field; that is, it strives "to abstract concepts and laws from the facts, being led in turn by those concepts and laws to further interpretation of the facts" (20). Like other researchers who propound this particular description of scientific method, Wundt fails to notice that he proposes a self-referential circle, a snake biting its tail.

Delbrück, by contrast, attempts to step outside the self-referential circle by taking a relativistic position toward the enterprise Wundt defines as "scientific psychology." Delbrück sees disciplinary flux and uneven development where Wundt envisions fixity.[38] Freud's aphasia book can be read as shifting its position along a fluid boundary between those two versions of what science is. Delbrück, of course, has no need to defend the legitimacy of his old and established field. He traces the genealogy of psychological linguistics he finds most congenial: from Steinthal to Hermann Paul. Herbart's view of the unconscious, from which Steinthal's is derived, Delbrück describes as the place where *Vorstellungen* that have dropped out of consciousness are preserved, having sunk "beneath the threshold of consciousness, into the dark space of the unconscious, from which they surface again at the appropriate time" (*Sprachforschung* 28). Steinthal views the unconscious as a field of intertwined associations that drive and regulate the body and the mind; he also imagines, between consciousness and the unconscious, a transition stage in which language is still retained. This linguistic tradition provides a context out of which a theory such as Freud's early view on the preconscious could comfortably grow. Thus two disciplinary veins have by this point carried Steinthal's theories to Freud: the medical via Kussmaul and the linguistic via Delbrück.

Delbrück quotes most extensively, however, from Hermann Paul, the linguist to whose ideas he is most indebted, as is clear from the appearance of those ideas in the lecture Freud read. Delbrück quotes Paul on the importance for linguistics of Steinthal's theory of the active unconscious and on the association of psychic processes in the unconscious. Among the relationships retained in the subconscious, according to Paul, are syntax and sound patterns in association with their thought content. Delbrück goes on to quote Paul's view that "psychic organisms"[39] are the carriers of historical development. It is wrong, according to Paul, to maintain that a

---

38. Delbrück also adheres to a cultural relativism that imputes for the purposes of linguistics equal status to "a play by [Gerhart] Hauptmann," "the Veda," or "the Chinese or Hottentot language" (Sprachforschung 4). This view contradicts the cultural hierarchy assumed by other researchers consulted by Freud, such as Kussmaul and James Ross (see Chapter 3).
39. Delbrück, *Sprachforschung*, 30; from Hermann Paul, *Prinzipien der Sprachgeschichte*, reprint of the 7th unchanged ed. (Tübingen: Niemeyer, 1966), 28. The first edition of Paul's book was published in 1880; the second (1886) included significant changes. Later editions (third in 1898, fourth in 1909, and fifth in 1920) did not affect the first chapter, with which I am concerned here. Thus, in historical time, it would have been possible for Freud to have seen the second edition before he wrote the aphasia book. There is an English translation, *Principles of the History of Language*, trans. H. A. Strong from the 2d ed. (New York: Macmillan, 1889), whose usage, however, is outdated; I have therefore made my own.

word has evolved from an earlier form. Individual words as "physiological-physical" products disappear. Their traces, like the traces of sounds and the movements of speech, are retained and transmitted only in the "psychic organism." Beginning with language as "organized" in the unconscious, Paul has developed and named a concept, associated with mind, that encompasses the language function and serves as the only collective transmitter of language, and therefore as the carrier of history. Paul's "organism" is dynamic, undergoing in every individual a continuous process of change. In addition, each individual's version is unique, having developed differently and changed under varied influences, its components all the while entering into shifting "power relationships to one another." Every individual "organism" is "infinitely changeable," which means "necessarily" that language is infinitely changeable as well (Paul 28). Mutability and transformation are built in. There are family resemblances between Paul's still-inchoate "organism" and Freud's "language apparatus"—a neurological construct he offers as his main contribution to aphasia theory. The most important difference is that Paul is concerned only with the normal case, whereas Freud is concerned with pathology. To attempt to explain language pathology, neurological description is required; with its addition, the tension appears once again between indeterminacy as in Paul's model and the determinacy of a brain anatomic model.

The congruence of description between Paul and Freud extends further. It includes what might be called "scientific attitude," for example, Paul's acknowledgment that the infinite complexity of language relationships requires a humble recognition of the impossibility of final explanations, which is also Freud's attitude in the aphasia book toward language phenomena. It includes Paul's prescription for "self-observation" to learn about the "psychic" aspect of language activity (30), a prescription Freud follows in the aphasia book. Otherwise, Paul's prescription for analysis includes those methods, such as observing ordinary speech in living languages, set out by Delbrück in his lecture. It is not remarkable to find overlap among contemporaneous researchers in different fields. What is noteworthy is that, based on acceptance of the unconscious, Freud stands so much closer to the linguists Paul and Delbrück than to the psychologist Wundt.

Freud makes no reference to the unconscious in his aphasia book. Only several years later, in *Studies on Hysteria*, does his point of departure for his description of the organization of pathogenic material in his section

"On the Psychotherapy of Hysteria" revisit, in a transformed setting, the terms in which Paul describes the unconscious. Elucidating Steinthal's view, Paul describes the unconscious as "a highly complex psychic formation [*Gebilde*] that consists of manifold intertwined groups of *Vorstellungen*."[40] In *Studies*, Freud writes: "The psychic material of such a hysteria presents itself as a multidimensional formation [*Gebilde*] with at least three strata" (*SE* 2:288; *GW* 1:291). (I was unable to use the *SE* translation in this case, in particular because of the recurrence of the term *Gebilde*.) Freud is describing the pathology of hysteria; Paul is describing the form that language takes in the unconscious. In Paul's version, no *Vorstellung*, once introduced into consciousness through language activity, is ever lost. Given the proper combination of circumstances, it will become conscious again. Whether it be the sounds or the motor movements of speech, or meanings of words, or syntactic relations, or whole sentences, the "groups" established in the outside world "organize themselves" into richer and more complicated connections in the unconscious mind. Sayings, case endings, verb tenses, parts of speech, and so on form associations among themselves, *although not necessarily according to established grammatical categories*. This last point leaves an opening for other principles of association. All told, the Steinthal/Paul narrative of the linguistic unconscious fits quite comfortably into the discursive framework of Freud's later narratives, such as in *The Interpretation of Dreams*, *The Psychopathology of Everyday Life*, and *Jokes and Their Relation to the Unconscious*.

There is, nevertheless, a telling difference between Paul's narrative, on the one hand, and Delbrück's and Freud's on the other. Only Delbrück's and Freud's narratives are self-referential; that is, they reflect on their own language. In the section of *Studies on Hysteria* quoted above, Freud shows anxiety about the metaphorical nature of his descriptions. In the aphasia book he deals with the nontransferability of descriptive terminology, and he comments on his own discursive choices. Delbrück, like Hughlings Jackson, is sensitive to metaphor and to the arbitrary nature of descriptive choice in scientific discourse. With the reference to Delbrück so early in the aphasia book, Freud may have been—knowingly or not—preparing the ground for his own sense of how language works. Delbrück is mentioned even before Freud's lengthy critique of Meynert's theorizing from brain anatomy, and thus he belongs to the preparatory material rather than to the heart of Freud's argument. But Delbrück's critical interrogation of

40. Paul, *Sprachgeschichte*, 25. The excess of meaning in the term *Vorstellung* is indicated by Paul's footnote explaining what meanings he intends in his use of *Vorstellung* (26).

positivistic assumptions, his disciplinary relativism, and his adherence to the Steinthal/Paul view of language and the unconscious all made an appearance between the lines of the lecture Freud read and may answer the question Why Delbrück? by pointing beyond the aphasia book toward the future evolution of Freud's thinking.

3

TOWARD PSYCHOANALYSIS

James Ross (1837–1892), physician in Manchester and Fellow of the Royal College of Physicians, was author of a study called *On Aphasia*, to which Freud made three scattered references in his text.[1] All three of these references are in the notes, but in one case the note lacks a corresponding number in the text, so its exact location on the page is uncertain. The slightness of these references belies the closeness of the two men's views. After I describe Freud's references to Ross's book, I look at the Ross text in some detail because it seems as if the confluence between Freud's and Ross's thinking is considerably more extensive than Freud's references indicate. Ross's writing is lucid; his treatment of the issues, balanced and pragmatic; and his views, compatible with Freud's across a broad range of theory. The overlap is so significant as to suggest the question What did Freud add to Ross? That is, What spin did Freud give to the spiral of accumulating theory on aphasia to make his contribution his own rather than a recasting in the German language of Ross's views?

1. James Ross, *On Aphasia: Being a Contribution to the Subject of the Dissolution of Speech from Cerebral Disease* (London: J. & A. Churchill, 1887). Ross also wrote "the first large modern textbook in English" on diseases of the nervous system: *A Treatise on the Diseases of the Nervous System*, 1881. *The Dictionary of National Biography*, ed. Leslie Stephen and Sidney Lee, vol. 17 (London: Oxford University Press, 1921–1922), 265.

Ross is one of the canonical list of names that opened Freud's aphasia book. The first mention of Ross (*AA* 23) occurs where Freud mentions a type of sensory aphasia in which the patient, unable to speak a single comprehensible word, produces instead an "inexhaustible series" of non-sense syllables. Freud writes that this syndrome may be called "gibberish" or it may be called "jargon aphasia," as the "English authors" call it. The Ross note follows the words "jargon aphasia." Ross does indeed use this term and further clarifies it as a compound disorder (Ross 70). The second mention of Ross is in the footnote (*AA* 33) for which Freud (or the publisher) neglected to include a note number in the text. The most likely place for the reference is where Freud mentions cases of sensory aphasia in which the patient retains the capacity for spontaneous, but nevertheless incorrect, speech—a point that would make sense as a reference back to Ross's explication of jargon aphasia. The third mention is of one of Ross's cases (Ross 19), to which Freud refers as one of several examples in an informational footnote. Freud's version is an accurate rendering of Ross's report of the case (*AA* 88). All together, these references do not add up to a picture of significant influence.

A noteworthy error interjects itself into the Freud/Ross connection: Freud has an incorrect footnote reference to another leading British aphasia researcher, William Henry Broadbent.[2] Broadbent is the object of an apologetic reference in the preface to Ross's book. Ross explains that in the last part of his book he has leveled what amounts to a polemic against Broadbent, who is a "distinguished author" whose opinions Ross considers important. But, writes Ross, "he belongs to a school of psychologists which manifests a tendency to break up the human mind into numerous faculties, with their corresponding cortical centres, and it is as the highest exponent of this school that his views are here singled out for adverse comment."[3] In other words, Broadbent advocates the very principles that are the target of Freud's book. Broadbent also writes of "Idea Centres" and "Naming Centres" (494). He claims that "the set of cells called into action in the utterance of a given word will constitute . . . a 'word-group' " (492). This claim is refuted by Freud, Hughlings Jackson, and others.

2. Broadbent was a physician at St. Mary's Hospital; his "A Case of Peculiar Affection of Speech with Commentary," *Brain* 1 (1878–1879): 484–503, was discussed in Ross, then incorrectly cited in Freud.
3. There is a parallel to Ross's comment on Broadbent in the comment Freud made about Wernicke in the letter to Ludwig Binswanger in 1911 (see above, Chapter 2, note 2). Freud wrote about Wernicke that he "was a brain anatomist and could not refrain from dissecting the mind [*die Seele*] into sections like the brain." *Sigmund Freud, Ludwig Binswanger,* 86.

Although Freud, like Ross,[4] rejects these views of Broadbent's, he nevertheless uses Broadbent in an evidentiary capacity instead of including him among the opponents, just as he overlooked the diagram making and localizationist views of Bastian. Beyond that, Freud's footnote reference to Broadbent's article uses it to support the claim that Freud has taken from Hughlings Jackson, that language loss is by "dissolution" or reverse evolutionary order, with those features lost first which are the latest acquired, most specific, least generalized, least embedded in associations. Thus nouns tend to be lost first, followed by adjectives, then verbs. Broadbent presents an opposing theory, namely, that the parts of speech, such as nouns, are lost individually when the centers where they are located are damaged. Thus, in Broadbent's theory, there is no sequential loss according to part of speech; nouns are lost only when a lesion occurs in the "naming center."[5] Beyond the strangeness of an apparent misreading of Broadbent's views, Freud's reference is to a page in Broadbent's article (494) where the topic is not even treated. A possible explanation for Freud's error is the fact that Ross quotes extensively from this very page in Broadbent's article, and Ross's footnote lists page 494. Perhaps Freud knew Broadbent's work only or primarily through Ross's discussion. That possibility leaves unanswered, however, the question of Freud's misreading of Broadbent's main point. Freud may simply not have been attentive to the pages of quotation from Broadbent, or, the momentum of his agreement with Ross may have lead him to overlook the contradictory information from Broadbent.

Ross is a thorough researcher like Freud and draws on the same sources: Bastian, Bernard, Charcot, Exner, Graves, Jackson, Otto Kahler, Kussmaul, Valentin M. Magnan, Hermann Munk, Nothnagel, William Ogle, Arnold Pick, Spamer, Watteville, and others, including, of course, Wernicke and Lichtheim (although not Grashey or the Americans Hammond and Starr). He relies most heavily on Bastian, Jackson, and Kussmaul.

4. Ross writes: "We may at once state our disbelief in the possibility of parcelling out the nervous structure in the cortex of the brain, the activity of which is the correlate of the process of thought, into distinct centres, each having a separate faculty, such as naming, ideation, and propositioning" (123).
5. Ross presents the case as follows: "Is it true that an individual may lose the use of concrete nouns while the other parts of speech remain unimpaired? We do not believe it. The case described by Dr. Broadbent as 'loss of nouns,' and other similar cases, merely show that the whole structure of language has been damaged, and in such cases the only words left to the individual are those which have been most frequently used in his experience, and which have, therefore, become most deeply organised in him. In these cases there is a dissolution of language, in which the most special parts are the first, and the most general the last to disappear, and if concrete nouns disappear in greater degree than other parts of speech, it is chiefly because they form a very special part of language" (111).

From Kussmaul's book, Ross adopts a taxonomy of types of aphasia as well as Kussmaul's elegant diagram; from Jackson, the theory of dissolution of functions; and from Bastian, the theory that "words are revived in the cerebral hemispheres as *remembered sounds.*"[6] Ross continues in a footnote that Bastian's thesis stands

> in opposition to the hypothesis advanced by Bain, and adopted by Hughlings-Jackson, that the material of our recollection is a *suppressed articulation*. If the latter hypothesis were true, both the amnesic and so-called ataxic disorders of speech would necessarily be caused by lesion of the motor mechanism of speech; while, if the former be accepted, the amnesic disorders will be caused, as we now know they are caused, by lesion of the cortical cerebral centres. Dr. Bastian's theory is tacitly adopted throughout these pages; it has, indeed, become so much the common property of psychologists that we are apt to forget to whom we owe its first enunciation, or rather, its first application to the explanation of the phenomena of aphasia. The theory itself had already, as is acknowledged by Dr. Bastian, been briefly, but very distinctly, stated by Mr. Herbert Spencer. (114)

This encomium sheds some light on Bastian's prominence in Freud's book, but Ross's terms also suggest a network of ideas on aphasia which intersect differently in Freud's thinking. Yes, for Freud the auditory function is the key to language learning and remembering. Yet the term *suppressed articulation* to designate the opposing (i.e., Jacksonian) view suggests another element that could have had an impact on Freud's long-term thinking about language, memory, and repression. Finally, we are reminded once again that Spencer, although Freud never mentions him, echoes through the aphasia book as an ancestral presence.

Ross makes a definite distinction between a functional versus an organic brain injury. Like Freud, he believes that injury has regional, or sympathetic, effects that radiate beyond the specific site. Symptoms may occur which cannot be correlated directly with the lesion. Although Ross's description lacks the precision of Freud's and makes assumptions that Freud does not make, there is, nevertheless, in Ross's more rudimentary version, a clear anticipation of the basic concept that Freud develops in the aphasia book:

6. Ross writes that Bastian made "the next great advance in the appreciation of the differences between these two forms of speech disorder ['motor and apperceptive aphasia,' the latter being another term for sensory aphasia] in an altogether remarkable paper," which is Bastian, "Various Forms of Loss of Speech" (Ross 113).

The slightest consideration of the mechanism of speech will, however, render it manifest that the disability will not be limited to this faculty, but that all the faculties, the nervous mechanisms of which lie in front the the main lesion, will be thrown into disorder. . . . Interruption of continuity of any portion of these routes will damage not only the function of the local part injured, but will throw into disorder all the parts which lie anterior to the lesion. (12)

But although it is proved that lesion of the posterior part of the third left and in occasional cases of the third right frontal convolution gives rise to a motor aphasia, it does not follow that this disorder of speech may not be caused by disease of other parts of the brain. (59)

Differences between Ross and Freud are revealed by looking at the way Ross read an article by C. Giraudeau,[7] as opposed to the way Freud read the same article, which suggests by what kinds of strategies he arrived at his central hypothesis. Ross provides a reading and translation of parts of Giraudeau's case. Aside from several minor errors in translation (age of the patient as forty instead of forty-six, several plurals rendered as singular), Ross gives an accurate rendering of the introductory and "present condition" sections of the case. Yet he gives only a one-sentence summary of the autopsy findings and only the beginnings of an analysis of the nature of the patient's aphasia. His comments are so scanty that it is not clear why he felt it necessary to include the case at all.

Freud finds in the Giraudeau case definitive proof of his argument against Wernicke's and Lichtheim's distinction between injury to pathways and to centers. His method is to note that the expected consequences of a tumor at the location shown in Giraudeau's illustration of the brain section are not born out by the patient's actual symptoms. In the process of searching out what is suspect, that is, how visual evidence does not coincide with narrative expectations, Freud teased out unstated meanings in Giraudeau's article, meanings the author himself either did not detect or found of no interest. Freud accomplishes his analysis in a complex rhetorical setting of dismantling of authorities. In other words, the process of discovery is driven by motivations rooted in Freud's persona at this time: discovery is always implicated in a web of feelings, drives, and cultural values, masculinity being not the least of them. These imbrications, intri-

7. C. Giraudeau, "Note sur un case de surdité cérébrale (surdité psychique) par lésion des deux premières circonvolutions temporo-sphénoïdales gauches," *Revue de Médecine* 2 (1882): 446–452.

cate folds of cultural inspiration and meaning, offer both an explanation for Freud's departure from Ross in the Giraudeau case and the answer to the question I posed earlier: What did Freud add to the ideas of his intellectual mentors?

Freud's argument can be divided into four parts. First, before taking up the Giraudeau case, Freud describes the patient whose case supported Lichtheim's argument. To get the flavor of Freud's rhetorical positioning, it is necessary to look at exactly how he phrases his reaction to Lichtheim's evidence for a case that supports the notion, presented in Lichtheim's diagram, of a separate auditory pathway for speech. Freud's tone is definitely not detached, but highly inflected. His language is marked by qualifications, even sarcasm (indicated in the following quotation by my italics), while appearing to accept Lichtheim's results:

> I *confess* that in view of the importance of the "sound images" for the use of language, it has been extremely difficult for me to attribute to this subcortical sensory aphasia another explanation that would dispense with the assumption of an afferent auditory pathway aA [a reference to Lichtheim's diagram]. *I was already on the verge* of explaining this case of Lichtheim's through individual independence of other speech elements from the sound images, since Lichtheim's patient was a highly educated journalist. This, however, *would rightly have been seen as nothing but an evasion.*
>
> Thus I searched the literature for similar cases. Wernicke, in reviewing the Lichtheim paper, stated that he had made a completely analogous observation and would communicate it in the regular reports from his clinic. However, *I have been so unskilled as to be unable to find* this communication in the literature. On the other hand I did come across a case of Giraudeau's that at least strongly resembles the Lichtheim case. (*AA* 70–71)

From this point in the text, where he has set up Lichtheim for defeat, Freud goes on to his second part, summarizing the Giraudeau case in his own words, exposing certain failings in Lichtheim's report of his case but otherwise stressing the similarities between the two.

Next Freud turns to the autopsy results and makes two observations that constitute to last two parts of his argument. One is that Giraudeau's illustration of the location of the fatal tumor in the patient's brain is inconsistent with the extent of the patient's symptoms, which included difficulty in comprehending what was said to her. Freud has structured his treatment of this issue like a mystery, finally arriving at the telling evidence: "No one who glances at the drawing included in Giraudeau's communication would be able to suspect that this lesion caused anything other than the usual form of sensory aphasia with serious speech disturbance. But there is something else to be considered." One knockout blow is followed by a second: his observation about the nature of the tumor's growth and its easy separability from surrounding tissue. Thus Freud adds together the external and the internal evidence to arrive at a conclusion that supports his thesis: "I therefore believe I am justified in assuming that subcortical sensory aphasia is due not to a lesion of the subcortical pathway aA but rather to damage to the same area that is otherwise considered responsible for cortical sensory aphasia. However, I cannot completely explain the specific functional condition that I must presume to exist at the site thus affected" (*AA* 72).

The centrality of this argument, and thus of Giraudeau's case, to Freud is indicated by a very long footnote he added while reviewing the proofs of his book. There he adds evidence from another case published after he had submitted his manuscript. This evidence suggests further refinement of the diagnosis and supports Freud's interpretation. Much hangs on this question because on it rests the case for functionalism which is Freud's claim for the contribution his book makes to the field.

In his close reading and critical analysis of the Giraudeau case and its rhetorical positioning in his argument, as well as its structuring as a mystery whose solution proves Lichtheim the perpetrator of error, we can find the writing power that distinguished Freud from many of his fellows and mentors. Their longer works, such as Ross's, Kussmaul's, and Bastian's, were diffuse in argumentation and focus. They went in many directions at once, were often internally inconsistent, and failed to pursue promising lines of argument, as in the example of Ross's treatment of the Giraudeau case. Freud, however, forced the logic of his case, building it like a hard-hitting prosecutor who leaves no evidentiary stone unturned, trying to draw readers to his side by positioning himself as a humble truth seeker who stumbles almost fortuitously across errors.

Among the suggestive points Ross makes is that aphasia can also be "a well recognised symptom of hysteria" (51). Another is his notion of paraphasia, for which he uses the same example Delbrück did (published a year earlier), but, like Freud, proposes a rather simplistic interpretation compared with the complexity of Delbrück's linguistic theory. In this example the disciplinary gap prevails: "A person, for example, who forgets the name of 'scissors,' may say 'the thing you cut with,' or of a 'chair' 'that you sit on.' When a wrong name is substituted for the right one, the former is generally connected with the latter by similarity in sound or meaning, or by frequent association in the use of the objects represented by the words. The patient may, for example, say 'butter' instead of 'mother' " (Ross 80). Delbrück had used the scissors/cut example to prove the greater generalizing power of verbs and, therefore, their retention when the more specific nouns were lost, thus tying the manifestation of disease to grammar and syntax. Ross's use of examples for paraphasia, like Freud's, demonstrates that ignoring linguistic explanation reduces the analysis and makes it more shallow. The "butter"/"mother" example is not particularly convincing, either in terms of sound or association, and certainly not when compared with Delbrück's example of the melding of "Vater" and "Mutter" into "Vutter," with its suggestion of subconscious meaning.

Ross, like Kussmaul, does, however, show an informed and sophisticated interest in historical linguistics. As did Freud, Ross sees evidence for phylogony in ontogeny, the course of "civilization" in a development from animal and infant to adult. One of Ross's most "Freudian" linguistic examples is the sound "ma-ma," which Ross does not see as the infant calling the mother by a name. Rather,

> it is probable that it is associated in the infantile mind with the pleasant sensations which contact with the mother, and especially with the breast of the mother, brings along with it, and consequently the signification of the word *ma* in the mind of the infant is more nearly expressed by the imperative mood of the verb "to come" than by our general name "mother." The signals of the social animals teach us a similar lesson. (111)

This theory is part of Ross's refutation of the idea, prevailing "even amongst cultivated psychologists," that historically nouns originated before other parts of speech. Ross accepts the thesis of the "science of language" that "the language of aboriginal man consisted almost entirely of verbs, demonstrative pronouns, and a few adverbs of time and place" (112), with the naming of objects being a later development. With the example of "mother," Ross seems to be providing Freud with a suggestive entry point, via language, for the idea of the infant-object relationship into the web of diachronic and synchronic interpretation that combined brain anatomy and physiology with historical linguistics, archaeology, anthropology, and aphasia studies.

The "law of dissolution," as Ross calls it, or a process of clinical disintegration that reverses evolution, is a product not only of Darwin, philosophers, and neurologists but also of mid to late nineteenth-century Britain, its class structures, and its imperialist certainties. In view of this background of an idea with such wide-ranging effects, the question arises. How far did Freud follow its implications? Did he adopt for his aphasia book the full range of cultural associations? In the case histories reported by Ross, as well as by Hughlings Jackson and the other British aphasiologists, connections are invariably made between the patients' speech patterns and social class. Those patients are commonly working or servant class, sometimes middle class or artisan, rarely, if ever, upper class. Class distinctions were mirrored in language—in accent or dialect, vocabulary, and grammar. The manifestations of illness in language will necessarily be, among other things, a function of the patient's social class. Thus aphasia theory as developed in Britain must inevitably be inflected by a class component.

Freud seems to have recast the British class component in the terms of his own social setting. In the context of the case history of an attorney with aphasia, Freud wrote: "It is to be expected that some symptoms of aphasia will be manifested differently in highly educated persons from the way they are manifested in those who are less articulate" (*AA* 90). He made a similar observation with regard to one of Lichtheim's patients. I see the category "education" as one that overlays and disrupts the category of class for Freud, as it necessarily would for Jews in Vienna, whose road to eminence lay in education (if they were not supremely wealthy converts).[8] A Jew was outside the categories of inherited class; thus education had to take precedence over class as determined at birth. This situation would produce a kind of freedom from class-determined attitudes, at the same time making one exquisitely conscious of acknowledgment of merit.

Turning again to Ross, we can trace medical/scientific theory as it expands to an ever widening circle of implications or, viewed centripetally, as it shows itself to be the nucleus of an integrated system of cultural metaphors. His central assumption is that "the inroads of disease conform, both as regards structure and function, to the law of dissolution; the mode of invasion being from the complex to the simple, and from the special to the general." Ross takes this central thesis to the level of the cell:

8. Steven Beller writes extensively on this topic in *Vienna and the Jews, 1867–1938: A Cultural History* (Cambridge: Cambridge University Press, 1989).

On examining the structure of the cortex of the brain, it will be seen that it is composed of several super-imposed layers of cells; and that the cells near the surface are destitute of processes, and therefore do not form any definite connection with one another, while the cells of the internal layers have numerous processes, by means of which they become connected with one another, and some of them even with the motor ganglion cells of the medulla oblongata and the spinal cord. Now the nervous impulses regulating actions, *which are frequently repeated in the experience of the individual and of the race*, tend to pass more and more with each repetition through the caudate cells of the cortex, and these being, as we have seen, definitely connected with one another, the nervous impulses pass through them without meeting much resistance, and the less the resistance offered to the passage of the impulses, the less is the resulting action attended by consciousness. Such actions are sometimes called automatic and at other times reflex actions of the brain, but *they really are psychical actions* which are effected in an unconscious manner. But the impulses which regulate unaccustomed actions must pass through unused channels, or in other words, must pass through the round cells near the surface of the cortex which have not formed definite connections with one another. In passing through these cells, the impulses meet with a considerable degree of resistance, and much of the force generated is expended, not in effecting the desired action, but in producing a new organisation in the round cells of the cortex, and this is the process which is the correlation of consciousness. (102; my emphasis)

A metaphor of surface versus interior directs the opening of Ross's narrative. He observes what the theory of dissolution suggests, and the theory necessarily poses limits to his interpretive conclusions from observation. Two crucial moves Ross makes, and on which his larger cultural assumptions will rest, are: In the first sentence quoted above, he extrapolates brain physiology to support the theory of dissolution. Then, immediately, he expands the entire structure to apply to the "the race"—a conventional Lamarkian assumption of the time, which implies a "racial" consciousness. (Here the implication is "human race," which correlates, we will see, with "European race.") The repetitive passages of nervous impulses that create consciousness must, therefore, also inscribe a heritable memory trace in the history of the "race." By contrast Freud, in his aphasia book, is chary of connecting the psychic to brain physiology and suscribes, rather, to Jackson's insistence on the separated course of the two. But the description of nervous impulses, resistance, used versus unused channels, and force expended in the generation of consciousness, are all reworked in Freud's exploration of brain function and the psyche in his "Project" of 1895. The imagery recurs there as he attempts to explain the difference between perception and memory.

When Ross turns to the demonstration of dissolution in case histories, he makes explicit the implications in the theory: that dissolution from a higher to a lower level is equivalent to reverting from "the developed language of civilization" to "the first expressions of infancy, or of the thoughts which may be supposed to have been uttered by aboriginal man in his first attempt at articulate speech" (111). For the nineteenth-century scientists, "aboriginal man" also existed contemporaneously, in the guise of the "savage." The early stages of language development, comparable to the language of early childhood, also exist contemporaneously—according to Ross and his source, Max Müller[9]—in the Chinese language, which they see as similar in its construction to the aphasic patient's language that has undergone a process of dissolution.

Racism and imperialism inhere in the system of values that drives linguistic and scientific theory. Ross presumes three levels of development in human thinking capacity: from percept to concept to "thinking by abstracts" (125). The first level is shared with animals, infants, and the aboriginal humans of prehistory:

> Thinking, on the high level, has for its subject-matter the relations in which phenomena are presented to us when they are detached from all individual perceptions, and it can only be carried on by means of mathematical symbols and *abstract* nouns. It is quite manifest that thinking of this kind is beyond the reach, not only of the lower animals, but also of the lower races and the youth and uneducated of the higher races of mankind. Such words as "function" and "co-efficient" in mathematics, and "virtue" and "benevolence" in morals, are not even capable of being expressed in the languages of the inferior races, and can only have a vague meaning to all except those whose mental faculties are fully developed and highly educated. Thinking on the middle level is possible to

9. Ross quotes Müller in a footnote "The language of a child, which is in reality Chinese spoken in English . . . in which . . . the distinction between noun and verb . . . is not yet realised" (Ross's reference: Max Müller, "Lectures on the Science of Language," 2nd Series, Lecture 2, p. 84). Ross and Müller see Chinese as pregrammatical and at a earlier stage of development. Max Müller (1823–1900) was an influential popularizer of linguistic theories. Not only in his adopted home country of England, but also on the Continent, his views were accepted uncritically by some aphasiologists (e.g., Conrad Rieger; see the last section of this chapter).

every healthy man who has passed the age of early infancy, but not to any animal. . . . Aboriginal man, even before he had any general name for his fellow man, was, no doubt, able to form a perception of him as the lower animals do. (122)

Aside from the logical error of presuming that knowing a particular term or designation (in the English language) is the same as understanding mathematical or moral principles, we also find a replication of Kussmaul's type of example of the "savages" who know neither an alphabet nor counting and therefore have no use for Aristotle or Euclid. In England and on the Continent, science was practiced by men who had complete confidence in the superiority and right to domination of the culture they represented. It was "scientific" to draw conclusions about unknown peoples and to impose on the rest of the world a local hierarchy of values, at the top of which was mathematics. For both Ross and Kussmaul—operating inside of the metaphorical structure of levels—mathematics, virtue, development, and progress represent the highest level of humanity. These qualities could only be realized simultaneously in the white male scientist-citizen of the Western nations. Within this model, even the language of an ancient Asian high culture proved that culture to be on a lower rung of the ladder of development.

Like Starr, Ross notes that priority of discovery of several types of aphasia is erroneously attributed to Wernicke, when actually Broadbent (Starr writes "English authors") had published the results earlier (Ross 114). On the subject of the priority in time of the capacity to use verbs over the capacity to use nouns, Ross cites an early (1866) lecture of which he had not been aware: "Its perusal has convinced me that I have not done full justice to the share which my own countrymen have taken in differentiating motor and apperceptive aphasia" (112).[10] The nationalism in Ross, the overlap of assumptions of cultural imperialism in Kussmaul and Ross, the racism of which they both partook, the significance of Kussmaul's work to Ross, and of both to Freud suggest the complexity of intercultural transference, even within the circumscribed area of western Europe. Beyond the idea that Freud may (if unconsciously) have transmuted evidence of the English class system into more familiar, local distinctions, one is left with unanswerable questions about reading as such. To what extent is it possible to filter out cultural assumptions?

10. The reference is to a lecture by William Tennant Gairdner, "On the Function of Articulate Speech and on Its Connection with the Mind and Bodily Organs," in *Proceedings of the Philosophical Society of Glasgow* 6 (1868) 87–123, which was quoted extensively by Bastian

There is a group of texts that fell into a different category for Freud. One of these is a very brief report by Otto Heubner (1843–1926) to which Freud refers as often as to Hughlings Jackson, and more often than to other source texts with the exception of Bastian.[11] From it Freud had reprinted the only brain autopsy illustration he used in the aphasia book (*AA* 25). The Heubner case, as well as those of several other authors, are used exclusively for evidentiary purposes. These are reports of cases and of autopsies on which Freud relies heavily for support of his argument. They are different from work by authors such as Ross, Bastian, Kussmaul, or Hughlings Jackson, whose books or articles develop extended theoretical arguments. By contrast, the role of the evidentiary article is relatively clear-cut, usually depending, as in the Giraudeau case, on a disjunction between the nature and location of a lesion or lesions as predicted by a patient's symptoms, on the one hand, and the actual location as shown in the brain autopsy, on the other.

At the July 16, 1889, meeting of the Leipzig medical society, Heubner reviewed the case of a patient whom he had presented to the group in November 1888 and presented the patient's autopsy report. While the patient was alive, Heubner's judgment of the location of the brain lesion had been based on Wernicke's views. The autopsy, however, proved the location to be different from that predicted by these views. The result caused Heubner to raise a question about the theories of localization. This question, which is quoted in entirety by Freud, takes a bold and suggestive leap, raising the same fundamental objection Freud raises.

Heubner's conclusion (222) points to the discrepancy between the relatively small and confined area of the lesions and the patient's massive "functional disturbance." The main tumor surrounded and encased a small area of the cortex adjacent to the language regions of the brain, severing its cerebral connections on three sides, without damaging the encased area. A very small ("lentil-size") tumor was located in a different area. The patient, however, had suffered from loss of the ability to produce spontaneous speech, to comprehend speech, and to comprehend written language. He retained the ability to repeat spoken language, to write dictation, to write spontaneously, and to read aloud. Nevertheless, he had

"Loss of Speech in Cerebral Disease," 481, who used it to support the priority of "internal association of ideas" over "volition" in aphasics in explanation of "amnesic" (sensory) aphasia.

11. Otto Heubner, "Über Aphasie," *Schmidts Jahrbücher der in-und ausländischen gesammten Medicin*, vol. 224, ed. Paul Julius Möbius and Hugo Dippe (Leipzig: Otto Wigand, 1889), 220–222.

no grasp of the meaning of what he wrote or read. He also suffered from the inability to connect words with objects.

The problem Freud is addressing when he draws on Heubner is Lichtheim's theory of "transcortical motor aphasia" and "transcortical sensory aphasia," which attributes the syndrome described above to the interruption of two separate pathways. The small tumor in the motor area was too insignificant to have caused the massive symptoms. They can be explained only by the larger tumor located in the sensory area. Thus, contrary to Lichtheim's prediction, a "transcortical sensory lesion" (*AA* 25–26) that severs and isolates the sensory area also causes the loss of spontaneous speech (a "motor" defect), meaning that the two separate pathways Lichtheim proposes are actually identical, or "that speech is produced only via the sound images" (*AA* 26).

It is not possible to exaggerate the importance to Freud of Heubner's observations. Freud writes that he will refer to them again many times because of their great significance. He does so seven more times in the aphasia book, weaving them in again and again as evidence in support of his case. He concludes several pages of discussion with the summary observation:

> We now note that we have arrived at the point where we can explain a clinically observed form of language disturbance by a change in functional condition instead of by a localized interruption of a pathway. Since this step is so important for the entire understanding of aphasia, we want to repeat, for the sake of our own reassurance, that we were compelled to drop the localizing explanation because the autopsy findings (Heubner, Hammond) contradicted it. The assumption we have decided to make, along with Ch. Bastian, appears to us to derive naturally from the fact that [the capacity for] repetition always remains intact longer than [the capacity for] spontaneous speech. Later we will become acquainted with facts that will also demonstrate to us that the associative action of a center is less easily lost than the so-called "spontaneous" [action]. (*AA* 30)

Freud's rhetorical posture is that of the "victim of circumstances," or the purely objective scientist, who is "compelled" or "forced" [*genötigt*] by incontrovertible physical evidence (the autopsy) to relinquish the prevailing explanatory model. An important English theorist (Bastian) is marshaled in support, as well as the "natural" or "unforced" [*ungezwungen*] generation of new theory out of fact. Freud is approximately one-third of

Hel. Meisenbach Riffarth & Co.A=G, Berlin.   Verlag von Julius Springer, Berlin

Otto Heubner
from *Otto Heubners Lebenschronik*, ed. Wolfgang Heubner (Berlin: Julius Springer, 1927), title page.

the way through his book, but he has already presented the most telling evidence for his case. His strategy is to pause to make summary statements at crucial points, making sure that the impact of the evidence compiled thus far does not escape the reader. The importance of this strategy is shown when at the very end of the book he once again returns to the powerful Heubner/Bastian team of evidence and theory, calling Heubner's case "nothing short of an indispensable support for our views" (*AA* 103) and presenting for the second time Bastian's scale of three pathological conditions of a speech center which describe types of functional change in response to lesions that cause partial destruction.

Freud takes yet a second important lesson from Heubner's mere two-and-a-half pages of discussion. In the aphasia book's fifth section where Freud is constructing his case for the relationship between the physiological and the psychological, he again brings in Heubner's case as the evidence. That is, Heubner's brief presentation at a medical meeting becomes foundational for Freud's discussion of brain and mind. Freud elevates the report of a researcher nearly unknown in aphasiology to a main pillar of his argument. This expansion of the use of a piece of evidence from the more specific and limited to the more general application traces the path of Freud's entire argumentative strategy. In the aphasia book we see this writing strategy in microcosm, as if this intricate text were also the story of Freud's work to come. The more one looks at the aphasia book in terms of patterns of argument, the more one sees in it the entire Freud. As with Delbrück, however, the question remains, Why Heubner?

Freud was likely to have been alerted to the Heubner piece by a reference he saw elsewhere. But there is also a deeper connection, as in the case of Delbrück, of "elective affinities," [12] of unconventional, defiant, or even quirky patterns of thought that attracted Freud. Otto Heubner, who late in life was called to the chair of pediatrics at the University of Berlin, eventually became the most well known pediatrician in Germany, after a medical career that—typically for the time—included experience in various specialties. Initially his interest was primarily in brain and nervous diseases. He was even offered the chair in psychiatry at his home university of Leipzig but turned it down because of the miserable (and apparently irremediable) state of therapy in the clinics and hospitals he had visited.[13] Heubner had personal contact with some of the figures who played an important role for Freud—Lichtheim, for example, and Grashey.[14] For

12. This is the title of a Goethe novel with which Freud was very familiar.
13. All biographical information comes from Heubner's posthumously published autobiography, *Otto Heubners Lebenschronik*, ed. and condensed by his son Wolfgang Heubner (Berlin: Julius Springer, 1927). It is a modest work that confines itself to personal, family, and career matters but also inadvertently sketches a portrait of political and social change. Heubner, a Prussian patriot and conservative of the old school, is appealing in his passionate commitment to quality in medical care, to children, to music, and to achieving his goals, often against great odds in the byzantine (and Machiavellian) world of academic medical politics.
14. Grashey was director of a large mental hospital in Deggendorf (in the Bavarian Forest) when Heubner paid a lengthy visit in 1876 to study the patients there. In an interesting

Heubner it was not unusual to be in the position of having to fight against great odds to accomplish his goals (for example, the building of Germany's largest children's hospital in Leipzig). A man of strikingly small stature, he was an effective political infighter whose proposals and plans often went against the grain of entrenched political interests. His spirited stance is reflected in the paper Freud read; for there Heubner allows himself to be led by the evidence to undercut not only the prevailing wisdom but also his own previous convictions.

I close my discussion of Freud's Section 3 with William Hammond, whose case histories Freud used relatively often, but for limited purposes, and with Bastian's important 1869 report. William A. Hammond, who had been surgeon general of the U.S. Army, professor of diseases of the mind and nervous system at the City University of New York, and seemed to have been awarded every honor that could be bestowed on an American physician, was not a newcomer in Freud's work. In 1887, Freud had published "Remarks on Cocaine Addiction and Fear of Cocaine, with Reference to a Lecture by W. A. Hammond," in which he drew on Hammond to defend himself against the critics of his cocaine papers. Freud was particularly defensive because he felt vulnerable to the justified attacks on his support of cocaine.[15] Therefore the positive results of Hammond's cocaine experiments were very welcome. It is thus not surprising that Freud, who referred to Hammond as the "well-known foreign authority" (col. 930), would later also check the chapter on aphasia in Hammond's basic medical textbook.[16] The twenty-four-page chapter consists of definitions, a historical overview, and fifteen case histories, several of them only a few sentences long. Freud uses three of Hammond's cases: no. 1 and no. 3 in conjunction with the Heubner case to disprove Lichtheim's theses, and no. 15 toward the end of the book when he is presenting Hughlings Jackson's principle of dissolution.

Freud uses Hammond's patient no. 15, who was captain of a ship, to

<hr />

historical note, Heubner (103–104) mentions that Grashey was later to become successor to Bernhard von Gudden, the Munich psychiatrist who drowned in Lake Starnberg with [and probably as victim of] King Ludwig II of Bavaria.

15. Sigmund Freud, "Bermerkungen über Cocainsucht und Cocainfurcht, mit Beziehung auf einen Vortrag W. A. Hammonds," *Wiener medizinische Wochenschrift* 37 (1887): cols. 929–932. In the end, Freud advises against the therapeutic use of cocaine (except as an anesthetic) because of the unpredictability of its vascular effects. One strange feature of his paper is a parenthetic remark in the first paragraph to the effect that the use of cocaine as a means of withdrawal from morphine addiction was not tested on Freud himself but rather merely advised by him. A second noteworthy point is his report that Hammond successfully treated women afflicted with "melancholy" by injecting them with cocaine.

16. William A. Hammond, *A Treatise on the Diseases of the Nervous System*, 7th ed. (New York: D. Appleton, 1881).

show that frequently used professional terminology may be retained even when a patient has lost all other naming speech. The captain designated all objects with names for the parts of a ship. Hammond remarks that the captain had no problems with parts of speech other than the nouns and when presented with a knife, for example, said it was something to cut with.[17] Hammond, however, does not theorize on such matters. Beyond therapy, his primary interest is to establish "that the organ of language is situated in both hemispheres, and in that part which is nourished by the middle cerebral artery," although he also believes the evidence shows "that the left side of the brain is more intimately connected with the faculty of speech than the right" (206). Freud chose to report Hammond's case no. 1 because Hammond described the autopsy findings, and case no. 3 because the surgery performed supported Hammond's diagnosis. That is to say, "hard" evidence against the Wernicke-Lichtheim hypotheses required physical examination of the brain. Freud honed in only on those few examples that were most valid from an evidentiary perspective.

We also see him operating in a well-defined discursive space not subject to contagion from, for example, either Heubner's or Hammond's key terms. Heubner uses the prefix *Seelen-*(soul-) to describe manifestations of aphasia, for example, *Seelenworttaubheit* (soul word deafness), *Seelenblindheit* (soul blindness), and *Seelenlähmung* (soul paralysis). These apply to the level of comprehension, or sensory aphasia, as opposed to the motor ability required to produce words. Freud used the term *Seele* elsewhere, and it became central to psychoanalysis, but it did not play a role in his descriptions of aphasia. With the support of Heubner's case, Freud refutes prevailing views, but he does so in their own terms. Hammond's diagnostic designation for sensory aphasia is "memory of words" (loss of), as opposed to "faculty of articulation" (loss of) for motor aphasia. These terms also do not appear in Freud's text, probably because of his awareness of the enormous complexity of the notion of memory, which Hughlings Jackson wrote about as a preeminent example of an imprecise term that handicapped the advance of neurological science. Freud was acutely sensible of the obstacles erected by description that is not self-conscious: with reference to Hammond's two cases he writes that the lesions were " 'transcortical' only in the sense of the term that makes it so unsuited for use in the theory of aphasia. [The lesion] consisted in one case of a hemorrhage over the motor center, in another of a bone fragment which had lodged in it" (*AA* 27).

---

17. Aphasiologists' frequent use of the example of sharp implements and the verb *to cut* is remarkable and might lend itself to analysis in terms of psychology and culture.

Beyond disproving Lichtheim's pathways theory, Freud uses the types of lesion involved in the cases of Heubner and Hammond (and one by Valentin Magnan)[18] to draw a broader conclusion about language capacity, one that anticipates early psychoanalysis:

> We know that the portions of the brain whose pathology reveals itself in any way as symptoms, will always only produce local symptoms, whereby it is up to us to guess the diagnosis of the process on the basis of accessory circumstances [*Nebenumständen*] or from the course of the disease. However, the language apparatus [*Sprachapparat*] disposes over such a wealth of means of expressing symptoms that we can expect from it alone that it will betray not only the site but also the nature of the lesion by the type and manner of disturbance of function. Perhaps we will succeed one day in clinically distinguishing aphasias caused by hemorrhage from those caused by softening, and in recognizing a series of speech disturbances as characteristic for special processes in the language apparatus. (*AA* 29)

This passage marks the beginning in the aphasia book of Freud's acknowledgment of the rich, almost infinite possibilities of language.

In the last pages of Section 3, Freud refers again and again to Bastian's work, showing how heavily he relied on it. With the why and the how of Freud's readings of Bastian, we approach the core of Freud's intellectual operations. His relationship with Bastian's work is a peculiar one because, as I indicated earlier, Bastian can be classified as a member of the very school of thought Freud had set out to oppose. Bastian's 1880 neurological magnum opus, which Freud cited, makes his stand clear: "The error of massing together all the varieties of 'loss of speech' under one name, such as 'Aphasia,' and then altogether rejecting doctrines of Cerebral Localization, because the lesions in such dissimilar cases have not always been found in some one part of the Brain, is manifest and absurd, and yet it is one which has been too often repeated in recent years."[19] Bastian's polemic indicates that over a decade before the publication of Freud's aphasia book, some researchers had been doing work that at least to some extent anticipated Freud's. Reading this passage, Freud would have found his theory called erroneous and absurd. Yet he did not turn away from Bastian.

18. Valentin M. Magnan, "On Simple Aphasia, and Aphasia with Incoherence," *Brain* 2 (1880): 112–123.
19. H. Charlton Bastian, *The Brain as an Organ of Mind* (New York: D. Appleton, 1880), 673–674.

Another passage in Bastian's book indicates the peculiarity of Bastian's logic which allowed his views at the same time to oppose and attract Freud. Bastian suggests that aphasia may result from a lesion at a distance from what he considers the language center (because a strictly localized impairment he calls "Amnesia" can merge by gradations into aphasia). "And if this were so," he writes, "such cases might have been quoted with much apparent effect against existing doctrines in regard to 'cerebral localization' (685). In other words, Bastian, with apparent lack of self-awareness, suggests how his own dogma may be undermined.

Seven years later, in the lecture "On Different Kinds of Aphasia" so often cited by Freud, Bastian has arrived at less dogmatic views on localization, and in some respects he has moved closer to Freud's views on the centers. Even though he does present reductive diagrams, he qualifies them by stating that he is "not a firm believer in the complete topographical distinctness of the several sensory or perceptive centres in the cerebral hemispheres."[20] Bastian was what one might call a mercurial thinker, rather than a rigorous, consistent one. His arguments are not crafted, do not follow step by step in logical progression as Freud's do; nor does he develop rhetorical strategies. He often contradicts himself. Yet Freud, like a prospector, sifted through the writings of this quirky British scientist, dipping for the nuggets of insight.

From one of Freud's many references to cases quoted by Bastian we learn that he read yet a third treatise by Bastian,[21] in addition to the text he most frequently cites and *The Brain as an Organ of Mind*. Bastian quotes extensively from his two earlier texts in the 1887 lecture, and Freud read them carefully as well, which makes it necessary to explore beyond the lecture if we are to determine what special factors drew Freud to Bastian.

At the end of the third section of his aphasia book, the most interesting element for Freud is Bastian's tripartite categorization (originating with *The Brain as an Organ of Mind*) of the "excitability" of auditory and visual speech centers: they function either in reaction to external stimuli, or through a process of association (with another center), or by a "voluntary" recall. Under the influence of illness or damage, the capacity is lost in reverse order. That is, first a patient will be unable to recall language voluntarily; with more severe damage, ability to associate will disappear; and finally, the most severe damage will lead to incapacity even to respond

20. See above, Chapter 2, note 9; 933, col. 1.
21. Bastian, "Loss of Speech in Cerebral Disease."

to external stimuli (such as dictation or reading aloud). Freud uses these categories to explain the nature of the functional changes that result from less than completely destructive lesions. That is to say that Bastian provided Freud with an organizing principle that gives substance to his hypothesis. Without Bastian, he could have maintained that functional changes existed but not described them.

The power of Bastian's categories is demonstrated by Freud's direct reference in the "Miss Lucy R." case in *Studies on Hysteria:* "The fact that in looking for numbers and dates our choice is so limited enables us to call to our help a proposition familiar to us from the theory of aphasia, namely that recognizing something is a lighter task for memory than thinking of it spontaneously" (*SE* 2:111–112; *GW* 1:169). In an integrative gesture to bring together the theories on which he chiefly relies, Freud ties Bastian to Hughlings Jackson by pointing out that Bastian's categories "also represent to a certain extent degrees of disinvolution" (*AA* 135). This is a particularly notable move on Freud's part in view of the fact that Bastian took pains to distance himself from Jackson. We see Freud exercising creative control by selecting, manipulating, and combining according to his own lights. Sometimes, as with Bastian, Freud will disregard even a researcher's basic principles.

Freud's rhetorical procedures alert us to the importance of Bastian. Although Freud hardly ever used the first name of an author, he introduces Bastian in his second appearance in the aphasia book as "Charlton Bastian," and on several later occasions he still writes "Ch. Bastian." Later Freud christens Bastian's categories the "Bastianian modifications." Finally, we see that Freud, characteristically, is drawn to an idea that goes against the grain, that seems to subvert its own narrative home. He writes: "At first of course there is something strange about Bastian's assumption; it stands as something unexpected in relation to a thought process [i.e., Bastian's] that concerns itself with circumspect lesions and their effects" (*AA* 31). As with Heubner, Freud is drawn to an insight that stands out like a foreign body from the rest of the text. Where did the insight come from, when the author neither prepared for it nor explained it? Perhaps inspiration, like a separate intelligence, has welled up out of the unconscious. Freud might have had an eye for such a phenomenon, as he demonstrated in *Studies on Hysteria.*

Freud's comment on the unexpectedness of Bastian's thesis opens passages that show Freud translating Bastian's ideas from the context of aphasia to a context of psychoanalysis before the fact:

To begin with, one would think that a reduction in excitability of a center would not need to be explained by a lesion; it appears to us as a purely "functional" condition. That is correct and there may be conditions similar to transcortical motor aphasia which result from mere functional impairment without organic lesion. However, if one considers the relationship of "organic lesion" to "functional disturbance," one must understand that a whole series of organic lesions can only manifest themselves through functional disturbances, and experience shows that these lesions in fact do just that. For decades we have been guided by the attempt to utilize the disturbances we see in clinical practice for understanding the localization of functions and have become accustomed to expecting an organic lesion to completely destroy a portion of the elements of the nervous system, while leaving the other parts completely undamaged, because only then is it [the lesion] exploitable for our purposes. Only a few lesions fulfill these requirements. Most are not directly destructive and draw a larger number of elements into the region of their disturbing effects.

Furthermore, one must consider the relationship of an incompletely destructive lesion to the apparatus which it has afflicted. Two cases are conceivable which are also found in reality. Either individual parts of the apparatus are maimed by the lesion while the intact parts continue to function in the usual manner, or it [the apparatus] reacts to the lesion *as a whole in solidarity*, does not reveal the loss of individual parts, but rather proves itself to be weakened in its function; *it responds to the incompletely destructive lesion with a disturbance of function which could also come about through nonmaterial damage.* (*AA* 31–32)

This is an extremely important passage for several reasons. It opens with a distinction between "functional" and "organic." The clear boundaries fade, however, and meld into one another under the guise of a wholeness that melds into an option called "nonmaterial." Does "functional" mean "organic" (as in the remote effects of a brain lesion) or not? Apparently, the answer is both: *functional* is a transverse term that crosses over and unites body and psyche. The stage is set for a protopsychoanalytic interpretation of hysteria with the suggestion in italics that "nonmaterial damage" can cause a disturbance in function. With these deliberations, one could argue, psychoanalysis itself had come into being.

Freud revisits the issue in the now notorious Dora case history (written in 1901, published in 1905, and in which a reference to his stay in Charcot's clinic in 1885 and 1886 suggests that his own history of ideas was very much on his mind):

We must recall the question which has so often been raised, whether the symptoms of hysteria are of psychical or of somatic origin, or whether, if the former is granted, they are necessarily *all* of them psychically determined. Like so many other questions to which we find investigators returning again and again without success, this question is not adequately framed. The alternatives stated in it do not cover the real essence of the matter. As far as I can see, every hysterical symptom involves the participation of *both* sides. It cannot occur without the presence of a certain degree of *somatic compliance* offered by some normal or pathological process in or connected with one of the bodily organs. (*SE* 7:40; *GW* 5:199–200)

The term *somatic compliance* names the bridge and attributes an intentionality to bodily processes; the metaphor of "somatic compliance" stands for integration of mind and body. There is no parallel in the aphasia book to the idea of "compliance," but the question is raised there, and the outlines of an integrative answer are drawn.

The passage from the aphasia book is also significant for Freud's critique of the inertial tendency of normal science—continuing to theorize along lines of practical convenience. He shows how habitual theoretical contructs determine outcomes. Finally, the excerpt also demonstrates one rhetorical pattern characteristic of Freud's writing: opening with a concession to the merits of the conventional wisdom, followed by an argument that reveals its inconsistency, followed by a history of the conventional wisdom which implies pronominally that the author is among those who, however justifiably, had been led astray.

Freud next extends his view to the language apparatus itself:

The language apparatus appears to show in all its parts the *second* kind of reaction to nondestructive lesions; it responds to such a lesion in solidarity (at least partial solidarity), that is, with a functional disturbance. For example, it never happens that consequent to a small lesion in the motor center a hundred words are lost whose nature depends only on the site of the lesion. It can be shown every time that the partial loss is the expression of a general functional curtailment of that center. It is not, by the way, a matter of course that the language centers behave this way. The fact that they do will later assist us in arriving at a very specific idea of their structure. (*AA* 32)

The subject here is the loss of categories. Although he does not acknowledge it, Freud's description is of a process that certainly cannot be explained in terms of "the word." His later focus on "the word" as a "psychological" category of explanation contradicts the explanation of loss presented here. In this passage we can begin to see Freud's views about the language function growing out of a thesis of Bastian's.

Bastian's own version of language is an expansive one closely related to Kussmaul's. In *The Brain as a Organ of Mind*, Bastian commits himself to a definition of language taken from William Thomson's *Outline of the Laws of Thought:*[22]

> As Thomson says, "Language, in its most general acceptation, might be described as a mode of expressing our thoughts by means of motions of the [organs of the] body; it would thus include spoken words, cries [and] involuntary gestures that indicate the feelings, even painting and sculpture, together with those contrivances which replace speech in situations where it cannot be employed." (Bastian, 602; my additions are from Thomson's 1859 edition.)

Such views on language also map a route to psychoanalysis. Hysterical patients, after all, were specialized in "involuntary gestures that indicate the feelings" as well as "those contrivances which replace speech in situations where it cannot be employed." Not only Bastian, but also Hughlings Jackson, in writing about aphasia quotes Thomson. Thomson's book, first published in 1842, was widely read and influential. It is considered to have anticipated John Stuart Mill's *A System of Logic,* to which Freud refers in Section 5 of the aphasia book. Thus Thomson entered Freud's book via three separate routes.

Later Freud will transfer Bastian's "modifications" from Bastian's setting of physiological speech centers into a division among visual, auditory, and kinesthetic elements of the language apparatus, and he will map, for each of these elements, the descending grades of incapacity according to an amalgam of Bastian's and Jackson's views. In the course of developing his

22. William Thomson, *An Outline of the Necessary Laws of Thought: A Treatise on Pure and Applied Logic* (Cambridge: John Bartlett, 1859), 43. William Thomson was archbishop of York and one-time provost of Queen's College, Oxford. Information on Thomson is from *Dictionary of National Biography,* vol. 19 (reprint, 1963–1964), 756–759. Thomson was an early explorer of semiotics: "The telegraph, and the signals on railroads, are new modes of speech; and though an inexpert practitioner may have at first to translate such signs into common language, the skill which comes from practice soon prompts him to omit this needless intermediate step. The engine driver shuts off the steam at the warning sign, without thinking of the words to which it is equivalent; a particular signal becomes associated with a particular act, and the interposition of words becomes superfluous. . . . It is conceivable that we might learn to think by the telegraphic signals, so that 'red flag over blue,' seen with the eye or recalled by the memory, might be our *word* for happiness" (Thomson 59).

thesis, Freud reiterates that Bastian's modifications only apply when lesions are not completely destructive so that intact nervous tissue can take over and compensate for the damaged area. He points out that, necessarily, "no single individual nerve fiber and nerve cell is enlisted for a single language association function; rather, a more complicated relationship reigns" (*AA* 91). Freud's approach is to pay tribute to complexity, to recognize it where others had chosen not to.

One corollary that Bastian added to his categories Freud does not mention, but its relevance to his interests is striking enough to lead one to think that he is likely to have filed the idea away for future reference. In *The Brain as an Organ of Mind*, Bastian adds the category of "unduly exalted" excitability of the centers, by which he means states of the mentally ill, such as "hallucinations, illusions, and a wholly different class of defects" (616). Although Bastian does not pursue this idea, because he believes it would take him far afield, nevertheless, like the three categories themselves, this addition stands out as foreign to the flow of ideas, and thus is not likely that Freud overlooked it. It brought the topic of mental illness into immediate proximity to questions of aphasia and the nature of language functions, and it is interpreted as a variation in degree of capacity of language centers to be stimulated. The implication is that there is an intimacy via language between disturbances of an emotional nature and those resulting from brain lesions, an implication that adds a further dimension to Freud's notion of "nonmaterial damage."

The categorization that Freud found so fruitful was not merely an isolated feature in a single report, such as in the case of Heubner, but rather was one of a set of views the future psychoanalyst must have found deeply suggestive. In his 1869 article on loss of speech in cerebral disease, Bastian produced a description of protopsychoanalytic theory which also led him to disagree with certain of Jackson's views on language:

> Emotion, [here Bastian's note 1: "Using this in its broadest sense, so as to include the various appetites."] . . . is the motive power . . . and its dictates are so all-powerful when aroused, even in man, as not unfrequently completely to conquer any mere volitional strivings which may be opposed to them—as may be seen when a person is absolutely compelled to give way to laughter, even though he make the strongest efforts to restrain it, and all prudential reasons may be against the indulgence. (480)

This last remark, which anticipates Freud's thesis in *Jokes and Their Relation to the Unconscious* (1905), leads Bastian next to the conclusion that the

Henry Charlton Bastian
From Obituary, *Lancet*, November 27, 1915, 1221.

power of emotion enables aphasic patients to utter expletives, although they have been otherwise unable to speak, and this conclusion puts him at odds with Jackson's view that of the two distinct kinds of language, the emotional and the intellectual, aphasia impairs only the intellectual. Of these two explanations, Bastian's would ultimately be closer to Freud's views.

The program of Bastian's *The Brain as an Organ of Mind* is contained in the title and realized at the end of the book, when Bastian presents his arguments for the "natural" or material origin of consciousness and for its dependence on "the activity of certain related cell and fibre networks in the Cerebral Cortex" (688). "States of Feeling may . . . react upon Nerve Tissues so as to alter the molecular motions taking place therein. Feelings . . . thus have . . . an indubitable effect in modifying our Intellectual Operations, our Volitions, or our Movements" (689). Whereas Jackson provided Freud the theory of psychophysical parallelism which explained, for example, hysteria as independent from the nervous system, Bastian's alternative view offers an explanation of how states of mind, such as hysteria, realize their effects on the body, such as paralysis. On the one hand, the unity of mind and brain is a logical consequence of Freud's arguments on aphasia. On the other hand, those arguments are developed on the basis of Jackson's notion of parallel but separate systems. I contend that Bastian's arguments are the more powerful ones. The difference between the two is that Bastian was willing—as was his nature—to take great leaps of the imagination without having evidence for his conclusions, whereas Jackson, thinking, above all of the limits to neurological investigation, was unwilling to do so. In the relationship between these two great opponents on the most fundamental question is reflected the ambivalence in Freud's text, or the play between interpretation and reproduction. This does not mean that Jackson was a stranger to ideas of indeterminacy or "variability of representation." As I discuss in my next chapter, Jackson showed himself acutely sensitive to questions of *linguistic* representation. In other words, language, and thus disciplinary discourse, carries an excess of meaning which, he believed, put it in conflict with the purposes of science.

The common assumption that Jackson's work is the key to Freud's aphasia book needs to be qualified by a closer look at Bastian, the contradictions between Jackson and Bastian, and how they are transformed in Freud's reading. Freud left these contradictions unresolved in his aphasia book, as if to imply that there can be no closure when language—sui generis both mind *and* body—is at stake.

The brief fourth section of Freud's book is devoted primarily to a widely influential article by Hubert G. Grashey[23] which presents a case history

23. Hubert G. Grashey, "Über Aphasie und ihre Beziehungen zur Wahrnehmung," *Archiv für Psychiatrie und Nervenkrankeiten* 16, no. 3 (1885): 654–688. A translation by Ria De Bleser was published as "On Aphasia and Its Relations to Perception," *Cognitive Neuropsychology* 6, no. 6 (1989): 515–546, but translations here are mine. Grashey, as I mentioned in connection

that—in contradiction to Grashey's own conclusion—suggested to Freud the validity of one kind of claim for localization and thus provided evidence for his own two-pronged theory of aphasia. Grashey, like Bastian, Kussmaul, and Ross, is one of those "best minds" in neuropathology to whom Freud refers on the opening page of his book. Freud also lists him, along with Wernicke and Lichtheim, in his letter to Fliess as one with whom he "crosses swords" in the aphasia book. Although Freud will show that Grashey's theory, too, is incorrect, he uses it as another nail in the coffin of Lichtheim's theory, and when it comes to disproving Grashey himself, Freud uses Wernicke's arguments to do so.[24] He then proceeds to prove that Wernicke's idea is wrong as well. Thus Freud uses one of the most prominent aphasiologists (Wernicke) to dismiss the case made by another important researcher (Grashey), after the latter has served its purpose as a blow against a certain kind of localization. Having done this service, Grashey's article is used by Freud to support his second major thesis. Section 4 of Freud's book plays a political/rhetorical role, but it also reveals an additional source of views on language which Freud adheres to, although they are significantly flawed. However flawed his theories, Grashey's influence extends both in time and significance beyond the "secondary" findings for which Freud gives him credit.

Freud opens the section with a sentence whose rhetoric immediately alerts us to his posture toward Lichtheim: "At approximately the same time as the paper by Lichtheim that carries through with such consistency

---

with Heubner, was a prominent psychiatrist who served for a time (at least between 1876 and 1881) as director of a mental hospital in Bavaria and was for some time subsequently, according to the title page of his article, at the University of Würzburg. His later prominence is indicated by his being called in 1894 as an expert witness in a notorious trial involving seduction by hypnosis. The fact that his affiliation at that time is listed as Munich supports Heubner's statement that Grashey took over the practice of King Ludwig II's psychiatrist; see *Der Prozeß Czynski: Thatbestand desselben und Gutachten über Willensbeschränkung durch hypnotisch-suggestiven Einfluß* (Stuttgart: Ferdinand Enke, 1895). It has not been possible for me to find Grashey's dates.

24. Wernicke discusses Grashey's case at length in his 1885–1886 publication "Recent Works on Aphasia," in *Wernicke's Works on Aphasia*, 173–205. Ria De Bleser and Claudio Luzzatti write about Wernicke's reaction: "It had an enormous impact on Wernicke, who considered it the most important article he had read in the previous 10 years. It made him revise his thinking on reading and writing completely." "Models of Reading and Writing and Their Disorders in Classical German Aphasiology," *Cognitive Neuropsychology* 6, no. 6 (1989): 501–513, here 502. This is correct (although Wernicke actually refers to Grashey's article as "the most significant advance in the aphasia question in the last 10 years"), and, as noted by Freud, Wernicke finds a fundamental contradiction in Grashey's report. It is noteworthy that in this same article ("Recent Works on Aphasia") Wernicke used the term *Sprechapparat*, which Freud used one time only (and which I have translated as "speech apparatus"), then abandoned it in favor of *Sprachapparat*, which I interpret as the concept of language as opposed to the concept of speech and have therefore translated as "language apparatus." Might Freud have wanted to avoid adopting Wernicke's term?

the localizing explanation for speech disturbances, a lecture by Grashey became known which soon was credited with having fundamental significance for the understanding of aphasia, without, by the way, anyone's having since then continued to build on the foundation it created" (*AA* 34–35). The most revealing elements of this sentence are as follows: (1) its juxtaposition of Grashey with Lichtheim (without yet revealing why), foreshadowing Grashey's role as another arrow in the quiver to be launched against Lichtheim's views; (2) the verb *nachrühmte* (translated as "credited with"), which carries an ironic flavor, as it is commonly associated with eulogies for those who are gone; and (3) the final clause that undermines the notion of "fundamental significance," inasmuch as Grashey's paper had not turned out to be productive. It is possible that Freud is considering himself the next builder on Grashey's foundation.

After briefly summarizing the outstanding symptoms of Grashey's case of a young man whose brain was damaged in a fall, Freud shows how it demonstrates the lack of logic in Lichtheim's interpretation of the same kind of aphasia. He follows Grashey's reasoning, which is based on a diagram of speech centers connected by pathways (Figure 1), and gives Grashey credit for recognizing that were he to assume interrupted versus intact pathways in every case, he would be able to provide an easy explanation for any and all symptoms. Here Grashey shows, like Heubner and Bastian, the kind of thinking against the grain that appeals to Freud. Grashey investigates further and after extensive testing concludes that the patient's inability to retain the memory of an object long enough to associate it with a spoken word—while at the same time being able to make the association in the opposite direction—is a consequence of the fact that words are perceived letter by letter or sound by sound, so it takes longer to perceive the sound of words than to comprehend an object by sight. His conclusion about his discovery is that "there is an aphasia that depends neither on functional incapacity of the centers, nor on lack of capacity of the connecting pathways, but solely on a decrease in the duration of sensory impressions and the disturbance of perception and association that results therefrom" (Grashey 684).

Freud reports Wernicke's refutation of Grashey's analysis as consisting of two parts: The sound of a word is heard as a whole and only later, in conjunction with writing, is it broken into the sounds of the individual letters; and there were certain inconsistencies between Grashey's theory and the abilities of his patient. Wernicke's own explanation of the case depends on localizing the disturbance in the visual area. Freud offers an alternative explanation based on a case by Conrad Rieger, professor of psychiatry in Würzburg, whose patient, instead of reconstructing words letter for letter as Grashey's did, arrived at the entire word in a sudden, explosive process, indicating that the type of memory problem Rieger's patient shared with Grashey's patient may be connected to a different type of disturbance than the one extrapolated by Grashey. Rieger's monograph, published in 1888 as a response to Grashey (who also had been at Würzburg), is significant for its portrait of clinical methodology, its self-consciousness about the cultural situatedness of inquiry, and its proposals for a coherent disciplinary terminology.[25] For these reasons, and because Freud read the monograph with care, I discuss some of its noteworthy aspects below. In contrast to Grashey, and using Rieger's case as supporting evidence, Freud postulates a *localized* lesion in the "center for sound images" (*AA* 41), creating the situation described by Bastian's second category: a center that reacts only in association with others (or to sensory input). Freud also draws on cases presented by several other authors to support his interpretation.

Grashey finds developmental parallels for aphasic disturbances; that is, he draws conclusions about language functions from the stages of a child's language-learning process and reveals thereby the intimacy between scientific theory and cultural matrix. He distinguishes language learning among children whose native language consists of symbols that designate objects (presumably he is reflecting the prevailing assumptions about the Chinese language) from language learning "that is usual in our schools," in which there is no such connection between symbols and the images of objects. "Our written language," Grashey writes, is a phonetic one. Thus when a child is learning to write, he or she "makes the written sign for a sound image. The more writing practice [the child] has, the more he succeeds in immediately attaching the appropriate segment of the written image to every individual segment of the sound image, thus not first completing the sound image and successively creating the written image from the completed sound image, but rather completing sound and written image simultaneously" (664).

Grashey builds his theory of aphasia on this view of childhood learning, even though he gives a nod to cultural differences. He fails to note that a diagnosis that depends on a claim to universality based on brain function (pathways and centers, etc.) stands in contradiction to the dependence of

25. Conrad Rieger, "Beschreibung der Intelligenzstörungen in Folge einer Hirnverletzung nebst einem Entwurf zu einer allgemein anwendbaren Methode der Intelligenzprüfung," in *Separat-Abdruck aus den Verhandlungen der phys.-med. Gesellschaft zu Würzburg*, new ser., vol. 22 (Würzburg: Stahel, 1888).

that diagnosis on evidence derived from cultural particularity, namely, the phonetic quality of spelling in the German language. Grashey presumes that "the European peoples" all have phonetic languages (675). Yet even English-language learners, with the peculiarities of English spelling, would not qualify for the kind of learning process that Grashey extrapolates. In addition, he presumes that children assume a standard language intact, whereas studies have shown that the young child's version of language is distinctive and agrammatical. Grashey gives consideration neither to the uncertainties in grammar and syntax which mark early childhood language nor to differences in social class, type of schooling, or gender (at a time when, for example, girls' schooling was very limited). Grashey also draws a conclusion about language function which depends on level of education: lesser educated people tend to draw on a different pattern of pathways and centers when reading.

All in all, Grashey does not acknowledge the larger implication of these differences: that the brain is to some extent a product of cultural habit, as Kussmaul had implied in 1877. Grashey is of the opinion there might be people who have intentionally cultivated a pathway from point B to point D in his diagram, (Figure 1) although that pathway normally does not exist because it would exclude the sound-image center, point A. He also suggests that "deaf mute" people may also have "learned" to open a pathway (B→C→G) that permits them to compensate for hearing loss. Suggesting intentional alterations of brain functions is a bold step that brings mind and brain together—a step that Grashey fails, however, to acknowledge. Grashey's entire discussion, his work with his patient, and the theory he develops all depend on the assumptions of a literate culture. An advanced level of literacy is presumed, as are a preoccupation with the written or printed word and a shared familiarity with cultural signs and linguistic codes, in spite of differences in level of attainment. That is to say that his theory of aphasia is culturally specific. Grashey interprets symptoms and postulates brain functions based on the culture he knows. Should we conclude that brain configurations in the electronic age will be altered as the fast-paced visual image becomes paramount? Grashey's ideas suggest that might be the case and that another culturally specific aphasia theory would be developed, just as new testing procedures elicit different responses from aphasic patients and thus, inevitably, a different description of their condition.

How does Freud respond to Grashey? He also believes that the pathology of aphasia repeats features of normal language development in children but interprets this process in the context of association among

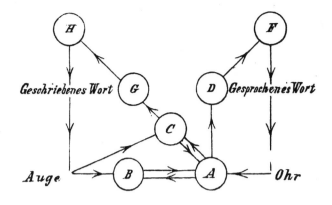

Figure 1. *A*   center for sound images,
B   center for object images,
C   center for symbols, i.e., for cursive or printed letters, words, and numerals,
D   center for motor images of speech,
F   nuclei of nerves for phonation and articulation,
G   center for motor images of writing, and
H   nuclei of motor nerves functioning during writing.
The centers *A* and *B* and the centers *A* and *C* are connected by two pathways that conduct in opposing directions, as indicated by the arrows. From Hubert G. Grashey, "Über Aphasie und ihre Beziehungen zur Wahrnehmung" (on aphasia and its relations to perception), *Archiv für Psychiatrie und Nervenkrankheiten* 16, no. 3 (1885): 656.

language centers (as opposed to Grashey's concentration on pathways). The difference between the normal and the pathological, according to Freud, is that in the course of the normal learning process in childhood, the various centers assume their functions according to a developmental hierarchy that determines their order: "first the sensory-auditory, then the motor, later the visual, finally the graphic" (*AA* 43). By contrast, in the case of aphasia, damaged centers draw for assistance on those that have remained healthiest (irrespective of developmental order). Freud has not attended to Grashey's assumptions about schooling and differences determined by different native languages (although he does mention education in another context).[26] Driven by his own agenda of theory construction, Freud does not let himself be distracted by such issues. As in his reading

26. That is Louis Victor Marcé's case of an attorney with aphasia, as recorded by Bastian, "Loss of Speech in Cerebral Disease," 222; Marcé, "Mémoires sur quelques observations de physiologie pathologique tendant à démontrer l'existence d'un principe coordinateur de l'écriture et ses rapports avec le principe coordinateur de la parole," *Comptes rendus des séances et Mémoires de la Société de Biologie,* ser. 2, vol. 3 (1856): 93–115, here 103.

of Ross's study, Freud excises direct mentions of cultural meanings and distinctions. Nevertheless, they are inherent in the materials he knew intimately.

Finally revealing the message concealed in the rhetorical formulation of his opening statement, Freud points out that though Grashey's report did not retain the significance for which it was initially given credit as a refutation of localizing theories, it had proved valuable for its secondary findings, of which he lists three:

> It was the first to explore again the true relationship of the speech centers to one another and their dependence on the center for sound images; it was the first to convey to us an idea [*Vorstellung*] of the complicated and multiply geniculated [*vielfach in seiner Richtung geknickten Ablauf*] course of associations in the speech process; finally, by providing proof that all reading is done by spelling, it established unshakably the correct point of view for judging reading disturbances. (*AA* 44)

There is much to be said about this passage. Rhetorically, it is the fulfillment of the promise of the opening passage about the nature of Grashey's paper. But most important are Freud's second and third points. His key terms for describing a pattern of associations are to be found again in the "Psychotherapy of Hysteria" section in the *Studies on Hysteria* (slightly varied as *vielfach abgeknickten Weg*). The pattern I have rendered as "multiply geniculated" is to be found in a passage that describes "the arrangement of psychical material." Because, with this reappearance of terms in a writer as meticulous as Freud, we have arrived at a notable feature of his work, it is necessary to quote the passages from *Studies* to see just where, by a roundabout path, Grashey's paper may have made its appearance once again:

> A third kind of arrangement has still to be mentioned—the most important, but the one about which it is least easy to make any general statement. What I have in mind is an arrangement according to thought-content, the linkage made by a logical thread which reaches as far as the nucleus and tends to take an irregular and twisting path, different in every case [*der einem in jedem Falle besonderen, unregelmäßigen und vielfach abgeknickten Weg entsprechen mag*].[27] This arrangement has a dynamic

27. German from *GW* 1:293. The German in the aphasia book is *"von dem komplizierten und vielfach in seiner Richtung geknickten Ablauf"* (*AA* 44).

character, in contrast to the morphological one of the two stratifications mentioned previously. While these two would be represented in a spatial diagram by a continuous line, curved or straight, the course of the logical chain would have to be indicated by a broken line which would pass along the most roundabout paths from the surface to the deepest layers and back, and yet would in general advance from the periphery to the central nucleus, touching at every intermediate halting-place—a line resembling the zig-zag line in the solution of a Knight's Move problem, which cuts across the squares in the diagram of the chess-board.

I must dwell for a moment longer on this last simile in order to emphasize a point in which it does not do justice to the characteristics of the subject of the comparison. The logical chain corresponds not only to a zig-zag, twisted line, but rather to a ramifying system of lines and more particularly to a converging one. It contains nodal points at which two or more threads meet and thereafter proceed as one; and as a rule several threads which run independently, or which are connected at various points by side-paths, debouch into the nucleus. To put this in other words, it is very remarkable how often a symptom is determined in several ways, is 'overdetermined.' (*SE* 2:289–290; *GW* 1:293–294)

The arrangement that resulted in the concept of overdetermination is intricate and quite distinct. The two patterns—zigzag and the ramifying system of lines—also describe Freud's method of research, that is, how he read and absorbed each author's work, or parts of it, into his own ongoing construction, letting the material find its way again into shaping and being shaped by later products of his pen. Are these two patterns also descriptive of the exploratory research process in general, linking the evidence of how Freud worked and thought to how a mind typically pursues such an investigation? Might these patterns reflect a specifically European cultural heritage or are they patterns of brain function? If they are both, what is their interrelationship? Such questions are not only suggested by Freud's writing but also are posed, for example, by Kussmaul and by Grashey, who presumed the possibility of the intentional development of nervous pathways. The link in Freud's "logical chain" of association through his writing in this case consists of the repetition of key words used to describe a functional pattern of associations but also to suggest a pattern in the brain itself.[28] The Freud who wrote the section in *Studies on Hysteria* wants the reader to know that he is fully aware of the metaphorical nature of

28. For further thoughts on this topic, see my "Tangled Patterns."

such description. Nevertheless, the descriptive passages in both of Freud's texts clearly slip from one sphere of investigation to another and back again.

How might Grashey's article have served as one inspiration for the idea of overdetermination? A sense of Grashey's project can be gained through the descriptive titles of the sections of his article:

1. The relation of object images to sound images
2. The relation of sound images to the language pathway
3. The relation of object images to the language pathway
4. The relation of sound images to symbols
5. The relation of object images to symbols
6. The relation of symbols to the language pathway
7. The relation of symbols to the writing pathway
8. The relation of sound images to the writing pathway
9. The relation of object images to the writing pathway

The result is a dynamic web with multiply connected intersections, each of which may engage with the others in various ways and along various routes. Whether the subject is an individual patient's peculiar combination of speech abilities and disabilities, or whether it is a matter of an undamaged language-learning process in a child, Grashey's descriptions map each function (e.g., comprehension of spoken words, recognition of written words or letters, association of names with pictured objects, etc.) as if it were commuting to and from various traffic hubs and, thus, show those hubs and those functions as multiply determined. Grashey also traces through his diagram (Figure 1) an example of how multiple determination serves to make a particularly intricate route (among centers and pathways) "decisively more secure" for the aphasic patient ("the successively associated parts of a sound image are not only retained through pronunciation, but also through writing movement" [680]).

Freud included Grashey's diagram among the few in his aphasia book.[29] Could Freud have committed this diagram so firmly to memory that it reappeared as a metaphor for "psychical processes" four years later? Such a translation and reuse would not conflict with what appear to have been his work habits. The character of a nodal point or hub is determined by its position as a destination and a source, leading to the idea of a feature or a function that is *"mehrfach determiniert, überbestimmt"* (GW 1:294),

---

29. The version in Freud's book (AA 36) is lacking Grashey's pathway from *"Auge"* (eye) to center C, and the arrow pointing in the direction of C. This is most likely a printer's error, as the diagram does not make sense without this pathway.

which is the phrase Freud uses in *Studies on Hysteria:* "determined in several ways, is 'overdetermined.' " As Strachey (*SE* 2:212) and others have noted, Freud introduces *"überbestimmt"* in the aphasia book, Section 6, where it appears in a discussion of language learning which Strachey considered so significant as a foreshadowing that he retranslated it and added it as an appendix to his translation of "The Unconscious" (*SE* 14), along with another passage, from Section 5 of the aphasia book.[30]

The third and final point for which Freud gives Grashey's paper credit is for proving "that all reading is done by spelling." The letter of the alphabet is a central dogma for Grashey. Not only do children learn to read by associating individual letters with sounds, but in the brain each individual letter in a "printed or written word" stimulates the particular sound image that belongs to it (Grashey 661). According to Grashey, "There exists in the healthy person a direct connecting pathway between the centers 'C' and 'G' for conducting letters of the alphabet" (667). In agreement with Wernicke and other aphasiologists, Freud accepts this view, which he asserts "established unshakably the correct point of view for judging reading disturbances," although he does allow for certain exceptions in cases of persons with language disturbances who are unable to spell and instead read a word as a whole unit. Freud will use the dogma about spelling in his own theory of language learning, even though in the Rieger monograph he cited with approval, Rieger found that reading does not proceed letter by letter, or even word by word, but rather by combining elements into groups. (Rieger's patient never spelled but arrived, after a delay, at whole words.) Why did Freud not accept this commonsense conclusion, especially when self-observation would have confirmed it?

Beyond the critique of Grashey that Freud found in Wernicke, he would have found a more extensive critical treatment in Rieger's monograph, which is aimed particularly at Grashey's report. Rieger's monograph provides a comprehensive narrative of psychiatric testing and explanation as it relates to aphasic disturbances, even though Rieger himself did not use the term *aphasia* in the main body of his text. Rieger, who provides neither schematic drawings nor neuropathological findings, is concerned primarily with an "inventory of human intelligence" he developed in 1885 as a testing mechanism and which he applied to the case at hand of a sculptor who suffered multiple skull fractures in a train accident in 1886. Freud

30. These two passages, along with Strachey's translation of them, are examined below in the sequence in which they appear in the aphasia book. Freud's own reference to the idea of overdetermination in the aphasia book appears in his letter to Fliess of December 6, 1896 (*FB*, 217; *FL*, 207).

read the Rieger study carefully enough to locate the pages where Rieger presents the finding that shows that Grashey made the mistake of basing general conclusions on one unique case. Freud does not seem to have otherwise utilized Rieger. (It may be that Rieger's focus on testing "intelligence" rather than "aphasia" was a disincentive to Freud.)

Yet Rieger, to whose study Wernicke refers in a posthumously published article as "Rieger's famous case" (*Wernicke's Works* 244) may have played a more important unacknowledged role for Freud. Whether or not this is true, it is possible to show at least where Freud might have chosen to distance himself from prevailing psychiatry and where Rieger's thinking might have intersected with Freud's at a later time.[31] Freud would have seen his own name in Rieger's text under circumstances bound to attract his attention: a footnote refers to the German translation of Charcot's lectures by "Freund" (53); later, a second footnote corrects this "overlooked missprint" with the correct name of "Freud" (117). At the site where Freud's name is corrected, Rieger quotes Charcot at length, only to refute his views. He opens with Charcot's explanation (in Freud's translation) of the word, which "at least among educated individuals" consists of four elements: auditory mnemonic image, visual mnemonic image, image of articulatory movement, and image of movement of writing. These are the four elements Freud presumes in his discussion of the word in the aphasia book. Freud and Rieger both reject completely, however, Charcot's line of reasoning that a consequence of this division of the word into four elements is that individuals will favor one or the other of those areas —they will be an auditory, visual, or motor type—which means that they are most seriously affected by damage in that particular area. Charcot also believes that (the capacity for) any one of the four elements can be lost without affecting the remaining ones. Rieger (117) calls Charcot's conviction that each of these capacities can be localized in the brain "a mythologogical perspective."[32]

Rieger, who, like Ross, relies on the views of linguist Max Müller, compares the theory of language "centers" in the brain to the ideas found in a famous fifteenth-century treatise on witchcraft and attributes such ideas to the general human tendency to mythologize. Although Freud is not ready in the aphasia book to accept such comparisons, especially as the very use he makes of Grashey is to support one kind of localizing

31. Reiger's importance as a representative practitioner in the field is indicated by his being the founder of the psychiatric hospital at the University of Würzburg in 1888–1889, as he reports in a foreword to the second section of his monograph (p. 71).
32. Wernicke also did not accept Charcot's hypothesis.

explanation, he will in later years be happy to diagnose mythologizing in several contexts.[33] The key step Müller takes, as he is quoted by Rieger, is to reverse the logic of localization. He argues that although it is true that we can neither see without the eye, nor hear without the ear, nor speak without "the third convolution of the left anterior lobe of the brain," nevertheless it is also true that by themselves the eye cannot see, nor the ear hear, nor the "third convolution" speak. They require the cooperation of many other elements and, in particular, of the willing "self."[34] Though Freud could not accept Rieger's polemical antilocalizationist views, he could well have found Müller's logic congenial to the functional side of his own theory, and Müller is also providing a possible bridge toward understanding the physical manifestations of hysteria and neuroses.

Freud would have found in Rieger's text a self-conscious treatment of language and metaphor in disciplinary discourse. Rieger proposed that language has an algebraic structure involving selection, order, and combination. He argues for adopting the mathematical terminology as the most precise and useful in diagnosis of intelligence defects, as long as the distinction is preserved that nonalgebraic combinations relate to the real world and thus cannot be tested on the basis of formal correctness only. For Rieger, the key diagnostic terms are *identification* and *combination*. He equates his term *combination* with "thinking," a notion he derives from Müller, but he prefers to use the term *combination* because of international agreement on its meaning. In the struggle to establish well-founded criteria for evaluating intelligence in a patient with massive language deficits, Rieger felt the need to develop terminology for an analytic linguistics of psychology. His attempt to establish a precise and generally acceptable discourse is analogous to a similar attempt by Hughlings Jackson (discussed in the next chapter), with the major difference that although Rieger rejects algebraic formalism, the certainty of numbers pervades his entire investigation and leaves no room for a theory that could admit of indeterminacy.

Rieger, like Delbrück, pays special heed to language as a situated cultural phenomenon. When testing for word associations one must consider local conditions. For example, in Würzburg one could expect normal subjects to respond to "Pontius" with "Pilate," and to "Sodom" with "Gomorrah." Classically educated subjects will be able to make the expected combinations such as saying "Remus" in response to "Romulus"

33. Freud uses Müller's work in *Totem and Taboo* (1913).
34. Rieger, "Beschreibung der Intelligenzstörungen," Rieger's footnote refers to Müller, *Das Denken im Lichte der Sprache*, trans. E. Schneider (Leipzig, 1888), 186.

(Rieger 30). He tests the patient's deficits by the difference between the knowledge the patient demonstrates after the injury and the "elementary" "common core" of knowledge shared by everyone on "our level of culture" (5). These cultural suppositions determine the form that testing of patients takes. They are extended to other geographic locales as well and show thereby how off the mark such interpretive certainty can be. Under the category of "recognition by indentification," Rieger distinguishes extralinguistic indentification from identification of a sensual impression with a linguistic concept. He notes that one finds the two confused in the "naïve thinking" that is characteristic of "lower levels of culture."

An example is a "charming" and characteristic anecdote reported by E. B. Tylor: "Perhaps this state of mind was hardly ever so clearly brought into view as in a story told by Dr. Lieber. 'J was looking lately at a Negro who was occupied in feeding young mockingbirds by the hand. "Would they eat worms?" J asked. The Negro replied, "Surely not, they are too young, *they would not know what to call them.*" ' " (Rieger 105). Apart from the possibility of misunderstanding and inaccurate reporting, the account of this anecdote also reveals one of two kinds of ignorance on the part of the reporter (Lieber, Tylor, or Rieger): either of the meaning of birdcalls as recognized by an expert field observer or of the possibility of irony and humor.

In the aphasia book, Freud shows almost no concern with the cultural situatedness of the testing situation (only refers in passing to level of education and to profession). He is occupied with evidentiary considerations, with refuting powerful authorities, and with building a legitimate and strong argument. In later years, however, the kinds of concerns we find in Rieger's and Ross's texts do play a role for Freud, for example in *Totem and Taboo*, where he relies extensively, albeit also critically, on Tylor's writings. It is as if he bracketed the cultural narratives for later use. Instead of "anthropological" material in the aphasia book, he substituted illustrative anecdotes about himself. It is as if he had absorbed the negative lesson from Rieger and Ross and the positive lesson from Delbrück, leading him to conclude that the only story that could have evidentiary validity was a story to which he had direct and immediate access (if only through memory) in his own time and place and language.

One additional fact about Rieger's testing procedures needs to be mentioned, particularly in light of Heubner's above-mentioned decision not to go into psychiatry. Rieger's methods are notably cruel. They include subjecting the patient over and over again to extremely distressing experiences that take advantage of his loss of short-term memory. For example, the patient had repeatedly to smell noxious odors, and a pincette was repeatedly used to pinch his flesh "at a place where the skin was sensitive" until he screamed (Rieger 19). His mouth was held closed "with force" (23). No experiments with taste were carried out, however, so as "not to torture the patient too much" (19) and because the effect of aftertaste would spoil the experimental conditions. In confidence that the (educated) patient would not understand the Latin word, Rieger mentioned in front of him to an assistant that it would be merciful if the patient were "soon to be autopsied" (20). The patient reacted to this remark with agitation and anger. Clearly, with the exception of the last acknowledged mistake, Rieger is only reporting standard procedures and, thereby, is revealing much about the state of psychiatry. We can presume, by the therapeutic choice he made in developing psychoanalysis, that Freud would have found the standard methods as reflected in Rieger's report inappropriate and unappealing.

After using the Rieger case to help build his argument against Grashey, Freud reviews an earlier one that anticipated Grashey's and adds several in which the loss of one capacity (for example, the visual) in the language function was compensated for by means of an associated capacity. When the visual capacity has been lost, patients may be able to read only by writing the individual letters of the alphabet or by tracing them in the air, that is, by utilizing motor channels. These examples support Freud's explanation of normal and pathological language development whereby learning to read or write requires the support of a hierarchy of capacities (such as visual, motor, and auditory) that are used either as determined by the normal sequence of development or, in the case of aphasia, according to which of the capacities have remained functional. Several such cases were described in the Charcot lectures Freud translated and in a lecture by Carl Friedrich Otto Westphal, published in 1874.[35] I want to look closely at the Westphal lecture, Freud's brief mention of which belies its significance. Naturally, there is no way of knowing when, in the course of his writing, Freud read Westphal's paper. Whether it aided in the initial formulation of Freud's fundamental views is, however, less important than the fact that a researcher was thinking so early in the same terms as Freud about aphasia, although with two signal differences.

---

35. Carl Friedrich Otto Westphal, "Vortrag über Aphasie," *Zeitschrift für Ethnologie: Verhandlungen der Berliner Gesellschaft für Anthropologie, Ethnologie, und Urgeschichte* 6 (1874): 94–102. It is noteworthy that Westphal's lecture was published in the journal of the "Berlin Society for Anthropology, Ethnology, and Early History." There could be no better evidence for the broad, cross-disciplinary defining of aphasia.

Freud's specific reference is to a case presented by Westphal. More important than the case is that Westphal takes a skeptical position toward prevailing assumptions about relating injury to symptom and about categorizing aphasias. He suggests that aphasia can be a temporary phenomenon rooted in a "temporary functional disturbance of the brain (probably without gross anatomic changes)" (95). (From the idea of subtle and indistinct changes, it is not far to raising the question whether there might be aphasia without organic changes, as Freud did.) Westphal, who read Hughlings Jackson, points to examples of patients whose presumptive injury—interruption of a pathway—was apparently circumvented when the patient was in a state of excitement and able to produce words fluently. Thus Westphal questions prevailing "formulas" he considers arbitrary and reductive and based on faulty or incomplete examinations. It is misleading, in his view, to place patients into distinct categories when examinations do not entail sufficiently varied questions or take into account the relative severity of specific symptoms. According to Westphal, the common assumption in "Germany and France" that Broca's area is the "center of speech" needs to be questioned; for an unprejudiced look at autopsy reports and case histories shows that there were cases of the "symptom complex" (also Wernicke's term) of aphasia when entirely different areas of the brain—sometimes distant ones—had been destroyed and Broca's area was intact. So, too, were there cases in which this area had been destroyed and *no* aphasia was present; likewise when the equivalent site in the *right* hemisphere had been destroyed and the typical aphasia *was* present. Westphal thus takes the same skeptical stand on questions of localization which Freud will later take, and based on the same kind of discrepancies between clinical symptoms and autopsy findings which Freud would discover. All told, Westphal's view anticipates the idea of "function," as hypothesized by Freud: "It is not always the lesion as such that determines the symptoms but, rather, the changes in its environment that may or may not be apparent to gross observation" (Westphal 101). By mentioning the German and French contexts of the assumptions he is questioning, Westphal demonstrates his distance from the nationalism at its height in the 1870s, adding an unspoken tilt toward British investigators by citing William Ogle (also one of Freud's citations) and Hughlings Jackson.

But their differences are also significant. The most important has to do with language theory. Westphal still assumed that there was a "speech apparatus" for spoken language and separate "psychic" or "mental" processes for internal speech or comprehension of language (i.e., as reflected later in the distinction between Broca's and Wernicke's areas, or between motor and sensory aphasia). It would be incorrect, therefore, to translate Westphal's term *Sprachapparat* as the more inclusive "language apparatus," as I have done in the case of Freud. Westphal's concept is illustrated by his choice of analogy to explain the "speech apparatus"—a choice that marks a another major difference from Freud. Westphal (101) chose "speech mechanism" *(Sprachmechanismus)*, which can be impaired in the way "an artificial mechanism can be put out of order by removing a screw or a spring from one or another location (not all locations)." We have seen Kussmaul's and Wysman's use of metaphors borrowed from technologies. Grashey (688) used an analogy with the telegraph to explain the simultaneous transmission of parts of words along a pathway that consists of mutiply connected conducting "centers." Although each of these is reductive to a different degree depending on the referent, Westphal's (101) clearly separates body from mind, or speech from "psychic processes." By 1891 not only Freud but other researchers, no longer theorized in terms of two separate realms, even though the distinctions between motor and sensory aphasia were maintained. The discourse on aphasia was thus maintaining a clinical distinction that was out of step with changing conceptualization.

Section 4 of the aphasia book concludes with a characteristic summary of territory covered and a preview of answers yet to come. The tasks Freud sets for himself in the coming sections are: (1) to establish by what criteria it can be determined whether a symptom of language disturbance can be attributed to functional change or to the directly destructive effects of a lesion, and (2) on the positive side, to offer a theory of language disturbances that is not subject to the objections raised against other theories.

At this point in Freud's text, a coherent view of language has not yet emerged, but some elements have been suggested, and others can be implied. It is clear that "sound images" are the central element around which other functions are grouped and on which they depend. It is clear also that understanding of language is enhanced by the relationship between language learning and the pathology of aphasia. That is, the analysis must proceed synchronically, via the study of aphasia patients, and diachronically, via the study of the normal learner. Freud has made it plain that the operation of language in the brain, as well as its possibilities of expression, are richly complex. So far, he has chosen, however, not to consider the explorations of language carried out by several of his source authors, in particular their attention to historical philology and anthropology, and the implications of cultural assumptions and technological metaphors. He has thus avoided the disjunction apparent in Grashey's text between the universal claims of neurological science in the study of brain function, on the one hand, and cultural particularity on the other.

4

TOWARD LANGUAGE THEORY ON A NEUROLOGICAL BASIS

Freud's fifth section is in some ways a culmination of the preceding ones, but it also expands his case to a new level of argument, introduces new perspectives, includes the last "crossing of swords" with a main opponent (this time, his old teacher Theodor Meynert),[1] acknowledges several particularly influential researchers (including Hughlings Jackson), indicates that language as an artifact of culture and communication (beyond the medical perspective on aphasia) constitutes occulted subject matter of the book, and treats problems of language use in terms of disciplinary discourse.

The section opens with a critique of Meynert's views on brain anatomy, on which Wernicke's theory of aphasia was largely based. Wernicke had written in his pathbreaking *The Aphasia Symptom Complex* (1874) that it was an attempt to provide "a practical application of Meynert's teachings of brain anatomy to the study of normal speech processes and the disorders generally recognized as aphasia . . . [and that] . . . whatever merit may

---

1. The relationship of Theodor Meynert (1833–1892) to Freud was a conflicted one over the long term, but Meynert's theory of the development of the "motor speech image" from a "primary" or reflex and subcortical stage to a "secondary" or conscious and cortical level has been generally considered a source for Freud's distinction between primary and secondary processes.

be found in this work ultimately reverts to Meynert."[2] Freud's argument concentrates on exposing inconsistencies in Meynert's interpretation of the anatomic evidence. In other words, he supports his arguments against Wernicke's views of centers and pathways by showing that they follow from Meynert's erroneous assumptions about brain anatomy. In this instance Freud wants to deal with the normal brain to show that his opponents are in error in the very foundations on which their aphasia theories are based. He takes advantage of the opportunity to deal a blow to Meynert's reputation and does so with a certain amount of sarcasm.

First he reviews Wernicke's theory, which involves specific sites in the cerebral cortex where nerve cells "somehow" contain the images [*Vorstellungen*] which are the basis of the speech function:

> These *Vorstellungen* are residues of impressions which arrived via the pathway of the visual and auditory nerves, or which originated in speech movements as a sensation of innervation or perception of the movement that was carried out. Depending on their origin from one of these sources, they lie together in the cerebral cortex, so that one site includes all "word sound images," another all "word movement images," [such as of the mouth and tongue] etc. These distinct cortical centers are connected by masses of white fibers (association bundles), and between the centers is "unoccupied territory" of the cortex, called "functional gaps" by Meynert. (*AA* 46)

Freud mentions that this last point of Meynert's was not adopted by Wernicke. The description Freud chose is important as a starting point because it organizes his response. A diagram of the brain from Wernicke's textbook follows, then a long and detailed discussion of brain anatomy directed toward showing Meynert's version (and Wernicke's by association) to be fundamentally wrong. The first assertion Freud disproves is that the cortex receives from the peripheral nerves a point-by-point accurate "projection" of the body. Relying partly on self-contradictions in Meynert's own texts, Freud goes to great lengths to prove this notion false, including drawing on the latest work of a series of prominent experts, among them Charcot, and even Wernicke himself.

Freud's reference to Charcot in this context is a reminder of his ambivalence toward his once-admired teacher. It is apparent in the several times in the aphasia book where he draws on Charcot's work, once with critical

2. *Wernicke's Works on Aphasia*, 92.

distance to a theory he then seems to relegitimate in a backhanded way by quoting a statement of Hughlings Jackson's which might be construed as supporting a related position. The discussion is clear evidence that Freud had withdrawn from the enthusiastic admiration indicated in letters to Martha Bernays from Paris five years before (an enthusiasm already tempered by then). The brain anatomic study presented in these pages of the fifth section is evidence of the fallacy of assuming that the time with Charcot marked a "turning point" for Freud from anatomy to psychology.[3] Developed ideas, long-held convictions, disciplinary allegiances based on experience do not shift at "turning points" except as viewed from a distance. The aphasia book shows a thinker who remains immersed in all significant areas that have engaged him. What shifts or "turns" are aspects, points of emphasis, directions in a pattern of ideas that is always evolving. That pattern here and in his major works of the next decade or so reconfigures original narratives that can be labeled "neuropathological" or "neurophysiological." What has not changed, however, is Freud's defiant attitude toward authorities, as he explains at length in a letter to Martha which also suggests (admittedly under the influence of cocaine) that given the right circumstances, he could perhaps achieve as much as Charcot someday.[4] These letters, written five years before the publication of the aphasia book, suggest a thread that helps to explain the extent and the tone of his attack on the theories of his one-time supporter Meynert.

One important consequence of Freud's line of argument is to deny the absolute dominance of the cerebral cortex in favor of an integrated cortical and subcortical brain, meaning that there is no such thing as a sharp division between the faculties of reason and the emotional faculties.[5] Having disproved the idea of a "projection" of the periphery of the body in the cortex, Freud offers his own substitute term, *representation*. The anatomic evidence shows that the image of the periphery is reconstituted as the nerve fibers that convey it follow paths—for example, from muscles to

---

3. As did Strachey, for example, *SE* 1:4 (reprinted in *GW, Nachtragsband,* 32). Commentators have drawn their conclusions from Freud's official report to the authorities who awarded him his fellowship for Paris. In reporting to our benefactors, however, we naturally would stress the signal importance of the experience their largess provided. But even in Freud's report there is already a hint of a critical attitude toward Charcot (*GW* 1:39; *SE* 1:10).
4. *Sigmund Freud: Brautbriefe,* 136.
5. Ingeborg Meyer-Palmedo (in Freud, *Zur Auffassung der Aphasien,* 91–92) provides a supportive reference to Freud's preface for his translation of Hippolite Bernheim's *Suggestion* (1888), where Freud states (in the context of hypnosis) that it is unjustified to oppose the cerebral cortex to the rest of the nervous system, because profound functional changes in the cortex are bound to be accompanied by changes in the other parts of the brain and because consciousness cannot be localized to any particular part of the nervous system. For Freud's remarks, see *GW, Nachtragsband,* 119; *SE* 1:84.

spinal chord—in which they are redirected, interrupted, and their quantity reduced or increased, the image thus appearing in a necessarily changed version in the cortex. Meynert, by contrast, sees the fibers as fundamentally unchanged, which means, in today's terms, that the information they convey would be fundamentally unchanged. In presenting this conflict of views and working out his own thesis, Freud's reasoning leads him to suggestive statements and a remarkable analogy for the transformation of nerve fibers as they traverse different territories on their way to the cortex.

If one were to follow a nerve pathway on its multiply altered and branching course through gray matter, one would have to conclude, according to Freud, "that a fiber on the way to the cerebral cortex has changed its functional significance [or "meaning," *Bedeutung*] after every new emergence from gray matter." He follows with an example of the course of the optic nerve in relation to retinal impressions, proposing that the changed (he writes "new") version of the nerve fiber has assumed more complex functions, or a "change in significance [or "meaning"; *Bedeutungsänderung*]." With regard to the transfer of skin and muscle sensation, the change in meaning, he speculates, must be even more complex; "we have as yet no idea which elements join together in the new content of the transmitted stimulus" (*AA* 54–55). In this discussion, which is central to the aphasia book, Freud has used the terms *meaning* and *content*. Just as the message or information transmitted by nerve fibers must undergo a process of translation, Freud's usage here reveals a translation of brain anatomic terms into a linguistic and literary discursive sphere. In continuing, he makes the translation explicit:

> We can surmise only that those fibers which arrive in the cortex after permeating the gray matter still contain a connection to the periphery of the body but can no longer produce a topically similar image, just as—to take an example from the subject that occupies us here—a poem contains the alphabet in a rearrangement [*Umordnung*] that serves other purposes, in manifold connections among the individual topical elements, whereby some may be represented repeatedly, others not at all. (*AA* 55)

To help clarify the condition of nerve fibers, Freud selected the analogy of a poem, which he calls "an example from the subject that occupies us here," without indicating what "subject" he has in mind—the possibilities include poetry, literature in general, the alphabet, or most likely, language per se. Aphasia, neuropathology, the aphasic patient, for example, are not among the possibilities. Has the careful writer allowed himself a "Freudian slip"? Is this in fact a book concerned above all with language as such? The remainder of the sentence deepens the mystery, as it is not possible to determine whether it is meant to apply in particular to poems or to nerve fibers; starting with the term *Umordnung*, the language melds disciplinary discourses so completely that it at once describes poems and nerves. The analogy itself stands out, and the ambiguity with which it concludes suggests an integration of different spheres of thought that has generally not been ascribed to the aphasia book. It seems as if an unacknowledged layer of meaning erupts in different forms and at different points in an ostensibly purely neuropathological text. In that sense, Freud's scientific work, like that of his colleagues, is prelapsarian: even when it is about brain anatomy, it is also about a culture on the verge of being separated into irreconcilable disciplinary parts, but not yet finally there. Freud's later work seems a holdover from this time when discourses still intermingled. When extracting from his source materials Freud tended to focus on the striking idea that did not fit smoothly into the expectations generated by the text. Following his lead, we as readers may be inclined to take his striking idea as a particular kind of truth telling— the kind that happens irrespective of one's intentions. The analogy from nerve fibers to poem also suggests a second analogy to the idea of sources that in Freud's case are translated, like the nerve fibers, and transformed as they are subjected over the years to various redirections, interruptions, and so on in his evolving oeuvre.

Freud's analogy assumes that the irreducible elements of a poem are the rearranged letters of the alphabet. In agreement with Grashey and other aphasiologists, Freud takes for granted that the letters of the alphabet are the fundamental building blocks of language. Thus the *Umordnung* is a "rearrangement" of the order of the alphabet, or a scrambling of letters. Why not postulate a scrambling of phonemes, or units of meaning, or syllables—which might be analogies that fit more comfortably into the explanatory framework of neurology? The answer to that question may lie in the hidden shape of language in their medical thought: in contrast, for example, to the present time, the educational system produced in those who were formally educated an unconscious breadth and mastery of language as a social object. The ancient languages, the writings of canonical philosophers and literary figures, the books and newspapers, the theater, lectures, and discussions, the necessity of being a literate, articulate talker and writer—were absorbed and required in order to function successfully. Thus it would follow that the weight of analysis, when language was at stake, would (unawares) be on language as it had been imbued in the researchers. The letter and the poem were local phenomena of reading and writing, transferable only by analogy to brain physiology. That is, the gap that has been diagnosed between the neurological and the linguistic study of aphasia is not a separation between two halves. The setting in which both were formed made it a matter of course that medical researchers would operate within deep cultural assumptions about language, just as researchers in any other discipline would. It would, in other words, be difficult *not* to concentrate on the letter as the ultimate unit.

The passage with the poem analogy carried so much weight for Freud that five years after publication of the aphasia book he wrote about the idea to Wilhelm Fliess, using the very same term, *Umordnung*, which he had repeated twice more on the same page of the aphasia book. In the letter Freud credits the aphasia book with the first description of nerve paths subject to "rearrangement," or "retranscription," just as "memory traces" are "several times over"; that is, they are over-determined (*FL* 207; *FB* 217). In the German edition of the letters to Fliess, a footnote instructs us that the letter of December 6, 1896, serves as a bridge from "The Project" to Chapter 7 of *The Interpretation of Dreams* and that the same ideas recur later in *Beyond the Pleasure Principle* (1920) and "A Note upon the 'Mystic Writing Pad' " (1925), "in a form that connects the early to the later theories" (*FB* 217). Freud also provides in the letter to Fliess a schematic drawing that divides the functions of neurons into four categories preceding consciousness: perceptions; indication [or signs] of perception (arranged according to association); unconsciousness (arranged perhaps causally); and preconsciousness—the "third transcription" of perceptions, "attached to word presentation[s]" [*Wortvorstellungen*]: About the fourth category, he continues, "This secondary *thought consciousness* is subsequent in time and is probably linked to the hallucinatory activation of word presentations, so that the neurones of consciousness would once again be perceptual neurones and in themselves without memory."[6] I propose that the divisions set up here by Freud show the influence of Bastian's categories, which were central to Freud's thinking in the aphasia book. Bastian categorized the degree of "excitability of centers," but Freud reworked the categories for his own purposes, and I believe they reappear in this attempt to reconcile discourses of neuronal activity and psychology. The first category, like Bastian's, depends on input from external stimuli;

6. The translation is from *FL* 208 (*FB* 218), from which I have selected those terms needed here. "Presentations" is the *SE* equivalent for *Vorstellungen*, which I have elsewhere translated as ideas or images. (I have made one change in the translation from singular to plural, as in the original.)

the second, on associations; the third is internally generated; and the fourth—also a suggestion by Bastian—is linked to "hallucinatory activation." Freud has taken the categories that played so prominent a role in his thinking as he composed the aphasia text and speculatively reshaped them to suit his evolving theories.

Freud concludes his brain anatomic argument by integrating it with his theory of function, showing the coherence of his plan that has combined evidence from anatomy, pathology, and clinical symptoms:

> If one could follow in detail this rearrangement that takes place from the spinal projection on to the cerebral cortex, one would probably find that the principle is a purely functional one and that the topical aspects are maintained only in so far as they coincide with the requirements of function. Since there is no evidence that this rearrangement is reversed in the cortex in order to produce a topographically complete projection, we may surmise that the periphery of the body is not at all *contained topically, but only according to function* in the higher parts of the brain as well as in the cortex. (*AA* 55)

Thus, in the end result, Freud has preempted objections from the field of anatomy.

The statement that follows is, like the poem analogy, one that does not fit comfortably into the flow of the argument. He points out that animal experiments would of course mask the functional state because they can show topographical relations only. This statement needs to be read in connection with critical references to Hermann Munk, whose laboratory Freud visited in Berlin on his way home from Paris in 1886. Freud refutes Munk's views on two occasions, the second time by showing that a conclusion of Meynert's was based on experiments by Munk, which themselves are based on Meynert's theories. Munk's writings report and expressly defend particularly gruesome animal experiments, not only his own but those of Jean-Pierre-Marie Flourens (1794–1867), whose crude methods entailed slicing away sections of the brains of birds and dogs while they remained awake and sensible.[7] Freud's one brief sentence questions the claim that such activities produced useful insights. Michael Molnar has

---

7. Hermann Munk, *Über die Functionen der Grosshirnrinde*, 2d rev. ed. (Berlin: August Hirschwald, 1890), esp. the Introduction. On Flourens, see Restak, *Modular Brain*, 18–19, and Harrington, *Medicine, Mind, and the Double Brain*, 9–11. On the basis of these activities, Flourens decided that the brain was a uniform whole; there were no specific sites for specific functions.

explored Freud's emotional connection, in particular, to dogs.[8] There are references in Freud's texts which show how seriously he thought about nonhuman species. For example, in "The Unconscious" (1915), he suggested that investigation was needed on the significance of the unconscious in animals (*GW* 10:288; *SE* 14:189). In "Psychoanalysis and Telepathy" (1921), he equated "human and animal minds" *(Menschen- und Tierseele)* (*GW* 17:27; *SE* 18:177). In *An Outline of Psychoanalysis* (1940), he wrote that his "schematic picture of a psychical apparatus may be supposed to apply as well to the higher animals which resemble man mentally [*dem Menschen seelisch ähnlichen Tiere*]. . . . Animal psychology has not yet taken in hand the interesting problem which is here presented" (*SE* 23:147; *GW* 17:69). Freud was by no means alone in considering such matters.[9]

With the comment "After this digression we return to the interpretation of aphasia" (*AA* 56), Freud concludes the section devoted to anatomy and shows how Meynert's theories form the basis of the erroneous hypothesis that "word images" *(Wortvorstellungen)* are contained in individual nerve cells. Why he refers to the pages on anatomy as a "digression" is not immediately clear, as they do provide foundation for his theory. This seems to be another case of self-revelation through indirect self-criticism: readers may note the polemical tone of this section and consider the discussion more extended than necessary for the topic of aphasia. Beyond their rhetorical positioning, however, the ten pages on anatomy also explore ideas that have implications for Freud's patients and for the theories he was developing with Breuer (to whom the aphasia book was dedicated). The discussion of the "rearrangement" and "change in meaning" of nerve fibers yields links to Freud's clinical theoretical section in the *Studies on Hysteria* but also to the other major work of 1895, "The Project," which can be seen as a further development and elaboration of questions in the aphasia book, with a shift in site and terms. On the one hand, "The Project" seems to be removed from the aphasia text because it represents

---

8. Michael Molnar, "In hündisch unwandelbarer Anhänglichkeit," *Werkblatt* 33 (1994): 82–93; English trans., "Of Dogs and Doggerel," *American Imago*, 53 (fall 1996): 269–280. For years Freud received an annual birthday poem (composed by Anna) from the family dog. These poems are in the collection of the Freud Museum in London. Freud's devotion to his chows is well known and documented. His diary entries in the last ten years of his life testify to his deep attachment to the dogs until the very end of his life. See *The Diary of Sigmund Freud, 1929–1939*, trans. and annotated Michael Molnar (London: Hogarth, 1992).

9. See, e.g., Paul, *Prinzipien der Sprachgeschichte:* "Culture," as opposed to the "objects of pure natural science," is defined by the activity of psychic factors; "therefore we must of course also acknowledge an animal culture, and include among the sciences of culture [*Kulturwissenschaften*] the developmental history of the instincts for art [*Kunsttriebe*] and the social organization of animals" (6).

a new discourse, a micro (i.e., neuronal) interpretation of phenomena discussed on a macro (whole-nerve) level in the aphasia book; that is, its discourse might be called "neurobiology" rather than the neuroanatomy and pathology of the aphasia book. It includes exploration of consciousnes; of the self *(das Ich)* [10] of wishes, desires, and drives; of the role of pain; and of communication *(Verständigung)*, all of which had been conspicuously missing from the aphasia book. That is to say, "The Project" stands fully within the concerns of psychoanalysis. It also depends primarily on models from physics [11] and makes liberal use of the machine metaphor. On the other hand, despite the different character of the two works, there are significant connections.

First, "The Project" continues the struggle to capture language in terms of neuroanatomy. The brain anatomy on which Freud's analysis depends in "The Project" is the anatomy he developed in opposition to Meynert. It requires two "systems of neurons," one with direct peripheral connections and one without them. The latter is identified in "The Project" with his system (psi), which is the memory system, in contrast to the phi system of permeable neurons connected with the periphery. The character of these neurons is established according to their location and their connections. As, in the aphasia book, he had extrapolated regarding whole nerve fibers, Freud proposes in "The Project" that the surroundings determine the character of the phenomena. He writes, "A difference in their essence is replaced by a difference in the environment to which they are destined" (*SE* 1:304; *GW, Nachtragsband*, 396). The beginnings of the distinctions made in "The Project" between the endogenous and exogenous sytems are to be found in his response in the aphasia book to the notion, taken from Meynert, that there is a direct projection of the periphery in the cortex. There cannot be such a projection because the nerve fibers that carry an image from the periphery undergo a transformation in quality and quantity, according to their environment in the nervous system. The most that can be said is that there is a "representation" in the cortex of the peripheral body.

Second, the idea of the periodicity of neuronal activity, which Freud

10. Freud defines *das Ich* as a "a constantly cathected mass of neurones" (*SE* 1:360; *GW, Nachtragsband*, 451). Because of the nature of this early definition, I believe that the Standard Edition translation as "the ego" in "The Project" is misleading and that "the self" is more accurate.
11. For an exploration of Freud and physics, including "The Project," see my " 'A Piece of the Logical Tread . . .': Freud and Physics," in *Reading Freud's Reading*, ed. Sander L. Gilman, Jutta Birmele, Jay Geller, and Valerie D. Greenberg (New York: New York University Press, 1994), 232–251.

attributes in "The Project" to the laws of motion in physics, is related to Grashey's report. Grashey had explained his patient's symptoms by a difference of duration in time between "object images" and successive "sound images." [12] He believed that his patient's perceptive and associative capacity had been damaged by a reduction in the duration of sensory impressions. As the patient's memory returned, the duration of his sensory impressions increased. In "The Project," Freud poses the question Where do differences in periodicity derive from? He answers: "Everything points to the sense-organs, whose qualities seem to be represented precisely by different periods of neuronal motion. The sense-organs act not only as Q-screens, like all nerve-ending apparatuses, but also as *sieves*; for they allow the stimulus through from only certain processes with a particular period" (*SE* 1:310; *GW, Nachtragsband,* 403). Freud also writes of the stimuli that reach the neurons from the outside world whose "quality" is "discontinuous, so that certain periods [I prefer 'periodicities'] do not operate as stimuli at all" (*SE* 1:313; *GW, Nachtragsband,* 406). With these passages, something resembling Grashey's thesis has resurfaced in the neuronal context of "The Project."

Freud seems to have spun out in "The Project" the implication in Delbrück's lecture that syntax was hard wired in the brain. Freud's version there assigns parts of speech to a neuronal discourse: "It [language] will call neurone *a* the *thing* and neurone *b* its activity or attribute—in short, its *predicate* (*SE* 1:328; *GW, Nachtragsband,* 423). Language itself is the independent actor and namer in this situation.

Third, the central issues of association, perception, and memory in "The Project" also owe much to their earlier exploration in the aphasia book. One example is the important concept of "association through si-multaneity" (*SE* 1:319; *GW, Nachtragsband,* 411; in *SE* it is translated as "by simultaneity"), which revisits the argument in the aphasia book for the simultaneity of associations and *Vorstellungen* (contradicting those aphasiologists who attributed them to different locations in the brain). Equally important is the concept of attention as it relates to perception. Attention was a determining element in Freud's interpretation of parapha-sia, as it was also for Kussmaul and for other authors. In "The Project," the concept is expanded and refined as it is filtered through the neuronal context and assigned a role in the intricate process of reality testing. Although any tracing of the genealogy of ideas is bound to be speculative, the terms of the struggle to relate language and neuroanatomy seem to

12. Grashey, *Über Aphasie,* 679.

have had their earliest full formulation in the aphasia book, their further development in "The Project."

James Strachey chose to translate pages 56 through 58 of the aphasia book and publish them as Appendix B to his edition of "The Unconscious"; for he saw these pages as a forerunner of that 1915 essay, which he considered the most important of Freud's theoretical writings. He titled the extract "Psycho-Physical Parallelism" and regarded it, among other things, as revealing Freud's debt to Hughlings Jackson (*SE* 14:206–208). Strachey also translated a longer section from Freud's Section 6 and appended it to "The Unconscious" under the title "Words and Things" (*SE* 14:209–215). These excerpts raise the question Why, having established a terminology, did Strachey not continue and translate the remainder of the aphasia book? The answer may lie in his prefatory remarks to the second selection, Appendix C:

> It may be of interest, . . . to reproduce here a passage from that work which, though not particularly easy to follow in itself, nevertheless throws light on the assumptions that underlay some of Freud's later views. The passage has the further incidental interest of presenting Freud in the very unusual position of talking in the technical language of the 'academic' psychology of the later nineteenth century. (*SE* 14:209)

Strachey thought the aphasia text difficult to read and, more significantly, regarded it as representing a bygone era, both as to discipline and as to what is most important about Freud's work. The terms *incidental interest* and *unusual position* are revealing. Strachey seemed to want to sever Freud from his origins (even though Strachey himself considers the aphasia text important enough to be quoted extensively as a forerunner of "The Unconscious"). In particular, he wanted to make Freud purely a figure of the twentieth century, one who created a magnificent—and above all, modern—edifice of thought out of whole cloth, leaving his "academic" (read: central European) origins behind. To associate Freud with what is outmoded would diminish his contribution and might cast doubt on his transcendence of national boundaries.

For Strachey to see Freud's discourse in the aphasia book as reflecting the academic psychology of the later nineteenth century is a misreading of a text that, in point of fact, was in the process of breaking with that discourse. Freud is analyzing, from a distance, the discourse (he calls it *Sprachgebrauch*; Strachey misleadingly translates it as the narrow and technical term *nomenclature*) of academic psychology. As far as Freud's writing is concerned, one need only compare the aphasia book with related contemporary and predecessor texts to realize that it is a significant departure. It is as if Strachey wanted to erase origins where they did not suit the history he had in mind. His negatively inflected term *technical language* leads us to a significant error in translation of the pages from Freud's Section 5. A key term for Freud is *Kunstwort*, on which his entire argument in these pages is constructed (*AA* 56). Though the first noun in the compound is "art" (the second is "word"), the term is more accurately rendered in English as "artifice"; that is to say, the term *Kunstwort* means an "artificial"—an invented or made up—word, which has a very different inflection from Strachey's translation "technical term." The problem Freud presents is that theorists of the sort (and generation) of Meynert have adopted words from psychology, in which sphere those words designate a limited concept, and applied them to distinct areas of the brain, where they are to describe phenomena of enormous complexity and must necessarily fail to do so. Freud is recognizing a lag behind while a paradigm is shifting. The topic is, indeed, language: he is arguing with, setting himself off from, an older discourse (which also includes, for example, Kussmaul, with the difference that Freud shows no defiant affect toward him), as did the writers he studied closely: Heubner, Bastian, Grashey, and, at this advanced stage in the development of his argument, Hughlings Jackson also.

After giving back-handed credit to Wernicke for at least declaring that only individual sensory "presentations" *(Sinnesvorstellungen)* could be localized at the end of the peripheral nerve that received the impression, Freud continues with three rhetorical questions:

> But shall we not be making the same mistake in principle, whether what we are trying to localize is a complicated concept, a whole mental activity, or a psychical element? Is it justifiable to take a nerve fibre, which for the whole length of its course has been a purely physiological structure and has been subject to purely physiological modifications, and to plunge its end into the sphere of the mind [*ins Psychische*] and to fit this end out with a presentation [*Vorstellung*] or a mnemic image? If 'will,' 'intelligence,' and so on, are recognized as being psychological technical terms [*Kunstworte*] to which very complicated states of affairs correspond in the physiological world, can we feel any more sure that a 'simple sensory presentation' [*Sinnesvorstellung*] is anything other than a technical term [*Kunstwort*] of the same kind? (*SE* 14:206–207; *AA* 56)

There are two major thrusts to this passage: the tie to Hughlings Jackson's theory that the mental (or psychic) and the physiological consist of separate, though parallel, processes, which Freud will explain and elaborate below; and the idea of the *Kunstwort*, or word that has been invented as a discursive convenience, a heuristic tool, ultimately a convention, irrespective of its evidentiary value or of how well it may lend itself to definition. All disciplines need to operate with such discursive conventions, even more consciously so in their early stages. Freud objects to the presumption that such concepts could be usefully translated into a disciplinary context where completely different rules, procedures, and standards of evidence apply. We saw in Delbrück's *Introduction to the Study of Language* a preview of the same concerns with language in the disciplines. Delbrück felt himself situated at a juncture of uneven developments when a great shift was occurring in the sciences, including his own of linguistics, and with this shift arose the problem of a disjunction in disciplinary discourses. From Franz Bopp's applications of terminology from the natural sciences to linguistic phenomena, a practice Delbrück considers to have had only metaphorical meaning, to August Schleicher's identification of the methods of linguistics with the methods of comparative anatomy, false discursive moves could have consequences for the new discipline and its claims for legitimacy and independent standing.

The next stage in Freud's argument hones in on one particular word, *Vorstellung*. A term that carries complex philosophic baggage, it is an example par excellence of the kind of transfer with which Freud quarrels. The impossibility of settling on a consistently satisfactory translation into English indicates the polyvalence of the term. Freud presumes the "physiological corollary" of a *Vorstellung* to be a process that *can* be localized in the brain. Once this process has run its course, it leaves behind a "modification," which he calls "the possibility of memory" (*AA* 58). Freud's brief exploration here of memory is related to the same topic as he will explore it several years later in "The Project." Finally, he delves even more deeply into issues of meaning in disciplinary discourse, seeking to separate, categorize, and define ill-defined terms. He is not a linguistic revolutionary, proffering a brand new vocabulary of *Kunstworte*; rather, he means to delimit existing terms:

Is it possible, then, to differentiate the share of "sensation" [*Empfindung*] from that of "association" in the physiological corollary of sensation? Evidently not. "Sensation" and "association" are two names that we apply to different aspects of the same process. We know, however, that both names have been abstracted from a unified and indivisible process. We cannot have sensations without immediately associating them; no matter how strictly we may separate them conceptually, in reality they are attached to a single process which, beginning at one site in the cortex, is diffused over the entire cortex. The localization of the physiological corollary is thus the same for *Vorstellung* and association, and since *localization of a Vorstellung means nothing but the localization of its corollary*, we must reject putting the *Vorstellung* at one point in the cortex and association at another. Rather, both originate from one point and are at no point at rest.

(I interrupt the passage before it reaches its well-formed conclusion to point out that Freud is considering "sensation" to be subsumed under *Vorstellung*.[13] I have not translated *Vorstellung* because of the inadequacy of available choices in English for purposes of this text.)

With this refutation of a separate localization for *das Vorstellen* [a verb used as a noun] and the association of the *Vorstellungen*, a primary reason for us to differentiate between centers and pathways of speech has been ruled out. At every site in the cortex that serves the language function we can presume similar functional processes, and it is not necessary for us to call upon white fiber masses to which we delegate the association of the *Vorstellungen* found in the cortex. We even have an autopsy finding which proves to us that association of *Vorstellungen* occurs through pathways that lie within the cortex itself. I refer again to Heubner's case, from which we have already learned *one* important lesson. (*AA* 58–59; my italics except for Freud's "*one*")

These paragraphs can be said to have drawn a thread—like a nerve fiber being transformed along its pathway—through the entire book—through

13. The term for sensation, *Empfindung*, is embedded in psychological thought of the time. Gustav Fechner, Wilhelm Wundt, and Ernst Mach are associated with its exploration. Mach's area of research at one time overlapped with Breuer's, and Breuer refers in a footnote in his theoretical section of *Studies on Hysteria* to Mach's *Outlines of the Theory of the Motor Sensations* (1875) (*GW, Nachtragsband*, 269; *SE* 2:210–211). Though Freud only refers to reading this book in a letter to Fliess of June 12, 1900 (*FB* 458; *FL* 417), it is possible that through Breuer he became acquainted earlier with that aspect of Mach's thought. Mach, although primarily a physicist, also belonged to the network of important philosophers and psychologists of the time. A committed antivivisectionist, he was deeply interested in the psychic life of animals. In addition he shared with Freud a commitment to Lamarckian principles. Freud and Mach came together on a public issue when, in 1911, Freud (along with Einstein and other

anatomy, physiology, and psychology, and through issues of meaning in language, leading to a disrupting of conceptual certainties on all those levels of inquiry and ultimately back to an evidentiary origin in Heubner's paper. Freud proceeds to discuss the paper again in some detail, giving full credit once again to Heubner's insight, as well as adding support from an 1891 article by Arnold Pick (on Hughlings Jackson and epilepsy) which confirms Freud's conclusion from Heubner's results.[14] Before turning to Hughlings Jackson and Pick, however, I would like to propose that even to Freud's senior colleague in Brücke's laboratory, Sigmund Exner, the self-conscious questioning of disciplinary discourse and a sense of its historical contingency were not unfamiliar.[15]

In a lengthy note at the end of Section 5, Freud gives Exner and Josef Paneth credit for papers that provided the stimulus for the aphasia book, correcting the presumption he assumes most people will make, that he depended on the work of Nothnagel and Naunyn.[16] There is no doubt that Exner's and Nothnagel's and Naunyn's work draw conclusions that anticipate Freud's. On the basis of pathological evidence, Nothnagel refutes the prevailing theory of "psychomotor centers," raising questions about how to define "localization" in an anatomic sense. In the context of what he calls "functional processes" (131), Nothnagel also proposes that in certain cases of recovery from the effects of lesions, the paralysis they caused must have been "indirect" as a result of "effects at a distance" *(Fernwirkungen)* (127).

Naunyn, whose report concerns itself directly with aphasia and with language, builds a methodical, logical case for locating the aphasias in or near Broca's and Wernicke's areas. He uses brief summaries of seventy-one clinical descriptions and autopsy reports by various researchers and maps the results onto a schematic drawing of the brain to determine where there is the most overlap among the lesions. Although Freud shows several flaws in this reasoning (see below at n. 36), Naunyn's results were clearly

---

prominent thinkers) signed a "positivist manifesto" generated and published to support Mach's philosophy. Information on Mach is from John T. Blackmore, *Ernst Mach: His Work, Life, and Influence* (Berkeley: University of California Press, 1972).

14. Arnold Pick, "Über die sogenannte Re-Evolution (Hughlings Jackson) nach epileptischen Anfällen nebst Bemerkungen über transitorische Worttaubheit," *Archiv für Psychiatrie und Nervenkrankheiten* 22 (1891): 756–779.

15. Freud wrote of Sigmund Exner (1846–1926) as one his "models" along with Ernst Brücke and Ernst Fleischl von Marxow (*SE* 20:9). Exner succeeded to Brücke's professorship and institute directorship.

16. Nothnagel and Naunyn, "Ueber die Localisation der Gehirnkrankheiten," 109–132 (Nothnagel's report) and 132–162, including Tables I.II and III.IV (Naunyn's report).

Some earlier explorations of language by Exner may have resurfaced in Freud's arguments about the transfer of certain terminology, in particular, the above-mentioned examples of "sensation" *(Empfindung)* and "association."It is useful initially to take note of Exner's magnum opus, the *Outline of a Physiological Explanation of Psychic Phenomena*,[19] published in 1894 and considered to have been a stimulus for Freud's taking up the same challenge in his "Project" the following year. Some light is shed on the context of Freud's deliberations by Exner's chapters, which include one devoted to "Sensations," one to "Perceptions," and one to *"Vorstellungen."* Much of Exner's discussion revolves around determining definitions that serve to establish the relationships of these concepts among one another, with *Vorstellungen* being the more general one, to the makeup of which the others contribute. *Vorstellung* is translatable in Exner's text as "impression" (of an object or a word, for example) or "idea," or sometimes even the faculty itself, such as "imagination." That Freud puts quotation marks around *Vorstellung* one time and around "sensation" and "association" twice draws attention to these as "names" that have been "abstracted" to artifically produce a separation where unity exists.

In 1875, when Freud was a medical student and about to take three courses with Exner,[20] Exner published a paper on vision which opened with a four-page critical excursus on disciplinary terms as introduction to his argument that recognition of movement depends on sensation rather than perception.[21] The problem Exner encountered is that there were "no good usable definitions of these concepts" (156). He writes that the situation is similar in the case of the definitions of animal and plant: the definitions exist, but it can be difficult in special cases to categorize an object as animal or plant. He wants to keep away from any definitions that contain the word *soul* (or "mind": *Seele* and its compounds) because it is impossible to determine where the author of such a definition draws the line between the material and nonmaterial processes.[22] Therefore Exner would like to stand by Helmholtz's definitions, but he finds that there are

19. Sigmund Exner, *Entwurf zu einer physiologischen Erklärung der psychischen Erscheinungen,* pt. 1 (Leipzig: Franz Deuticke, 1894).
20. The courses were "Medical and Physiological Demonstration" and "Spectral Analysis" (1876) and, most important, "Physiology of the Senses" (1876–1877). See Siegfried Bernfeld and Susanne Cassirer Bernfeld, *Bausteine der Freud-Biographik* (Frankfurt am Main: Suhrkamp, 1981), 179–180.
21. Sigmund Exner, "Über das Sehen von Bewegungen und die Theorie des zusammengesetzten Auges," *Sitzungsberichte der mathematisch-naturwissenschaftlichen Classe der kaiserlichen Akademie der Wissenschaften* 5, no. 72, sec. 3, 1875 (published 1876): 156–191.
22. This statement takes on a special meaning with regard to Freud's avoidance of the term in the aphasia book and his later use of *Seele* in the psychoanalytic writings.

views were among the other English aphasiologists; whether in agreement or disagreement (as, for example, Bastian), they are among the most commonly cited. Freud was but one of relatively many who were stimulated by Jackson's ideas, in particular "concomitance" (or psychophysical parallelism), dissolution, and speech residues. The two often-discussed theories that appear in the aphasia book are: (1) the parallel but separate course of physical and psychic processes (Freud uses the English term *dependent concomitant*) and (2) the notion of the dissolution of the speech functions, the idea—borrowed from Herbert Spencer—of evolution in reverse, whereby the first functions lost are the "higher" ones, that is, those Jackson considered to have been acquired later, and thus to be less organized, as compared with those acquired earlier, which have become automatic, more tightly organized in the brain. The first of these theories is of particular importance to Freud in the section we are dealing with; he turns to the second in the last section.

The first mention of Hughlings Jackson had been early in the book, when Freud referred to those often-cited patients of Hughlings Jackson who, though otherwise unable to speak (motor aphasia), nevertheless occasionally and unpredictably uttered a curse or some other, more complicated speech fragment. The theories Jackson developed about this syndrome of speech residues or "recurrent utterances" were the third element that Freud integrated into his argument. For Freud, this syndrome was the apparent exception that actually proved the rule that the ability to imitate was never lost by itself but, rather, always remained intact if the capacity for spontaneous speech remained intact; for Hughlings Jackson's patients were unable to spontaneously repeat the uttered phrase. Thus these cases helped Freud to prove one of his early points, but they reappear at a more crucial point in Section 5, where Jackson's role has grown considerably more significant, or at least been given more direct acknowledgment.

Sulloway interprets Freud's position in the aphasia book as a "dualist

---

impressionistic translation. Stengel makes several historical errors in his pioneering article. He maintains that Freud "stood almost alone in immediately recognizing the importance of Hughlings Jackson's contributions to the study of aphasia" (348). As we have seen, nearly every English-speaking author Freud drew upon recognized the relevance and significance of Jackson's ideas earlier than Freud did. Mark Solms and Michael Saling make the same incorrect assumption in their discussion of Hughlings Jackson, *A Moment of Transition: Two Neuroscientific Articles by Sigmund Freud* (London: Karnac, 1990), 125. Stengel also incorrectly states, "While none of the leading authorities in the field of aphasia escaped Freud's criticism, he quoted Jackson with unqualified approval" (349). As we have noted, Freud spared other leading authorities as well, for example, Bastian and Kussmaul; nor was Freud's approval of Jackson's ideas unqualified.

position on the mind-body problem within the more general context of his support for J. Hughlings Jackson's doctrine" (50), which I see as a misreading of Freud's position in general and of his nuanced presentation of Jackson's views. Freud's writing on this topic is marked by qualifiers and modifications that put his own stamp on the theory, altering it from Jackson's version, which is itself nuanced and complex. I have added italics to the following quotation to indicate Freud's qualifier: "*It is probable* that the chain of physiological events in the nervous system does not stand in a causal connection with the psychical ones" (*SE* 14:207; *AA* 98). Freud's description continues, following generally along the lines of Jackson's views, and concludes with the English term in parentheses and quotation marks—"a dependent concomitant."[25]

There is an additional qualification in Freud's discussion of *Vorstellung* and its physiological corollary which concludes with the proposal of a "modification" in the cortex which he calls "the possibility of memory." Here his every word plays a role in suggesting nuanced views: "It is highly doubtful whether there is anything psychical that corresponds to this modification either. Our consciousness shows nothing of a sort to justify, from the psychical point of view, the name of a 'latent mnemic image.' But whenever the same state of the cortex is provoked again, the psychical aspect comes into being once more as a mnemic image" (*SE* 14:208; *AA* 58). The qualifications are in "doubtful," "our consciousness," and "but," which means in this case "however" and determines some kind of connection between a "state of the cortex" and a "psychical aspect" without knowing how the connection is made. The problem is ignorance of what the intermediate stages might be. It is as if Freud's language were porous, leaving openings for revisions of the views presented.[26]

There follows a biologic analogy that inflects the discussion toward complexity, in particular, expanding Freud's point about the complexity of physiological phenomena: "Of course we do not have the slightest idea how animal tissue is able to manage undergoing and keeping separate such manifold modifications. But that it is able to do so is proved by the example of the spermatozoa,[27] in which the most varied and detailed of

25. All references to Jackson are from *Selected Writings* (see Chap. 2, n. 8). The term *doctrine of concomitance* is found in Jackson's "Evolution and Dissolution of the Nervous System" (Croonian Lectures delivered at the Royal College of Physicians, March 1884)(72), which means that Freud read those lectures as well as the ones referred to in his footnotes.
26. Otto M. Marx agrees that "he [Freud] did not succeed in a consequent application of the principle of psycho-physical parallelism." "Freud and Aphasia," 822.
27. Some rather obvious points could be made about Freud's choice here of sperm alone.

such modifications lie ready to develop" (*AA* 58). This example also undermines the idea that Freud truly accepted a strict psychophysical parallelism; for the developing embryo carries the entire human potential. The cortical "modifications" responsible for memory find their parallel in the "modifications" of the developing embryo, joining the fascination with complexity for its own sake that showed itself in Freud's poem metaphor and his conviction that a "wealth of means of expression" is at the disposal of the language apparatus. The common denominator here might be the idea of language. It is possible to trace it from "wealth of means of expression" to "manifold connections among the . . . elements" of poem and nerve fiber, to the multiplicity of modifications in the course of laying down a memory, to the manifold modifications in the course of the development of an embryo. If we take this speculative leap, we can picture Freud on the verge of imagining a genetic language. In any case, he once again brings in a noteworthy analogy for which the text does not prepare and which draws our attention to other comparable moments in the text. These moments seem inflected by and toward language—as Freud wrote, "the subject that occupies us here."

Freud included a footnote with a quotation from Jackson, which he introduced by noting that "Hughlings Jackson warned most sharply against such a confusion of the physical with the psychic in the language process" (*AA* 58): "In all our studies of diseases of the nervous system we must be on our guard against the fallacy that what are physical states in lower centres fine away *into* psychical states in higher centres; that, for example, vibrations of sensory nerves *become* sensations, or that somehow or another an idea produces a movement."[28] It is clear that Jackson provided Freud with significant support in the attack on the localizing theories that make facile assumptions about ideas and nerves. This passage is quoted by several of the commentaries on the aphasia book, but no attention is given to the fact that it is excerpted from Jackson's discussion of disciplinary language. It is instructive to look at the preceding and succeeding material in Jackson's article. By examining this and several other Jackson articles both for his ideas on language and for the manner in which he expressed them, it is possible to add some further dimensions to the prevailing views on his role for Freud.

The article from which Freud took the quotation opens with extensive credit given to the researchers in aphasia whose work has brought an

28. John Hughlings Jackson, "On Affections of Speech from Disease of the Brain," 156.

"*embarras des richesses* in material," then it proceeds to a list of thirteen British researchers, including Bastian and W. T. Gairdner, with special recognition to Broadbent and to Kussmaul's just-published book (the English version), which is called "very complete and highly original." Freud's book does not mention all the names on Jackson's list, but there is enough overlap to underscore their mutual ties to the international aphasia community.

After making his acknowlegments Jackson states that "it is very difficult for many reasons to write on Affections of Speech" (the term he prefers to aphasia). One difficulty is the amount of material available; the other is (to a reader) rather peculiar: "The subject has so many sides—psychological, anatomical, physiological and pathological—that it is very difficult to fix on an order of exposition." In other words, he is worried about how to organize a narrative. The obstacles are located in the conventional discourse: confounding physiology with pathology, using "the vague term 'disease,' " ignoring anatomy in favor of morphology by "saying that words 'reside' in this or that part of the brain" (155). Jackson's concerns about these matters are reflected in his frequent use of quotation marks to highlight a word or a phrase about which he is skeptical. His remarks are characterized by an attempt to establish boundaries of discourse, to set limits on naming. In the section immediately preceding Freud's quoted passage, Jackson writes:

> A method which is founded on classifications which are partly anatomical and physiological, and partly psychological, confuses the real issues. These mixed classifications lead to the use of such expressions as that an *idea* of a word produces an articulatory *movement*; whereas a psychical state, an "idea of a word" (or simply "a word") cannot produce an articulatory movement, a physical state. On any view whatever as to the relation of mental states and nervous states such expressions are not warrantable in a *medical* inquiry. (156)

There is obviously a close parallel to Freud's writing on this topic. The term *idea* would be the equivalent of *Vorstellung* in Freud's discussion. It is also obvious that Jackson is so acutely conscious of language per se, as a "thing" with its own rules and qualities, that he can hardly write without questioning his every abstraction, in almost a Nietzschean sense. Jackson's immediate concern is with classifications; he is prescribing how inquiry should be *described* if it is to be medically legitimate (and at the same time, necessarily legitimate a medical discipline). Behind that concern lies a highly developed and sophisticated critical sensibility for language. As a young man, Jackson apparently once considered leaving his medical career to become a writer.[29] Such an inclination would help explain the depth of his interest in language issues; his footnote quotations of Coleridge, Locke, and Lewes; and references to various literary magazines and reviews. It leads him so far as to suggest that neurological discourse might depend on metaphor: "It so happens that different morbid processes have what, for brevity, we may metaphorically call different seats of election" (157).

Jackson's definition of speech sets him apart from nearly all the other aphasiologists (with the exception of Kussmaul) because it crosses that seldom-breached border between the medical and the linguistic territories. Roman Jakobson claimed Jackson "among the precursors of modern linguistics . . . [who] . . . launched many ideas which later were developed in the science of language.[30] As Forrester has noted, Jackson's idea of language entails a structure and a syntax. Jackson writes: "To speak is not simply to utter words, it is to propositionise. A proposition is such a relation of words that it makes one new meaning; not by a mere addition of what we call the separate meanings of the several words; the terms in a proposition are modified by each other. Single words are meaningless, and so is any unrelated succession of words. The unit of speech is a proposition" (159). He goes on to explain that a single word—yes or no, for example—may be a proposition, depending on the speaker's intention. The aphasic, or "speechless," patient's residue of words may or may not be propositional, according to whether the patient utters it with a meaningful intention. More structured recurrent utterances, a command, for example, may just as well not be propositional, because the patient utters them irrespective of the occasion, "every time he tries to speak." In sum, "loss of speech is loss of the power to propositionise" and "Speechlessness does not mean entire Wordlessness" (160). Unlike other aphasiologists, Jackson

29. The evidence for this is an account by the physician Jonathan Hutchinson (1828–1913), a close friend of Jackson's: "When Dr. Jackson and myself first made acquaintance he had been some two or three years in the profession, and, in the belief that it did not offer attractive scope for mental powers of which he was not unconscious, he was on the point of abandoning it, intending to engage in a literary life. From this I was successful in dissuading him, and for many years I plumed myself upon this most successful achievement of my long life. Of late, however, I have had my misgivings, and have doubted whether—great as has been the gain to medicine—it might not have been a yet greater gain to the world at large if Hughlings Jackson had been left to devote his mind to philosophy." Quoted in Greenblatt, "John Hughlings Jackson," 354–355.
30. Roman Jakobson, "Linguistic Types of Aphasia," Brain Function, vol. 3, Proceedings of the Third Conference, November 1963, "Speech, Language, and Communication" (Berkeley: University of California Press, 1966), 67–91, here 81.

focuses neither on the word nor on the letter of the alphabet as the foundational unit. He does offer a division of language into intellectual and emotional language, which seems to muddy any definitional clarification he is trying to achieve. (Bastian, as already noted, did not accept that division.) His examples of defects of speech that fit the category of dissolution—a patient who uses "worm-powder" for "cough-medicine" or "parasol" for "castor oil"—would seem to be better explained by Delbrück's views than by the idea of dissolution.

When proposing a division of aphasia into three degrees (at the time noting that each case is also unique), Jackson writes, "We have to consider degrees of affection of Language, of which speech is but a part" (161). Thus his categories are: defect of speech (something like paraphasia), loss of speech, and loss of language (the most profound, which entails loss of all ability to communicate, including gestures). He makes the distinction between language and speech which cannot be made in German because of the ambiguity in the word *Sprache*. Jackson's distinction supports rendering Freud's terminology as "*language* apparatus" when the broader category is immanent.

Jackson writes that "words are in themselves meaningless, they are only symbols of things or of 'images' of things; they may be said to have meaning 'behind them' " (165). Whereas Freud does not write that words are meaningless—on the contrary, he focuses on the word as such—he does rely on the compound nouns with "image," such as *Wortbild* (word image), *Klangbild* (sound image), *Schriftbild* (written image), and *Bewegungsbild* (kinesthetic image). (Such compounds belonged to the standard German scientific terminology of the time.) Jackson's remarks privilege the category of "things," just as Freud privileges "objects" over words. Jackson's "images of things" are equivalent to Freud's *Vorstellungen* (or *Bilder*) that take the place of direct experience of an object. John Stuart Mill's writing on perception and language is evident here in Freud's and Jackson's concepts and formulations (see Chapter 5).

In a footnote Jackson discusses the term *image*, concluding that "the expression 'organised image' is used briefly for 'image, the *nervous arrangements for which* are organised,' correspondingly for 'organised word,' etc." (165). If "image" depends on or arises out of "nervous arrangements," then—even in Jackson's writing—there is no longer a strict division between the physical and the psychic. Jackson, who associates words and images, both expressly as psychic phenomena, here allows "image" to refer to the setting of "nervous arrangements." There is a drift, a porosity, in his discourse which makes it less definitive than supposed by those who rely only on Freud's quotation from Jackson on psychophysical parallelism.

Yet another important area for Freud would have been Jackson's discussion of consciousness versus preconscious states. Representing the generally held view about Jackson's role for Freud, S. P. Fullinwider claims that "with the aid of Jackson's theory, which associated consciousness with speech, Freud entered into his work with neurotics" (155). Jackson's views are actually not as clear-cut as that statement implies. Furthermore, Fullinwider attributes to the aphasia text ideas about consciousness versus unconsciousness which Freud would not articulate until later. As Jackson continues to try to explain aphasic patients' language capacity, he writes: "Words are required for thinking, for most of our thinking at least, but the speechless man is not wordless; there is an automatic and unconscious or subconscious service of words." His footnote to this statement shows how untenable fixed borders or absolute binaries were to Jackson:

> The expression *"un*conscious reproduction of words" involves the same contradiction as does the expression "unconscious sensation." Such expressions may be taken to mean that energising of lower, more organised, nervous arrangements, although unattended by any sort of conscious state, is essential for, and leads to, particular energisings of the highest and least organised—the now-organising—nervous arrangements, which last-mentioned energising is attended by consciousness. I, however, think (as Lewes does) that some consciousness or "sensibility" attends energising of all nervous arrangements (I use the term subconscious for slight consciousness). In cases where from disease the highest nervous arrangements are suddenly placed *hors de combat*, as in sudden delirium, the next lower spring into greater activity; and then, what in health was a subordinate subconsciousness, becomes a vivid consciousness, and is also the highest consciousness there then can be. ("On Affections of Speech" 167)

He also writes: "It is, I think, because speech and perception are preceded by an unconscious or subconscious reproduction of words and images, that we seem to have 'faculties' of speech and of perception, as it were, above and independent of the rest of ourselves" (167–168). This statement is reminiscent of Freud's speculation in *Studies on Hysteria* on the feeling the analyst has that there are times when an independent intelligence—the unconscious—is operating in the patient. But combined with the note above, it is testimony to a struggle, or at least a lack of resolution, in

Jackson's thinking about the relationship between language and the unconscious. If Jackson is a source of Freud's views, then Freud later refined (or reduced) that relationship with a certainty foreign to Jackson.

Jackson's statement is also a testimony to his continuing struggle with his own language. "Now-organising" is an example of the neologisms he coined in the course of a sustained effort at description that would reach beyond the prevailing discourse—like a James Joyce of neurology. Although Freud coined a new name for one type of aphasia, he did not otherwise take such leaps in 1891. The first segment of Jackson's article (printed in three parts) concludes with thoughts on loss of speech among patients who do not show any disease of the nervous system. He writes: "Let us state the facts. The patients are nearly always boys or unmarried women. The bearing of this is obvious." Uniquely among Freud's sources, Jackson is proposing a sexual etiology for hysterical speech symptoms. This must indeed have caught Freud's attention, as by this time he had already treated Frau Emmy von N. without the benefit of this insight and with disappointing results. Jackson's thought is strikingly liberated and unconventional, and he was inclined to make suggestions that strike us as insightful a century later. One insight that Freud probably preferred not to take into consideration was Jackson's belief that such patients "might be 'cured' by faradisation of the vocal cords, or by a thunderstorm, or by quack medicines, or appliances, or by mesmerism, or by wearing a charm, or—not speaking flippantly—by being 'prayed over' " (170) (even though, in *Studies on Hysteria*, Freud did compare the therapist with the priest).

The second installment of Jackson's tripartite series "On Affections of Speech from Disease of the Brain" consists of reports of cases of patients who manifested recurrent utterances. The class distinctions are often clear in these cases (more than one patient lives in a workhouse), and one has the impression that the practice of physicians who saw aphasic patients did not include member of the higher classes, which circumstance may be relevant to the kinds of utterances Jackson is able to report and theorize. Showing his close reading of Kussmaul's book, Jackson includes in the body of his text a reply to Kussmaul's misreading of questions asked of a patient by Jackson and a colleague. Kussmaul reported that the two English physicians asked patients questions "designed to make them angry" (Jackson 177). What they actually did was ask questions such as "Are you 100 years old?" to see if patients could be stimulated to say "no." Kussmaul's misinterpretation must arise out of different cultural practices, possibly different notions of courteous discourse, certainly different assumptions about the clinical situation. When language is at issue, social signals inevitably enter the diagnostic situation, even though the aphasiologists (including Freud) do not acknowledge it.

Jackson does not build arguments as Freud does in logical or rhetorical sequence; rather, his style is to cast ideas scattershot throughout his papers. For that reason it is necessary to comb them for the nuggets that apply especially to Freud and language. The third installment of "On Affections of Speech" is particularly arresting with respect to the problem of essential concepts. For example, in a footnote devoted to exploring the meanings of the term *dissolution,* Jackson incidentally mentions that the word *consciousness* is itself a reductive abstraction: "Our highest, latest, ever-changing mental states, the abstract name for which is consciousness, there being really a series of consciousnesses."[31] He is even more adamant about the invalidity of the term *memory,* which he uses with the support of an extensive footnote that adds to the series of notes that serve— occupied as they are with the existential impossibility of truth-telling in language—as a running deconstruction of his text: "The use of such highly technical expressions as 'memory,' in 'explanation' of complex symptomatic conditions, seemingly definite and authoritative, is largely to blame for our remaining with our ideas on nervous diseases out of focus" (186).

Clearly, when Jackson writes of "technical expressions," he is writing about the terms Freud refers to as *Kunstworte,* that is, made-up words, words to which cling the sense of "artifice." In Jackson's lexicon, however, *all* the central terms in the professional discourse which he is obliged to use are *Kunstworte,* and as a literary person he must continually assuage his acute dissatisfaction with them and with their pernicious effects. In later years, Freud demonstrated that he shared this sensibility. One example is found in the essay "The Unconscious," where Freud struggles with the "ambiguity" of the terms *conscious* and *unconscious* (*GW* 10:271; *SE* 14:172). Accounts of Jackson's work do not explore questions of linguistic representation and indeterminacy. They make his views seem fixed, when he was really calling them constantly into question from the sidelines, like a dissatisfied fan. Freud may have responded several years later to the unspoken question in Jackson's note: What does "memory" really mean? With great intensity, he struggles with this question in "The Project."

This segment of Jackson's article brings the two cases Freud chose to report in his aphasia book, after explaining that they were borrowed from

---

31. Jackson, "On Affections of Speech," 185. Jackson's definition is reminiscent of a modern neurobiologist's definition of the self: "a perpetually re-created neurobiological state." Damasio, *Descartes' Error,* 100.

Hughlings Jackson, "on whose views I have based almost all the preceding remarks, in order to dispute, with their help, the localizing theory of speech disturbances" (*AA* 63). Beyond the commonly retained "yes" and "no," patients who have lost speech may often repeat a formulaic curse. Freud reports Hughlings Jackson's view that this type of utterance is also classified in the healthy person as belonging to emotional rather than intellectual speech. He recounts Jackson's case of a man who sustained a brain injury in a brawl and was left with the recurrent utterance "I want protection" and that of a clerk left with only the words "list complete" subsequent to a brain episode and loss of speech that occurred after working hard on a catalog (*AA* 63; "On Affections of Speech" 188). Why, of the cases reported by Jackson, did Freud choose these two? As in his other choices (e.g., from Hammond), the cases Freud selects have special features. First of all, he will use them in the last section of his book to illustrate one kind of speech that survives the process of dissolution: retention of what is most intensely associated—that is, where the degree of emotional involvement in the speech fragment is what counts (in contradiction to theories of localization).

But there is yet a second level of involvement in these cases on Freud's part. He speculates that these are "the last words which the speech apparatus had formed before falling ill, perhaps with a premonition of what would occur." This mystical note introduces a personal anecdote. Freud seemed to attach a certain mystique to aspects of his own life experiences, even before what has been called the building of his legend. He continues that he would like to interpret these two "modifications" (he means the recurrent utterances) as deriving from "their intensity at a moment of great inner excitement" (*AA* 63). He remembers on two occasions having suddenly believed that he was in mortal danger and thinking, "Now it's all over with you," while hearing those words as if they were being yelled into his ear and simultaneously seeing them as if printed on a fluttering slip of paper (*AA* 63–64).

The anecdote is striking because, of course, it is *not* related to Jackson's cases of recurrent utterances that were the only bits of speech left to brain-damaged individuals who repeated them compulsively and without meaning. It does, however, coincide with Jackson's hypothesis of an "unconscious or subconscious reproduction of words and images." With this anecdote Freud seems to be reacting to something that is never addressed in his aphasia book: Jackson's views on language and the unconscious. More than a story about himself, Freud's anecdote sounds like the compulsive recurrent utterances of patients, such as Frau Emmy von N., whom he treated several years before publishing the aphasia book. Originating in trauma, such statements would recur in inappropriate settings divorced from the original contexts.[32] The anecdote is of the kind one is accustomed to from Freud's later works. In the aphasia book it marks the chapter where Freud is developing expanded considerations on language, going beyond the more strictly neuroscientific ones of the earlier sections. With the extended attack on Meynert, the resistance to authority has been spent. Now that the rhetorical clash of blades is no longer necessary, the narrative has taken on a more personal quality.

Jackson's writing is most remarkable for its self-reflexiveness on language. In an early article, "Notes on the Physiology and Pathology of Language" (1866) he wrote: "It need scarcely be said that words, especially such as 'mind,' 'sensory,' 'motor,' etc., fetter our thoughts as well as define them"—a condition fully grasped by Freud. Jackson's struggles with this condition are realized in his attempts to get as many degrees as possible away from definition without settling on a neologism. He writes, in this article, "It is the nervous system of the nervous system" (121); in the tripartite article I have been discussing, Jackson wrote, "Written words are symbols of symbols of images" (166), drawing close, in 1878, to the ideas of Nietzsche, for example, in that Jackson, while seeking grounding, does not seem to believe in its possibility. Jackson's writing seems to have carried into Freud's ken the conflict of "determinate meaningfulness" with "variability of representation,"[33] perhaps less as a "conflict" than as the idea of their necessary coexistence, even in a neurological context—a kind of legitimating of the flux and play of brain and language, of reproduction and interpretation.

In the 1866 article, Jackson states: "Damage near the corpus striatum affects language and thought, not because any so-called faculty resides there (or anywhere, except in the whole brain or whole body) . . ." (125). In his earlier years he seemed to demonstrate a flexibility and an unconventionality in his thought that was a function of his critical fascination with language. Had he read this statement, Freud would have read of the incipient psychoanalytic "talking cure," which depends on the idea that language and thought "reside" in the whole brain and whole body. He would also have read of "Dr. William Thomson, the present Archbishop

32. In her discussion of Hughlings Jackson and Freud, Anne Harrington (237–238) interprets Freud's anecdote in terms of the several ways in which recurrent utterances foreshadow later psychoanalytic theory.
33. Richard Terdiman, *Present Past: Modernity and the Memory Crisis* (Ithaca: Cornell University Press, 1993), 307.

of York" (from whose book *Outline of the Laws of Thought* Bastian took his definition of language), and his view that for the "deaf and dumb" who "must use . . . the remembered images of hands in the various combinations of finger-speech *as the symbols of their thoughts*" ("Physiology and Pathology of Language" 126–127; italics added by Jackson)—ideas that have an obvious connection to the body's language of symptoms as noted by Freud in his early psychoanalytic patients. After his quotation from Thomson, Jackson writes: "Of course, we do not either speak or think in words or signs only, but in words or signs referring to one another in a particular manner, . . . Indeed, words in sentences lose their individual meaning—if single words can be strictly said to have any meaning—and the whole sentence becomes a unit, not a word-heap" (127).

The observation that meaning depends on context to so great an extent that "words in sentences lose their individual meaning"—in other words, that context is everything—takes Jackson far beyond other aphasiologists' preoccupation with the letters of the alphabet or the individual word which set the limits of their understanding of linguistic phenomena. It takes him all the way to Saussurean linguistics and late-twentieth-century language theory. Jackson's fellow aphasiologists did demonstrate interest in his ideas on recurrent utterances, dissolution, and dependent concomitant; but they generally ignored his thoughts on language itself. In the aphasia book, Freud too seems to adhere to the more common circumscribed views. After the excitement of Jackson's struggle with language, Freud's explorations seem limited and conventional. Although he does not appear to have attended immediately to Jackson's most provocative insights, they may well have had consequences for the psychoanalytic writings. In my reading of Jackson's role for Freud, I am taking a recognized connection and suggesting that there is more to it than has met the eye up to now. It is inevitable that texts like Jacksons's would impart more than the three theories (psychophysical parallelism, dissolution, and recurrent utterances) by which Jackson's relationship to Freud is generally defined. There would have been translation and transmission in the broadest sense —a product also of the fecundity of the texts in a time of disciplinary ferment—to a sympathetic, receptive reader.

In the context of the further elaboration of his main point, Freud arrived at the formulation that

> at every site in the cortex that serves the language function, we can presume similar functional processes, and it is not necessary for us to call upon white fiber masses to which we delegate the association of the

John Hughlings Jackson
From *The Founders of Neurology*, 2d ed., ed. Webb Haymaker and Francis Schiller
(Springfield, Il: Charles C. Thomas, 1970), 457.

Vorstellungen found in the cortex. We even have an autopsy finding which proves to us that association of *Vorstellungen* occurs through pathways that lie within the cortex itself. I refer again to Heubner's case, from which we have already learned one important lesson." (*AA* 59)

We saw that that first lesson was to disprove Lichtheim's theory that patients who presented the same syndrome as Heubner's patient were victims of a *trans*cortical aphasia. This second lesson is a far broader one. Freud has shifted the focus from Lichtheim's erroneous views to the larger issue of association. Freud's argument has traversed this issue, beginning with a circumscribed focus on detail, all the way to questions of meaning in language, on the way deconstructing (or reconstructing) terms, finally returning to the starting point with an enhanced and enlarged interpretation of Heubner, the argument having traced a transforming path like Freud's description of nerve fibers on their path from periphery to cortex. Again Freud credits Heubner with having recognized the significance of the finding, and he also credits Arnold Pick with having drawn the same conclusion from Heubner's article. Freud adds the Pick reference at the last moment; for Pick's article was published in 1891.[34]

The article, an account of a case of epilepsy, is steeped in Hughlings Jackson's views, in particular the idea of regular progression according to the model of evolution. The term *re-evolution* described stages of recovery from a seizure that entailed inability to recognize words (*Worttaubheit,* or "word deafness"). In addition, Pick subscribed to Hughlings Jackson's concept of psychophysical parallelism. He believed at the same time, however, that the sensory aphasias formed a connecting link between somatic and psychic processes and that, in the course of re-evolution, psychic conditions followed stages parallel to conditions in the brain, "in the sense of monism" (757). Pick's statement, then, also contradicts those interpretations of Hughlings Jackson's views which emphasize the strict separation of the processes into mind and body. When he takes the side of Hughlings Jackson, Pick comes into conflict with Wernicke's views, although he nevertheless does make the standard assumptions about centers versus pathways. Pick reports on Heubner's results with approval and realizes that they contradict Wernicke and Lichtheim, but he uses Heubner only to clarify the process of re-evolution: that it follows an "intracortical" (as opposed to transcortical) path (774). By no means does Heubner's

---

34. Pick, "Ueber die sogenannte Re-Evolution nach epileptischen Anfällen." Pick's later work became influential and is still cited today in studies on aphasia.

work assume as central a role for Pick as it did for Freud. What is a rather dramatic affirmation for Freud, however, is the fact that Pick brings together Hughlings Jackson and Heubner, finding in the Heubner case evidence for the regular stages of recovery as a step-by-step return to "territories" (774) in the brain. Freud must have been drawn by Pick's adherence to Hughlings Jackson's parallelism, perhaps especially by Pick's version that saw it as "monism."

Unfortunately, Pick's article is so badly written as to be nearly incomprehensible. The writing lacks clarity and control as well as the sense of how to construct a modulated sentence, how to clarify and present an argument, let alone how to make a rhetorically persuasive presentation. Freud's writing stands out in particular relief against such a style, reminding us of his qualities as a master communicator who delineates sharply, expresses his views clearly, and rhetorically highlights points of particular import. His highly crafted style has often been remarked on. Even his most "technical" or scientific writing, such as in the aphasia book or the earlier articles, seduces readers with narrative craftsmanship the way a good story does.

When Freud next mentions Pick, it is again in association with Heubner's findings, and in reference to a case of "transitory word deafness following epileptic attacks" (AA 85). This case history, published by Pick in 1889,[35] shows him as belonging to the same aphasia network as Freud, which included Hughlings Jackson and Ross, Broadbent, Spamer, Charcot, and, of course, Wernicke and Lichtheim, although Pick's approach to them differs from Freud's. The treatment of Lichtheim in this and Pick's 1891 article reminds us that Lichtheim was the prominent, established authority whose diagrams were accepted as a matter of course in German-speaking circles. Thus it also reminds us what it meant for Freud to take on Lichtheim as the prime target of his argument.

Pick's 1889 case reports in heart-rending detail the story of progressive deterioration from brain disease of a 35-year-old illiterate, mentally retarded, unmarried, unemployed prostitute named Marie, mother of three children, who was picked up by police after a history of bizarre behavior that culminated in begging in the streets in winter until her feet froze. Of course none of these details appear in Freud's reference, which has only to do with the patient's manifestation of "asymbolia," or break in the connection between the idea of an object (Objektvorstellung) and the idea

---

35. Arnold Pick, "Zur Localisation einseitiger Gehörshallucinationen nebst Bemerkungen über transitorische Worttaubheit," *Jahrbücher für Psychiatrie* 8 (1889): 61–193.

of the word for it *(Wortvorstellung)*, even while the object is seen and the word itself can be repeated but without comprehension.

We are reminded again of how distant Freud's study appears to be from actual patients and their circumstances. Their stories would detract from the logical force of his argument and the import of his presentation. We are also reminded by Pick's case that aphasia was basically untreatable. All the cases Freud refers to, unless involving a surgically treatable injury such as Hammond's cases, merely report the presentation, history, and progress of a condition for which there was neither therapy nor cure. Although to the onlooker, aphasic symptoms may give the impression of being comic errors, they always represent a tragedy for the victim, even if sometimes only temporary, as in cases where there is eventual recovery from a head injury, for example, or from aphasia of unknown cause. While diagnosis and understanding of brain function and malfunction has progressed enormously in our time, treatment has not, and case histories of aphasia remain primarily accounts of manifestations of damage for which there is no medical relief. Freud, of course, made the choice in his own practice to treat patients for whom therapy had greater prospect of success.

Before he can present his own proposal for the structure of the "language apparatus" in the brain, Freud needs to dispense with Meynert's thesis that there are areas of the mature brain that are "empty," that is, without function until such time as, for example, a new language is learned or those areas are needed to replace the functions of damaged areas. He points out that Meynert's view rests on the findings of pathological anatomy but that this particular question cannot be decided on that basis. He offers the example of overlays drawn by Naunyn on the basis of lesions in seventy-one cases of aphasia. By tracing where the lesions overlap, it was thought possible to establish where the speech centers are located. Freud objects to this conclusion for the following reasons: (1) There may be additional sites in the cortex which serve the speech function but whose destruction does not have as noticeable an impact on speech. These would not appear on Naunyn's charts. (2) There is the possibility that damage to the speech function has been caused by action at a distance from the site of the lesion *(Fernwirkung*—as discussed, for example, by Nothnagel and also named by Bastian). (3) Sites outside of the overlapped areas may still serve speech without being either indispensible or continuous.[36]

---

36. The *New York Times* (May 30, 1995, B5–B6) reported on work like Naunyn's done by Nina Dronkers, who mapped the lesions of patients with Wernicke's aphasia (sensory aphasia) and found that they indeed overlap at the area identified by Wernicke. Hanna and Antonio Damasio have mapped intersections of lesions to find, for example, regions for

Meynert sees the limits of intellectual capacity in the limits of memory capacity set by the cells of the cortex. Freud concludes that Meynert believes not only that development in childhood entails the "occupation" of previously "unoccupied" areas of the cortex but that this process applies to later intellectual acquisitions as well, such as learning a new language. He contends that the situation is precisely the opposite from Meynert's presumption. Whereas the language function does make extraordinary new acquisitions—such as reading and writing—damage to which can, indeed, be localized because they entail visual and chiromotor elements—all of its other new acquisitions, such as foreign languages, are not to be found in previously "empty" territory but at the same site as the language learned first. The key to the dispute between Freud and Meynert lies in the distinction between functional and spatial interpretations. Meynert envisions a space with strict borders and with limits, so to speak, on the numbers of its population (of cells) and what they can do. Freud makes a proposal that does not lend itself to being envisioned, meaning that it is theoretically denser and more difficult to follow. His notion is defined not by place where but by processes accomplished, and the capacity he proposes does not have distinct topographical limits.

Freud makes Meynert's hypothesis slightly ridiculous by taking it to its ultimate geographic implications, comparing it to a city expanding beyond its walls (see Chap. 1 at n. 37) to "previously unoccupied land." The metaphor as a rhetorical choice serves to inflect toward the pejorative Freud's next statement referring to Meynert's "earlier remark" that empty areas take over the functions of "centers" that have been destroyed "experimentally or otherwise"—a conclusion based on Munk's experiments, which are themselves "rooted" in Meynert's theories (*AA* 61). That is to say, the metaphorical devaluation can also be understood as part of Freud's negative investment in the kind of experiments he found scientifically invalid and, on another level, perhaps even offensive. Munk certainly stood in the tradition of Flourens, whose sadistic experiments "proved" that no part of the brain had a specific function, so that when a part was destroyed, the remaining areas would take over its functions. There can be, after all, no relevance of animal experiments to the questions Freud wants to address here—the acquisition of reading and writing and foreign language skills.

---

concepts of objects. Such research no longer requires autopsy material; it is carried out noninvasively with brain scanning and computer processing. It is tempting to wonder whether Freud's trenchant objections might not still stand in relation to the investigations being carried out in our time.

Freud continues in a conspiratorial tone: "Thus we have now learned with what intention the presumption has been made of 'functionless gaps' in the cortex, and we can move ahead to test its usefulness for understanding speech disturbances" (AA 61). It is, of course, quite clear to the reader what the outcome of the "test" will be. The test has to do with language learning and brings another occasion for self-observation, although Freud does not mention himself directly but does switch to the first person singular:

> Whether I learn to understand and speak many foreign languages, whether in addition to the alphabet learned first, I master the Greek and the Hebrew alphabets, and in addition to cursive writing I use stenography and other scripts—all of these accomplishments (and the number of memory images [*Erinnerungsbilder*] employed for them can exceed by multiples those used for the original language) are obviously located at the same sites that we know as centers for the language learned first. It never happens that an organic lesion causes the mother tongue an impairment from which a language acquired later would escape. (AA 62)

For Freud to acknowledge the personal nature of this observation directly would be, in the case of such an impressive list of skills, excessively prideful (at least according to the conventions of scientific writing). Beyond the demands of theory, he seems to be seeking an explanation for his own exceptional linguistic abilities.

From this point Freud launches into comments on foreign language learning (and by implication, teaching) which have not lost their validity and which show how seriously he occupied himself with analyzing skills that were already highly and consciously developed in himself as a young man and a product of the classical-humanist educational system. He writes that the evidence shows that the keys to language retention are age at acquisition and practice, with age at acquisition being the overriding factor. In cases of impairment of the polyglot's language capacity, there is never a relationship among the losses of languages that could be explained by localization at different sites in the brain: "It is apparently true that the language associations with which our language capacity [*Sprachleistung*] works are capable of a *superassociation* which we clearly perceive as long as we carry out the new associations only with difficulty, and that the *superassociated — irrespective of where the lesion is located — is damaged before the primary-associated*" (AA 62). The background to this thinking becomes clear as Freud continues with the discussion that gives credit for "all preceding remarks" to Hughlings Jackson and cites his cases of speech remnants—such as "yes" or "no" or the last words before injury—in aphasic patients. Those speech remnants are examples of what Freud calls the "primary-associated" (such as his own example of seeing the phrase "It's all over for you" in two life-threatening situations). Out of Hughlings Jackson's ideas, perhaps also Jackson's belief that surviving speech remnants are examples of emotional (as opposed to intellectual) language, Freud has forged an analytic model that will serve him in the clinical setting of psychoanalysis. In his 1893 article on the distinctions between organic and hysterical disturbances of speech, distinctions he developed in the aphasia book reappear: (1) The inevitable loss of the foreign and later-acquired language before the loss of the mother tongue is symptomatic of the organic lesions only; the hysterical patient (such as Breuer's Anna O.) is perfectly capable of losing the mother tongue while retaining the use of foreign languages. (2) The retention of speech remnants as recurrent utterances is a symptom of organic disorder; the hysterical aphasic patient "utters not a word" [ne profère pas un mot].[37] In addition, Freud had already contrasted organic and hysterical aphasias in medical dictionary entries of 1888.

Now at last, two-thirds of the way through his book, Freud introduces his own scheme of organization for the "language apparatus":

> Accordingly, we reject the assumptions that the language apparatus consists of separate centers which are divided by cortical regions that are without function, furthermore that the *Vorstellungen* (mnemic images) [*Erinnerungsbilder*] that serve speech are stored at particular cortical sites which are to be called centers, while their association is provided exclusively by subcortical white-fiber tracts [*Fasermassen*]. After that, it only remains for us to state the view that *the language area [Sprachgebiet] of the cortex is a coherent cortical region* within which the associations and transmissions upon which the language functions are based take place with a complexity that is beyond comprehension. (*AA* 64)

Freud's scheme for the language area is not new, nor is this the last version in print: essentially the same version had appeared in a medical dictionary entry of 1888 and would reappear in yet another dictionary in 1893.[38] The

37. Sigmund Freud, "Quelques considérations pour une étude comparative des paralysies motrices organiques et hystériques," *GW* 1:39–55, here 45; *SE* 1:157–172, here 164.
38. The 1888 (unsigned) entry, "Aphasia," appeared in Albert Villaret, ed. *Handwörterbuch der gesamten Medizin*, vol. 1 (Stuttgart: Ferdinand Enke), 88–90. It has been translated and edited by Solms and Saling in *Moment of Transition*. The 1893 (signed) entry appeared in

1888 version shows Freud already steeped in Jacksonian thinking: "One distinguishes between natural or emotional speech (gestural speech) and artificial or articulate speech, of which the latter succumbs to disturbances more frequently because it is acquired later" (Solms and Saling, 31; *Handwörterbuch*, 88). With regard to the 1893 entry, Kästle comments on the unusual circumstance that Freud was contributing to a general medical dictionary at such a late date, which Kästle attributes to Freud's self-categorization as a specialist for disturbances of speech and of language, an interest that Kästle traces back to Freud's medical student days (509). In the 1893 entry, Heubner's report is once again brought in as evidence, this time as offering the location for the lesion that causes pure asymbolia. The 1893 version derives, with some small changes, from the aphasia book, thus surpassing the 1888 version in complexity and sophistication while, nevertheless, carrying through the original vision of the language area in the brain. In the earlier article, Freud begins his analysis with the four elements of the word—two sensory and two motor—and from those derives the four principal types of aphasia and then the description of the relevant brain anatomy. In both the aphasia book and the 1893 entry, however, he makes an express distinction between the "psychological" description, which is the analysis of words and their associations with objects, and an anatomic description. In 1893, Freud provides an expanded and updated version of his schematic diagram from the aphasia book and adds a new, anatomic diagram that locates on a sketch of the left brain the description of the speech apparatus he introduced in the fifth section of the aphasia book. In his French article on organic and hysterical paralyses, written between 1888 and 1893, he refers to the aphasia study, where organic aphasia is explained "by the fact that we are dealing not with separate centres but with a continuous area of association" (*SE* 1:167; *GW* 1:49). Thus the thread that connects these different but closely related texts is his vision (from another point of view, we might call it a metaphor) of the organization of language in the brain. In both 1893 texts Freud draws extensively on his aphasia book. (Perhaps he wanted to encourage more readers to turn to it.)

In the aphasia book, his further elaboration of the language area allows

---

Anton Bum and Mortiz T. Schnirer, eds., *Diagnostisches Lexikon für praktische Ärzte*, vol. 1 (Vienna: Urban und Schwarzenberg), and was reprinted with commentary in Kästle, "Einige bisher unbekannte Texte von Sigmund Freud." Both entries are referred to by their editors as showing Freud's transition from neuropathology to psychoanalysis. When we add to that testimony the commonly held view that Freud's 1885–1886 visit to Paris marked a "turning point," we have a Freud "turning" and "in transition" for a decade or more, if one takes *Studies on Hysteria* to mark the beginning of psychoanalysis.

Freud to resolve the matter of "centers," including Broca's area and Wernicke's area with their distinct properties. (An illustration of the brain, which would serve his purposes at this point, because he mentions "the convex surface of a left hemisphere," is included not in the aphasia book but only in the 1893 dictionary entry.) His explanation is that what have been called "centers" lie at the outermost "corners" of the language "field" in the cortex, encompassing it between them. Language disturbances occur within this area. What distinguishes the "centers" is the fact that, external to the language field, they impinge on other crucial areas whose character can determine the character of a language disturbance. For example: Broca's area impinges on motor centers for bulbar nerves; Wernicke's area lies in the same area as the ending of the acoustic nerve; the visual center impinges on the location of the ending of the optic nerve.[39]

Freud's scheme builds on historical antecedents. One "diagram maker" central to Freud's theory was, of course, Bastian, who wrote in 1887:

> Although I am not a firm believer in the complete topographical distinctness of the several sensory or perceptive centres in the cerebral hemispheres, I consider it clear that there must be certain sets of structurally related cell and fibre mechanisms in the cortex, whose activity is associated with one or with another of the several kinds of sensory endowment. Such diffuse but functionally unified nervous networks may differ altogether from the common conception of a neatly defined "centre."[40]

In this article, to which Freud refers so often, were the germs of the following ideas: questioning the prevailing topography of centers while granting that some kinds of functional clusters must exist, confining them to the cortex alone, positing a functional unity, and above all, associating them with "sensory endowments." Here lie suggestions to which Freud responded, I propose, because they are products of a mind set that "may differ altogether from the common conception." Immediately above this statement in Bastian's article is his simple diagram (Figure 2) that, despite its crudeness, suggests the future outlines of Freud's language field. What Freud can be said to have done is to have taken Bastian's suggestions and applied them to the old, simple diagram, stretching it out in four directions and providing it with a second frame. Something of that nature

---

39. This is very close to Exner's scheme, as mentioned above, after n. 18.
40. Bastian, "On Different Kinds of Aphasia," 933.

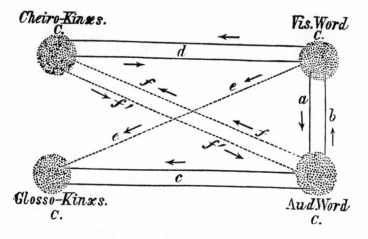

Figure 2. From H. Charlton Bastian, "On Different Kinds of Aphasia, with Special Reference to Their Classification and Ultimate Pathology," *British Medical Journal* 2 (July–December 1887): 933.

clearly crossed Bastian's mind, but in his typical fashion, he did not expand on or develop the thought.

After setting out his version of the language field as succinctly as possible, Freud turns to two of the figures who have accompanied him on route, standing to either side of his discussion: Wernicke, to whom Freud gives credit for coming closer to his view (although only in a limited sense) in a recently published paper,[41] and Heubner, who is introduced as a contrast to Wernicke with a "whereas" and whose entire question Freud quotes because it provides the foundation on which he can build his case.

Freud's unpacking of the language field, using it to explain aphasia, and finally completing his refutation of, in particular, Lichtheim, concludes with a return to the central problem of *Vorstellung* versus association. The logic of his argument has inexorably led to the neurological description presented in detail as follows:

> The association area of language which visual, auditory, and motor (or kinesthetic) elements enter extends for that very reason *between the cortical fields of those sensory nerves and the related motor cortical fields.* If we now imagine a lesion that can be moved within this association field, its effect will be greater (given unchanged dimensions) the closer it approaches to one of the cortical fields, thus the more peripherally it is located within

41. Wernicke, "Recent Works on Aphasia."

the language area. If it abuts directly on one of these cortical fields, it will cut off the association area of language from one of its tributaries: the language mechanism will be deprived of the visual, the auditory element, etc., since every stimulus for association of this kind originated from the relevant cortical field. If one moves the lesion further toward the interior of the association field, its effect will be indistinct; by no means will it be able to destroy all the possibilities for any one kind of association. In this way the sections of the language field that abut the cortical fields of the visual, auditory, and motor cranial nerves gain the significance attributed to them by pathology, which has led to their being put forth as centers for language. This significance, however, holds only for the pathology and not for the physiology of the language apparatus, since one cannot maintain that different or more important processes take place in them than in those parts of the language field which can better tolerate lesions. This view follows directly from the refusal to separate the process of *Vorstellung* from that of association and localize both processes at different sites. (*AA* 65–66)

With this statement Freud is presenting his vision in terms of anatomy. In its essentials, it is strongly reminiscent of Exner's brief outline. It remains for Freud to recast the language apparatus in the discourse of psychology and connect the two versions, which he will accomplish (or attempt to accomplish) in Section 6. He will provide an illustrative diagram when he is ready to formalize and elaborate his thesis.

Before attending to the psychological arguments, however, he deems it necessary address two potential objections. One has to do with the significance of destruction of the cortical areas (such as auditory, visual, etc.) that serve as the "corners" of the language area, which would seem to have just as severe implications for language as the situation described above. He argues that such damage does not produce language disturbances because, although language is organized in only one hemisphere, the other cortical areas are present in duplicate in the other hemisphere, thus permitting the necessary connection with the language area to be maintained. Especially characteristic of Freud's rhetorical strategy is the second "objection" he poses, which questions his entire project of denying language centers on the one hand while proposing on the other hand the equivalent of centers for the visual, auditory, and motor functions. His answer is that anatomic evidence, such as nerve endings, shows the connection of the visual, auditory, and motor functions to the periphery, whereas that is not true of the "association field of language," which lacks direct sensory and motor connections to the periphery of the body (*AA* 68). As did Hughlings Jackson, Freud faces here a problem in the language of description: how to escape the influence of terms that distort and mislead because they have become so deeply entrenched as metaphors for a fixed pattern, shape, or constellation. It is difficult to successfully challenge the conventional wisdom on "centers."

In the sixth and final section of the aphasia book, Freud's theory will achieve full independence, be provided with its own illustrations, and be buoyed by some new supporters. Up to this point, Freud has, on the one hand, proved himself a discerning critic of scientific method, both of experiments (testing) and of the logical coherence of conclusions. He has proved himself a skeptic in relation to the value to his interests of the animal experiments that were a staple of neuropathologists. He continues to work toward a discourse of his own, shaping and borrowing from others as he goes along. And he has completely integrated into his thinking a trio of authorities—Bastian, Hughlings Jackson, and Heubner—that make an unconventional choice when compared with those with whom he has argued. On the other hand, contrary to the view of many commentators on the aphasia book, he has not completely rejected localization. His theory is in fact constructed of both interpretations: functional and localizing. In the last section, Freud joins the "diagram makers" with his own schematic drawings. Most important, language as an idea and a construct has shown many faces, shuttling between cortex and culture, recuperating unity in the social meanings of aphasic patients' speech patterns, in metaphors of poem and embryo, and in anecdotal narratives about Freud himself—not, however, in Freud's expressed theory; for there he believes that he is holding separate the physiological from the psychological. In point of fact, the effort is less than completely convincing. Freud knew more about language than he let on directly, probably more than he knew he knew, or cared that he knew at this time. Nevertheless, he reveals what he knows.

5

TOWARD LANGUAGE THEORY ON A "PSYCHOLOGICAL" BASIS

Section 6 opens with a recapitulation of the conclusions in the preceding section. Freud expressly accepts the anatomic location that Wernicke ascribed to the language apparatus in his paper of 1874, indicating the evolution of Wernicke's status in this text toward increased acceptance and a more deferential treatment, and marking the dialectical engagement with Wernicke in the aphasia text. In his recapitulation Freud adds that "we have earned the right" to reject the distinction between the so-called center, or cortical, aphasias and the conduction aphasias and to state that *"all aphasias are due to interruptions of association, i.e., conduction"* (*AA* 69). He feels, it seems, that the heavy work is behind him and he is satisfied with the result so far. He is left, however, with the problem of explaining subcortical aphasias such as those in cases described by Wernicke and Lichtheim. At this point Freud turns for evidence in support of his theory to Giraudeau's article (discussed in Chapter 3 at n. 7), with further material supplied by Arthur Adler's paper which Freud ran across while proofreading his manuscript.[1]

In concluding the discussion, Freud refers for the second time to a paper by Carl Eisenlohr, the Hamburg hospital director who had been

1. Arthur Adler, "Beitrag zur Kenntniss der seltneren Formen von sensorischer Aphasie," *Neurologisches Centralblatt* 10 (May 15 and June 1, 1891): 294–298 and 329–337.

cordial to the young Freud in 1885. Eisenlohr must have made an unusually favorable personal impression, because both times Freud mentions him with a compliment: in Section 1, where Eisenlohr's skeptical comment on Lichtheim's diagram is quoted, he is called "one of the most prudent German neurologists" (*AA* 10), and in the discussion of subcortical aphasia in Section 6, Freud refers to "several well-observed cases, most recently one of Eisenlohr's" (*AA* 74).[2] When in addition we consider, for example, the crediting of Exner and Paneth with the original inspiration for the book, we can see that Freud's professional loyalties could be as determined as his animosities and that in his strong attachments, the personal may be difficult to separate from the intellectual. There is no doubt, of course, that there would have been enormous appeal for Freud in the remark by Eisenlohr that Lichtheim's and Wernicke's diagrams have value for heuristic purposes rather than as an expression of the facts (Eisenlohr 737). Eisenlohr's analysis of the various cases presented in his paper does demonstrate a thoughtful, informed approach. A main interest of his is to establish a more precise nomenclature for the aphasias. He is in touch with the work of Wernicke and Lichtheim, Grashey, Naunyn, C.S. Freund, Giraudeau, and Charcot and his school. Once again, for Eisenlohr (739) as for other researchers, the results of Grashey's "exemplary analysis" are well known and accepted as a matter of course. Missing from Eisenlohr's paper, however, is any reference to British aphasiologists.

In conjunction with his translation of "The Unconscious," James Strachey chose to provide as an appendix a translation of pages 74–81 in this segment of Section 6. Strachey feels that the final section of "The Unconscious" "seems to have its roots" (*SE* 14:209) in the aphasia study, in particular, in Freud's early distinction between " 'word-presentations' and 'thing-presentations' " (*SE* 14:201).[3] There are complex relationships between the two works, even beyond those Strachey suggested. One is via Breuer, to whom Freud gives effusive praise in the later work and to whom the earlier one is dedicated. A second is the preoccupation with establishing a mental site for "the word," which remains in 1915 the focus of Freud's theorizing on language. "The word," of course, becomes associated with consciousness, a notion that may partly date back to Hughlings Jackson's related (although, as we have seen, qualified) thesis. So may the idea that a word can represent "a whole train of thought" (*SE* 14:199;

---

2. Eisenlohr, "Beiträge zur Lehre von der Aphasie."
3. In a footnote to "The Unconscious," Strachey comes to grips with the problems of translating *Vorstellung* (*SE* 14:201).

GW 10:298), which connects to Jackson's observations of patients with speech residues and is also an idea whose linguistic context is represented in Delbrück's lecture. The failure of "translation" into words is at the heart of the mechanism of repression, and we can also interpret the obstacle faced by patients with asymbolic aphasia as a failure of translation, which Freud describes toward the end of the segment Strachey translated:

> The pathology of disorders of speech leads us to assert that *the word-presentation is linked at its sensory end (by its sound-images) with the object-presentation.* We thus arrive at the existence of two classes of disturbance of speech: (1) A first-order aphasia, *verbal aphasia,* in which only the associations between the separate elements of the word-presentation are disturbed; and (2) a second-order aphasia, *asymbolic aphasia,* in which the association between the word-presentation and the object-presentation is disturbed. (*SE* 14:214; *AA* 80). The descriptions are of motor and sensory aphasia, respectively.)

In a broader sense, translation can be said to be the process that governs Freud's relation to the sources he read. Pursuing the idea of translation might lead to finding a connection between Bastian's tripartite division of levels of excitability of language centers and Freud's later tripartite division of the psyche. Bastian's least accessible state might be held to be a precursor of the unconscious, his state accessible by association would seem to be related to the preconscious in its mediating role, and his self-activating state equivalent to consciousness. Be that as it may, such connections would be devious and untraceable. One clear connection between "The Unconscious" and the aphasia book, however, lies in Freud's worry about separating the anatomic from the psychological, although in 1915 he no longer uses Jackson's terminology:

> Research has given irrefutable proof that mental activity is bound up with the function of the brain as it is with no other organ . . . parts of the brain [have] special relations to particular parts of the body and to particular mental activities. But every attempt to go on from there to discover a localization of mental processes, every endeavour to think of ideas as stored up in nerve-cells and of excitations as travelling along nerve-fibres, has miscarried completely. (*SE* 14:174; *GW* 10:273)

This passage could have been lifted directly from the discussion in Section 5 of the aphasia book. It serves well as a transition to Freud's presentation of his psychology of the speech apparatus, because the question still unanswered by science in 1915 had meant in 1891 that the psychology of the speech apparatus remained strangely detached from the surrounding discussion. That discussion gives the impression, compared with Freud's other theoretical deliberations, of being inadequately thought through, presenting, once again, the limited focus on "the word" which prevailed among most aphasiologists and, all told, appearing more significantly out of date than Freud's more strictly neurological discussion. Part of the fault is with Grashey's ideas about language, which haunt Section 6. Nevertheless, the discussion is significant in relation to Freud's development—as Strachey recognized—and to the aphasia book as a whole.

Having responded to his own satisfaction to the question of subcortical aphasias (for example, with the Giraudeau case), Freud launches the "psychological" version of his theory of the speech apparatus with an internally contradictory sentence construction—a chiasmus—that may indicate that some issues in this important section will remain fundamentally unresolved: "I now propose to consider what hypotheses are required to explain disturbances of speech on the basis of a speech apparatus constructed in this manner—in other words, what the study of disturbance of speech teaches us about the function of this apparatus" (*SE* 14:209; *AA* 74–75. Strachey uses "speech" were I have used "language"). Does he want to explain the disturbances of speech, or explain the apparatus? The first would appear to be the predominant goal of an aphasia study; the second seems to be in keeping with a second agenda as indicated in his poem metaphor and elsewhere, that is, language in and for itself. The syntax of this sentence tells a story of priorities: first comes the language apparatus, then aphasia. In tracing the subject of language, we have come upon some deeply personal associations and some preoccupations that do not lend themselves to explanation by the sole criterion of investigation of aphasia.

Freud sets out the frame of his discussion as follows: "From the point of view of psychology the unit of the function of speech is the 'word,' a complex presentation, which proves to be a combination put together from auditory, visual and kinaesthetic elements." Thus he sets a narrow limit for the scope of the consideration of language (and, for that matter, speech as well). He divides the topic into six parts illustrating "the probable process of association that takes place in each of the various activities of speech" (*SE* 14:210; *AA* 75): (1) learning to speak, (2) learning to speak the language of other people, (3) learning to spell, (4) learning to read, (5) learning to write, and (6) the later exercise of the individual language functions on the same association paths on which they were learned. The longest part by far is the fourth one, on reading, which is largely taken up with an observation of Freud's own reading habits. Freud's first two categories touch on the development of language in childhood, but only superficially (as opposed, for example, to Wernicke who seems to have thought more deeply on the subject). The most problematic aspect is Freud's attempt to correlate description that is ostensibly "psychological" with explanation from physiology and pathology, despite his having promised to keep "the psychological and anatomical sides of the question as separate as possible" (*SE* 14:209; *AA* 75). A disjunction bedevils Section 6 which seems to be an effort to cast a bridge over a gap that Freud had wanted to leave unbridged. He had wanted to leave it unbridged, not only because he subscribed to Hughlings Jackson's psychophysical parallelism but also—perhaps primarily—because scientific investigation could go no further, the obstacle to which he refers again and again.

The category of spelling depends on Grashey's view that what is learned is the sounds of the individual letters of the alphabet. This is incorrect, of course, first because the sounds of the letters are not the same as those that make up words. As Jackson had indicated, the story of language is a story of contextual relations. Second, the description Freud offers of the learning process is a culturally specific one that depends on teaching methods. The idea that the way children are taught spelling, reading, and writing affects the sequence and manner of their learning, neither Grashey nor Freud chose to consider, although they did grant that there was a difference between learning the sounds of German and the process of learning nonphonetic languages.

Freud's discussion of reading is again based on spelling. He apparently never thought how long it would take to read a page, let alone a book, if one were to read each word letter by letter (instead of by the gestalt of familiar words and word sets, as well as the cues of grammar and syntax). Neuropathology (or neuroanatomy) sets the limits to his thinking on this subject, because it remains his evidentiary default option: "We shall also be prepared to find that disturbances of reading in aphasia are bound to occur in a great variety of ways. The only thing that decisively indicates a lesion in the visual element of reading is a *disturbance in the reading of separate letters*" (*SE* 14:212; *AA* 77). Tied as he is to the evidence of pathology and to the notion of the word, Freud is prevented from thinking on this topic beyond those boundaries. That is, until he recounts his own various reading experiences—proofreading for errors compared with correcting for style, reading a novel, reading aloud with or without attention

—all of which are "phenomena of divided attention," a concept that was important for Kussmaul and recurs as a main concern in *The Psychopathology of Everyday Life.*

Finally, in the last sentence of the last category—almost an add-on—Freud suggests an alternate view of reading, one that is liberated from the explanatory model of pathology: "As regards reading, the 'visual word-image' undoubtedly makes its influence felt with practised readers, so that individual words (particularly proper names) can be read even without spelling them" (*SE* 14:213; *AA* 78–79, where "word-image" is in italics). Something as fundamental as the reading process depends on stage of literacy and level of education. Reading slips out of the explanatory model to become part of the private model of linguistic/cultural activity. When theorizing about reading, Freud himself is the preferred example, just as he was when theorizing about the neurological explanation for the mastery of different languages and scripts.

For the next step, to establish how a word "acquires its meaning," Freud turns for the only time in the aphasia book expressly to a philosopher, John Stuart Mill. He also turns for the first time to a schematic drawing of his own. The challenge of demonstrating the complex relationship between words and objects—leading to the introduction of his newly defined term *agnostic aphasia*—is so great that he must have recourse to philosophy and a visual aid. The discussion begins with a qualification that seems out of keeping with the thinking on language found in a number of Freud's sources: "A word . . . acquires its *meaning* by being linked to an 'object-presentation,' at all events if we restrict ourselves to a consideration of substantives" (*SE* 14:213; Strachey's italics; *AA* 79). To Delbrück, Jackson, Kussmaul, and Ross, such a restriction would suggest that no theory beyond a very narrow application could be developed. By taking a reductive point of view, Freud is, in effect, ignoring the clinical evidence that testifies to the role of the other parts of speech. Nouns are the most specific, the most limited in application, the part of speech lost first by aphasic patients, according to the reports Freud read and accepted.

The exclusive focus on nouns, however, makes it possible both to work out a schematic drawing similar to those of other aphasiologists and to suggest explanations that accord with pathology. The entire plan of "object associations" will not work with verbs, prepositions, or conjunctions, or even with abstract nouns, let alone with propositional speech (Hughlings Jackson). That is to say, Freud's theoretical construct rests, at this point, on only one part of speech:

The object-presentation itself is once again a complex of associations made up of the greatest variety of visual, acoustic, tactile, kinaesthetic and other presentations. Philosophy tells us that an object-presentation consists in nothing more than this—that the appearance of there being a 'thing' to whose various 'attributes' these sense-impressions bear witness is merely due to the fact that, in enumerating the sense-impressions which we have received from an object, we also assume the possibility of there being a large number of further impressions in the same chain of associations (J. S. Mill). The object-presentation is thus seen to be one which is not closed and almost one which cannot be closed, while the word-presentation is seen to be something closed, even though capable of extension. (SE 14:213–214; AA 79–80)

Mill writes of "an indefinite multitude" of "properties" "open to our knowledge."[4] But more important, he writes that it would "be absurd to assume that our words exhaust the possibilities of Being" (14). There are limits to naming. This association of "multitude" with what is out there, and limits with words, is reflected in Freud's view of "object-presentations" as open and "word-presentations" as closed. We can also see the philosophic underpinnings of the whole idea of of "presentations" (Vorstellungen), resting on the notion that "a Sensation is to be carefully distinguished from the object which causes the sensation."[5] Mill's Chapter 3, "Of Things Denoted by Names," in his System of Logic, and his Sir William Hamilton's Philosophy are both referred to by Freud in a footnote. Both are marked by an acute sense of limits in language—although the terms words and naming are used instead—of its ambiguity, "equivocality," and metaphoricity. In Logic, Mill writes, "The distinction which we verbally make between the properties of things and the sensations we receive

4. John Stuart Mill, An Examination of Sir William Hamilton's Philosophy, 3d ed. (London: Longmans, Green, Reader, and Dyer, 1867), 14.
5. John Stuart Mill, A System of Logic (New York: Harper, 1873), 34. The philosophic underpinnings as originating with Kant are discussed by Mill in Sir William Hamilton's Philosophy. It is noteworthy that in "The Unconscious," Freud refers to Kant on a similar matter of perception: "Just as Kant warns us not to overlook the fact that our perceptions are subjectively conditioned and must not be regarded as identical with what is perceived though unknowable, so psycho-analysis warns us not to equate perceptions by means of consciousness with the unconscious mental processes which are their object. Like the physical, the psychical is not necessarily in reality what it appears to us to be" (SE 14:171; GW 10:270). The fact that Freud utilized Mill in the aphasia book, and turned to Kant on the same topic twenty-four years later, does not mean that Kant was absent from the aphasia book. In addition to his presence via Mill, Kant was part of Freud's intellectual baggage, as were many other thinkers, to whom he would not have found it necessary to refer in the context of aphasia. It would be presumptuous to attempt to tease out from the aphasia book every strain of thought Freud had imbued.

from them, must originate in the convenience of discourse rather than in the nature of what is denoted by the terms."[6] Jackson is likely to have found in Mill a source for his thinking on the propositional nature of language, and he would have found much of his own ambivalence in Mill's discussion. Bastian was indebted to William Hamilton for his discussion of memory, which defines it as "the power of retaining knowledge in the mind, but out of consciousness," from which it is recollected according to the "laws" of "mental association."[7] Freud was deeply engaged with the British thinkers on several fronts. In a paper on Freud's translation of Mill's essays, Michael Molnar writes: "Mill's book on Hamilton, if not a direct cause of any specific subsequent development in Freud, at the very least gave him a ringside seat on some of the seminal intellectual debates of that era."[8]

Freud's scheme of word-presentations and object-presentations is infused with a philosophic narrative that was also carried over to "The Project." He transferred the idea of "closed" associations versus open ones. As he had attributed that idea, with reference to word associations versus object associations, directly to Mill, it would seem that at work in "The Project" is the unstated presence of philosophy, particularly as it treated perception. Freud then begins a discussion that takes him to the idea of communication as, for example, in a baby's cries for its desired object. Thus from the neutral "object" of the aphasia study (i.e., an unspecified external thing), whose role was to elicit naming, or the production of a noun, he moves to the object of desire or fear that stimulates cries. In the cries is information that characterizes the object. From there, he suggests, the next step is the creation of language. Within a discourse that Freud calls "biological development" (*SE* 1:366; *GW, Nachtragsband*, 456) he has delved back in time and cultural history as well. Although couched in the terms of "The Project," these ideas are familiar, in particular, from the version Freud read in Ross's book (quoted above, in the

6. Mill, *System of Logic*, 42. Mill also attributes (in Chapter 4) the capacity to detect ambiguities to the study of a "plurality" of languages, because one finds that "the same word in one language corresponds . . . to different words in another" and that "things which have a common name" may not have "a common nature" (53). These truisms would have been familiar to the polyglot Freud.
7. Bastian, "On Different Kinds of Aphasia," 931.
8. Michael Molnar shows how deep and long-standing was Freud's involvement with the associationist tradition of British philosophy; see "John Stuart Mill Translated by Siegmund Freud," in *Proceedings of the 1995 Conference on Freud's Preanalytic Writings* (Ghent: University of Ghent, forthcoming). Freud's teacher Franz Brentano lectured on Mill and assigned Locke and Hume, among others. Freud wrote about these early readings to his friend Silberstein; see his letter of March 15, 1875, in *Jugendbriefe an Eduard Silberstein*, 117–118, and 103–104.

second section of Chapter 3) where Ross writes about linguistic features of a child's first cries for its mother's breast. Several other sources, including Kussmaul and Delbrück, explored the history of language in anthropological and developmental terms, speculating on the origin of language in the expression of needs. Freud skipped over this material in his aphasia book but seems to have required it for the more ambitious program of "The Project."

Section 6 of the aphasia book brings to prominence the unease with language that we saw in Jackson. There is a disjunction between the message in Freud's diagram of word association in relation to object association and the informal message on language to be found at many places in the aphasia book. To find Freud's perspective on language, one must look at both strains in his narrative. Any theory of language we might attribute to him must consist, on the one hand, of the formal and schematic presentation that stresses limits and, on the other hand, of the elements inherent in the rest of his narrative which stress linguistic range and complexity. The former view allows him to draw conclusions compatible with his findings on aphasia as expressed in anatomic/pathological discourse. The latter seems to well up from another source, represented perhaps by his poetry metaphor, his attention to Delbrück's situated linguistics, and his own self-observations. Those observations pit a cultural narrative—such as his personal reading habits or his acquisition of different languages and alphabets—against a neurological one. In the neurological version, language is a brain function subject to damage. The tale is ahistorical, acultural, and individual. It attends only to the individual *producer* of language. The cultural narrative takes a more expansive view of language as a product and a function of community and communication, that is, as a phenomenon of time and place. Ironically, like Grashey's conclusions, Freud's diagram and analysis are admittedly based on local assumptions of a phonetic language. Thus, under the guise of universality, Freud presents a picture of the workings of language in a European language speaker.

Illustrations were a significant element of Freud's work, and to them he devoted considerable care. From his earliest precisely executed histological drawings, through the sketches he sent to Fliess, and the *New Introductory Lectures on Psycho-Analysis* of 1933 (for which there are five draft versions of an outline of the structure of the psyche),[9] they played an important role for him. For the complex topography he describes in the

9. As noted by Grubrich-Simitis, *Zurück zu Freuds Texten*, 200–201.

psychotherapy section of *Studies on Hysteria*, he makes several references to what a diagram might accomplish by way of illustration. Several years later, in a letter to Fliess, he included such a diagram *(FB* 263; *FL* 247). The title page of the aphasia book advertises "10 woodcuts"—apparently as an attraction to readers, which highlights the ambivalent role of the scientific illustration: it serves as a distillation and clarification but also as an alternative to the written text and thus inevitably as a potential subversion of it (e.g., by making a model that is meant to be "functional" appear to be "topographic"). Pictures offer a different and possibly superior model in so far as they appeal to readers with an alternative that seems more direct and easier to understand. There is at the same time a certain conservatism inherent in illustrations; they are conserving theory in fixed lines, as opposed to the fluidity of meaning in shifting and pliable language, at least as it is realized at the hands of masters such as Jackson and Freud.

Freud's illustrations no doubt served several purposes but, perhaps above all, a rhetorical one. He seemed to feel a need to imagine space in a way that the written narrative does not provide, transferring techniques of visualization from the laboratory culture to the theoretical text. But an illustration is also subversive in the sense of being a distraction, a foreign body, an interruption in the text, offering a new, often more conventional language. The illustration is a fixed "object," as opposed to multivalent language. If we compare Freud's diagram (Figure 3) to Grashey's (Figure 1, in Chapter 3), we see that Freud was imagining within conventional boundaries. Despite setting out to disprove the vision that saw language organized in the brain by centers and pathways, he drew a diagram that suggests just such a scheme. Freud thus lands ideologically somewhere between his initially bold project and a more cautious realization.

If we next compare Figure 3, from 1891, to its republication in 1893 (Figure 4), we can see that in addition to adding some dotted lines and a reversal in the location of the "acoustic" and "tactile" object associations, there has been a slight shift in the design, which results in two rhomboids. On the next page is the new illustration of the "language field" in the brain (Figure 5). Though the two illustrations are not parallel, there are similarities in the gestalt particularly the rhomboid form, and some overlap in localizations. As in the aphasia book, Freud's imagination remains linked to his notion of evidence, even, once again, to Heubner's article, which is the only authority he refers to in the 1893 article. The psychological, which he intends to be separate, continues to show the influence of the more powerful (or deep-seated) discipline. In his 1893 prescription for

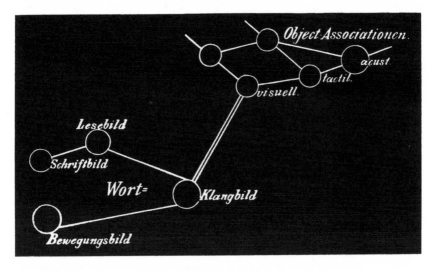

Psychological Diagram of a Word-Presentation [*Vorstellung*]

Figure 3. The word-presentation is shown as a closed complex of presentations, whereas the object-presentation is shown as an open one. The word-presentation is not linked to the object-presentation by *all* its constituent elements, but only by its sound-image. Among the object-associations, it is the visual ones which stand for the object, in the same kind of way as the sound-image stands for the word. The connections linking the sound-image of the word with object-associations other than the visual ones are not indicated. (*SE* 14: 214.) From Sigmund Freud, *Zur Auffassung der Aphasien: Eine kritische Studie* (Leipzig: Franz Deuticke, 1891), 79.

correct diagnosis of aphasia, Freud states that the first step is to "localize the lesion" on the basis of the symptoms. By 1893 he has become more accepting of the limits he had argued against two years before. (Naturally, a dictionary entry would also have posed different requirements.)

In the 1893 entry, Freud made two critical changes in his description of the relations shown in Figure 3: (1) He deleted entirely what had appeared in the aphasia book to be the indispensable term *Vorstellung*. (2) As a consequence, he was able to establish a direct relationship between the word and the symbol: "Between 'object' and 'word' there exist those relations that we call 'symbolic.' With every object a word is associated as a 'symbol.'"[10] The 1891 version of this description, embedded as it is in a philosophic matrix, insists on an intervening mental (or psychic) layer in the form of *Vorstellung*. What had been complex in 1891 was reduced in 1893. As already mentioned, Freud distinguishes between "a first-order aphasia, *verbal aphasia*," and "a second-order aphasia, *asymbolic aphasia*, in

10. Kästle, "Einige unbekannte Texte," 522.

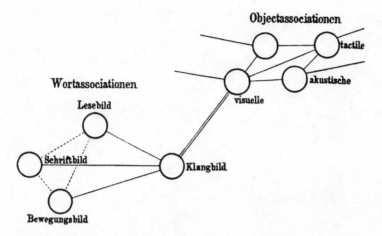

Figure 4. The word-presentation [*Vorstellung*] is shown as a closed complex of presentations, whereas the object-presentation is shown as an open one. The word-presentation is not linked to the object-presentation by *all* its constituent elements, but only by its sound-image. Among the object-associations, it is the visual ones which stand for the object, in the same kind of way as the sound-image stands for the word. *The connections of the word-associations among each other (other than with the sound-image) are indicated by dotted lines;* the connections linking the sound-image of the word with object-associations other than the visual ones are not indicated. (*SE* 14:214.) [I am using the Standard Edition translation because the legend is the same as for the related diagram in the aphasia book, with one addition, which I have translated and set off with italics.] From Freud's medical dictionary entry on aphasia, reprinted in Oswald Ulrich Kästle, "Einige bisher unbekannte Texte von Sigmund Freud aus den Jahren 1893/94 und ihr Stellenwert in seiner wissenschaftlichen Entwicklung," *Psyche* (Stuttgart) 41 (June 1987): 522.

which the association between the word-presentation and the object-presentation is disturbed" (*SE* 14:214; *AA* 80). The entire discussion that leads to the introduction of his new term *agnosia* turns on the notion of *Vorstellung* (Strachey's "presentation"). Freud could not have done without it:

I use the term 'asymbolia' in a sense other than that in which it has been ordinarily used since Finkelnburg, because the relation between word [-presentation] and object-presentation rather than that between object and object-presentation seems to me to deserve to be described as a 'symbolic' one. For disturbances in the recognition of objects, which Finkelnburg classes as asymbolia, I should like to propose the term 'agnosia.' (*SE* 14:214–215; *AA* 80)

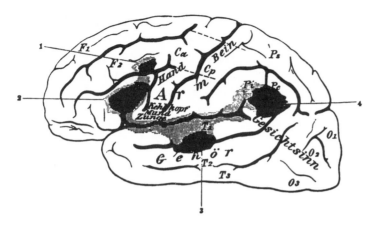

Figure 5. The areas with hatching correspond to the language field; the areas darkened over them correspond to the so-called language centers; and, in particular, *1* is the area where a lesion causes agraphia (the area bordering the center for the hand); *2*, Broca's area, where a lesion causes motor aphasia (adjoining the centers for muscles controlling speech and larynx); *3*, Wernicke's area, where a lesion causes word deafness (adjoining the field where the acoustic nerve or a part of it terminates); *4*, the area where a lesion causes alexia (directly adjoining the visual centers in the cortex). A large part of the *central language field* lies deep in the Sylvian fissure. From Freud's entry on aphasia, reprinted in Oswald Ulrich Kästle, "Einige bisher unbekannte Texte von Sigmund Freud aus den Jahren 1893/94 und ihr Stellenwert in seiner wissenschaftlichen Entwicklung," *Psyche* (Stuttgart) 41 (June 1987): 523.

The intervention of a mental or psychic filter (in the nature of a reader) is key to this idea. Without philosophy, word and object come together untranslated and unimagined. Freud was correct the first time around: the word is not a symbol of the object—which would imply a nonarbitrary or necessary connection—but rather the relationship is between the idea *(Vorstellung)* of the word and the idea of the object. In the course of casting off old philosophic baggage when he wrote the dictionary entry, he also cast off fine distinctions critical to his definitions, leaving them sounding more modern and more scientific but in reality less precise. Discursive rigor is purchased at the price of accuracy.

It may have been a Freudian slip that the term *Vorstellung* was left out of the diagram in the aphasia book (Figure 3)—Strachey added it in brackets—or perhaps it was a printer's decision. From the legend it is clear that it ought to have been there. The open-endedness of the object associations in the diagram seems not only in the one direction to derive from philosophic considerations but also, in the clinical direction, to be required by Freud's agnosia and the cases he quotes as examples. He shows that the disorder involving disturbances in recognition of objects can manifest itself through any of the senses through which an object may be perceived, and a patient may lose or retain any of the innumerable aspects of an object. Freud's diagram thus plays the role of mediator between philosophy and physiology (or psychology, as Freud would maintain).

There is a notable convergence between Freud's "Psychological Diagram of a Word-Presentation [*Vorstellung*]" (Figure 3) in the aphasia book and his drawing of the neuronal process of inhibition in "The Project" (*GW, Nachtragsband*, 417; *SE* 1:324), which looks like a twisted version of the 1891 diagram, one which has added the idea of motion, or a sense of flow, to the earlier one. This family resemblance is to be explained by the assumption in revised form of the ideas about language function expressed in the first diagram. Freud writes in "The Project" about neurons that serve sound images *(Klangvorstellungen)* and are associated with motor speech images. The scheme of association among speech functions which produced the word, as described in the aphasia book, has now been recast as a central explanatory feature in "The Project" discourse of neurons, the three systems (phi, psi, and *w*), memory, and discharge:

> These associations [speech] have an advantage of two characteristics over the others: they are limited [*geschlossen* = "closed"] (few in number) and exclusive. In any case, from the sound-image the excitation reaches the word-image and from it reaches discharge. Thus, if the mnemic images are of such a kind that a part-current can go from them to the sound-images and motor word-images, then the cathexis of the mnemic images is accompanied by information of discharge, which is an indication of quality and also accordingly an indication of the consciousness of the memory. (*SE* 1:364; *GW, Nachtragsband*, 456)

After adding further detail, Freud states that "this is conscious, observing thought" (*SE* 1:365; *GW, Nachtragsband*, 456). Although in the aphasia book he did not raise the question of whether or not language was essential to thought, authors whose papers he read for the aphasia book did grapple with it, arriving at different answers. In "The Project," Freud calls thinking in language the highest form of the thinking process (because it is a form of reality testing). Beyond equating the association process of language with thought, he adds another layer of significance: "In addition to making cognition possible, speech association achieves something else, of great importance" (*SE* 1:365; *GW, Nachtragsband*, 456): it makes memory possible. In other words, it is hardly possible to exaggerate the importance to Freud to "The Project," and, in the end result, to psychoanalysis, of a conceptual paradigm he had developed in the aphasia book.[11]

For his reference to Finkelnburg's terminology, Freud relied on its presentation in an older article by Carl Spamer.[12] For a number of reasons, both Spamer and Finkelnburg deserve special attention in relation to the aphasia book. Spamer's article is remarkable for the clarity of its presentation and language. He opens by pointing out that such an enormous amount had already been published on aphasia (as of 1876!) that one needed to have reasons to write about it beyond the presentation of a few more cases. (It is clear that Wernicke's paper in 1874 had unleashed a flood of reports and hypotheses on aphasia.) Spamer's reasons for writing are to provide an explanation and a taxonomy. He writes that Finkelnburg had supplied in his lecture of 1870 a comprehensive new organizing principle (Spamer calls it a "picture" [Bild]).[13] (Spamer adds that he had been prevented by the wars from reading Finkelnburg's lecture earlier. This is the only mention in the examined sources of an interference in the affairs of science by events in the world at large.)

Finkelnburg had presented patients who had lost the capacity to identify familiar symbols—for example, a religious Catholic and government official who no longer recognized the procedure of the Mass or the insignia of rank—and he named this syndrome "asymbolia" (461). Finkelnburg relied on Meynert's findings on brain anatomy and on Charcot's work, but he also took into consideration Kant and, to disagree with him, the influential linguist Max Müller. Finkelnburg presented two cases of the reevolution (without, of course, using Jackson's term) that later so interested Arnold Pick. In one case, a patient recovering from a stroke was able to add daily to his store of recognizable symbols and names for them, until they were completely restored to him. In another, a patient recovering from a seizure gradually added parts of speech to his repertoire, beginning with adjectives, then verbs, finally nouns and proper nouns. Although Finkelnburg does not theorize from these cases, their intersection with the entire complex of evolutionary thought in neurology and linguistics

11. Strachey acknowledges this connection in a detailed footnote that traces the ideas from the aphasia book to *The Interpretation of Dreams*, "The Unconcious," *The Ego and the Id*, and other works (*SE* 1:365).
12. Carl Spamer, "Über Aphasie und Asymbolie, nebst Versuch einer Theorie der Sprachbildung," *Archiv für Psychiatrie und Nervenkrankheiten* 6 (1876): 496–542.
13. Carl Maria Ferdinand Finkelnburg, Lecture on aphasia, in "Niederrheinische Gesellschaft in Bonn, Medicinische Section, Sitzung vom 21. März 1870," *Berliner klinische Wochenschrift* 7 (1870): 449–450 and 460–462; here 449.

(and philosophy) is obvious, irrespective of whether the episteme is founded on, precedes, or develops in tandem with the evidence.

In addition to the central European sources—Finkelnburg, Westphal, Meynert, Wernicke, Kant, and others—Spamer read widely among the French, British, and American writers: Broadbent, for example, and Bastian, as well as Maudsley's influential 1868 article in *Lancet*, which urges an understanding of language as the basis of understanding aphasia (quoted in Chapter 1 at n. 12). Spamer agrees with Maudsley. He also looks to the development of language through history, from speech to written language, finally to the language of gesture, and of symbols, such as the cross that "represents the sum total of the teachings of the Christian religion" (Spamer 525). For his notion of "symbolic knowledge," Spamer gives credit to Kant. He also notes the fact that after strokes, patients lose language in the order of proper nouns, common nouns, verbs, adjectives, prepositions, and conjunctions. His explanation is a physiological one, in terms of interrupted pathways.

Three additional points in Spamer's article draw our attention to this remarkable thinker. First of all, his paradigm metaphor for heuristic purposes is the steam engine and, in association with it, the railroad. He takes a metaphor from another author: that it is as useless to try to understand aphasia without understanding language as it is to try to explain the breakdown of a steam engine through a special coincidence without understanding its normal structure and the function of its individual parts. From here he carries the metaphor throughout the article as an explanatory tool. He also refers to the "language mechanism" (506) and to a damaged or healthy "machine" (520) and adds the sounds of trains as an example of stimulation of a concept via hearing. His fascination with technology is obvious, as was Westphal's in 1874, Kussmaul's with photography in 1877, Grashey's with the telegraph in 1885, and Wysman's with the phonograph in 1891 (in Java, no less!). Freud differs in this respect. He does not use technological metaphors in the aphasia book. They would not permit the kind of imagining that his poetry metaphor permitted, at least not at the technological and theoretical level of steam engines. (The telegraph and the phonograph would be better suited if used, not to illustrate brain function, as Grashey and Wysman did, but to indicate a transformation from organized to disorganized information and back again, i.e., the distinction between message and noise; but such metaphors lay in the distant future.) Freud's reach into another science is more likely to be into theoretical physics (optics).

Second, Spamer's vision of language in the brain is that the production of a word or a concept is carried out by "coordination centers," or groups of cells that connect and organize multiple impulses into proper sequence. A "concept" comes about when one of its elements is stimulated, calling to mind the others (e.g., seeing a loaf of bread brings to mind its taste, odor, consistency, etc.). These ideas relate to associationist psychology, but they also resemble neurological theories of concept formation in our time. Spamer developed them without the aid of any modern techniques to investigate brain function.

Third, Spamer offers, along with an elaborate, organic diagram of the "language mechanism," a theory of the role of scientific illustrations:

> I have attempted to draft a scheme of the language [or speech] mechanism which, I believe, corresponds in a straightforward manner to the observed phenomena. Even if it is soon replaced by a better one, I will consider myself to have been rewarded if I succeed at all in encouraging a schematic treatment of the question, since it is my firm conviction that such a scheme is best suited to conveying an exact and coherent idea [*Vorstellung*] of the language [speech] machine. It appears to me to be beyond doubt, however, that in the clash of opinions, the polemics that often digress and end without results could be significantly abbreviated and sharply defined at certain points. I might note in this regard that I have often seen an apparently irreconcilable, lengthy disagreement about the functions of the nervous system brought to a relatively speedy resolution once a scheme had been drawn on a blackboard or a table. (508)

In a footnote Spamer credits Wernicke with having taken just this step in *The Aphasia Symptom-Complex.* Spamer's interpretation of the role of diagrams raises them to the level of final answer, inhibiting the productive clash of opinions and argument. Here, once again, Spamer shows himself ahead of his time: Language is the culprit that interferes with understanding. Language means digression, polemics, conflict. Diagrams, apparently, lead to agreement. How pointless Hughlings Jackson's struggle with language appears, when he could have resolved the matter with a simple diagram. It is easy to see why diagram making would have gained in popularity and led to a loss in theoretical complexity. Freud might seem to stand somewhere between Jackson and Spamer; for he uses diagrams sparingly (only two of his own) in the aphasia book. Whereas Spamer's drawing seems to have been inspired by the organicism of romantic science, the second of Freud's two diagrams suggests modern physics.

It is clear from the physiological detail and from his description that

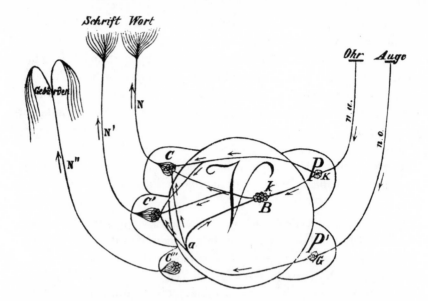

Figure 6. The circle in the middle of the figure, *V,* signifies the pathways for *Vorstellungen.* Stimuli enter the brain from the right side via the sensory nerves.

n.a. = acoustic nerve. *n.o.* = optical nerve

Pj and *P'* represent the sites where acoustic *(K)* and visual *(G)* perceptions take place. — When stimuli have arrived there, we have simple sensory perceptions, without connecting concepts to them. The connection with specific, corresponding concepts happens only when the stimulus passes on to *B,* the concept. From here the stimulus can be directed on—arbitrarily, it is said—to *C, C',* and *C",* into the coordination centers for speech and the movements of writing and gestures.

N, N', and *N"* are the motor nerves which are active during the respective symbolic expressions (speech, writing, gestures). At their terminations one sees them dissipate into fibers for individual muscles. From Carl Spamer, "Ueber Aphasie und Asymbolie, nebst Versuch einer Theorie der Sprachbildung," *Archiv für Psychiatrie und Nervenkrankheiten* 6 (1876): 507.

Spamer meant his diagram (Figure 6) actually to trace the course and function of nerves in the brain (he does not specify the cortex) which lead to ideas *(Vorstellungen)* and concepts. Kussmaul credits Spamer, (as well as Wernicke and Baginsky, as predecessors of his scheme (Figure 7), which, like Spamer's, means to show the location of ideas, although on a considerably higher level of abstraction than Spamer's scheme. But Kussmaul faults Spamer for having left out the "word images" as necessary mediators.[14] Reading Kussmaul's critique of his predecessors' diagrams makes one realize that Spamer's trust in the diagram to resolve disputes was misplaced.

14. Kussmaul, *Die Störungen der Sprache,* 183.

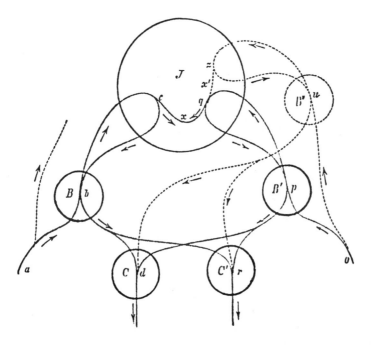

Figure 7. The circle *J* designates the ideational centre or centre of conceptions, in other words all that portion of the cellular network of the cortex in which ideas are produced as a result of impressions of the most varied description made on the senses (object- and word-images).

B and *B′* are the sensory centres for word-images, *B* for the acoustic (sound-images), *B′* for the optical (text-images).

C and *C′* designate the motor centres for the co-ordination of the sound-movements into spoken-words (*C*), and of the strokes produced in writing into written-words (*C′*).

a is the acoustic nerve, *o* the optic. Each of these nerves is seen to divide into two branches, one of which, however, is indicated only by points for the sake of clearness. — *a b c b d* is the collective acoustic motor track for spoken speech, *o p q p r* the optic motor track for written speech. The adjoining punctated lines and circles are intended to indicate that still other tracks lead from the nerves of sense through other image-centres to the centre for conceptions; the acoustic nerve, e.g., also conveys melodies, and delivers musical ideas and the sound attributes of object-images (song: the nightingale), the optic nerve brings gesture-images and physiognomic attributes (grimaces: the monkey). For the sake of clearness we leave out the tracks of the other nerves of sense, e.g., the nerve of taste, and the motor centres of co-ordination for all other voluntary expressions, except spoken and written words; the centre for pantomime is also left out.

a b d is the track for the imitative speech of children or parrots who repeated uncomprehended words; *o p r* is the track for the copying of uncomprehended words; *c b d* is the track for the utterance of the conceptions in spoken words; *q p r* for the writing down of the thoughts. The track *c x q* forms the connection between sound-images and text-images in the centre of conceptions, and renders feasible the change of spoken-signs into written-signs through the intervention of the thoughts.

b r and *p d* are the tracks between the centre for spoken-images and the motor centre for writing on the one side, and between the centre for written-images and the motor centre for speech on the other side. A person who writes down an uncomprehended word that he has heard, uses the track *a b r*; one who reads off aloud an uncomprehended written word, uses the track *o p d*. In writing down dictated words that are understood, the longer track *a b c b r* is employed; in reading aloud written words that are understood, the track *o p q p d*. From Adolph Kussmaul, "Disturbances of Speech," in *Cyclopaedia of the Practice of Medicine*, vol. 14, ed. H. von Ziemssen, trans. E. Buchanan Baxter et al. (New York: William Wood, 1877), 779–781.

There is just as much dispute among aphasiologists about the accuracy of diagrams as about the accuracy of descriptions in words. Wysman drew eight diagrams that, ironically, appear much closer to Spamer's metaphor of the machine than does Spamer's own plantlike scheme.[15] There is a clash of representations in Spamer's article between diagram and metaphor. One can easily image Wysman's drawings in motion and producing energy. The first depicts a simple single belt and pulley, the last a multiply connected three-belt arrangement (Figure 8).

Freud, however, chose the route of greater abstraction and borrowed neither from organicist traditions nor from the new mechanics (e.g., technology of the steam engine) but from theoretical physics, in particular optics, to represent an "anatomic scheme of the speech [language]-association field" (Figure 9). The diversity represented in these diagrams indicates why Spamer's views on diagrams are not convincing. First of all, when deciding on a new visual scheme, authors must look to different traditions and sources of inspiration, meaning that it may be necessary to look beyond disciplinary boundaries. Second, because diagrams are meant to persuade, they serve rhetorical purposes. In order to persuade, they must be acceptable aesthetically to the intended audience and represent a metaphor (e.g., organic, mechanical, or physical) that is legitimate and commands respect. Legitimacy depends on the prestige and wide acceptance of the disciplinary model selected. Third, diagrams may engage in argument with or contradiction of their own texts, as Spamer's does. Freud's diagrams do so in the larger sense that the thrust of his project is against the diagram makers. Fourth, they inevitably reduce and simplify, which many authors find desirable. From the authors' perspective, diagrams are intended as heuristic devices. Thus a reader may test herself: do I understand this concept better as a result of the diagram? Or does the diagram get in the way of a complex grasp of the material? It is noteworthy that Freud and the other aphasiologists did not let diagrams stand on their own but found it necessary to attach long and elaborate legends. Diagrams, in the end, are supposed to get closer to reality because they dispense with the interference of ambiguous words and address our major source of information—the eye—directly. By doing so, they necessarily partake of the limits and distortions of our visual capacity. There is a certain irony in using diagrams that depict an elementary and undisturbed wholeness for the purpose of trying to depict the complex disturbances, breaks, and gaps of aphasia.

15. Wysman, "Aphasie und verwandte Zustände," 31–35, 37, 45, and 48.

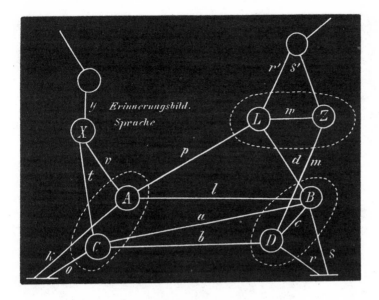

Key

Figure 8: Left side:
    Nuclei of nerves that function during writing
    Vorstellungen of writing movements
    Letter image
    Object image
Bottom line:
    Eye
    Ear
Right side:
    Nuclei of nerves that function during speaking
    Mnemonic images
    Singing
    Image of the sound of a word
    Image of sound
From J. W. H. Wysman, "Aphasie und verwandte Zustände," *Deutsches Archiv für klinische Medicin*, 47 (1891): 37.

Freud carefully prepared the textual ground for this diagram with two cases of agnostic aphasia, one reported by Farges, the other by Freund. In the first, the patient, blinded by a brain lesion, could use a full range of speech only when presented with the opportunity to touch, taste, or smell an object. For example, although she could not recognize her physician by the sound of his voice, she could by the touch of his hand. Freund's patient was able to recognize and correctly name objects only when allowed to hold them in his hands with his eyes closed. These cases are important to Freud because they provide evidence that agnostic aphasia

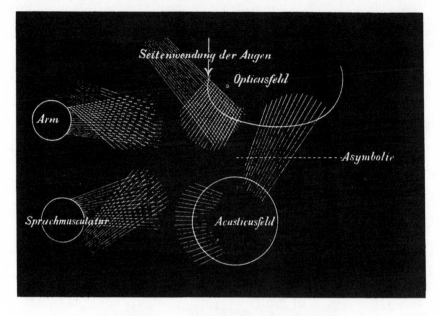

Anatomic Scheme of the Language Association Field.

Figure 9. In order to explain the appearance of language centers. The cortical fields for acoustic, optical, and arm muscles are schematized by circles; the association pathways that reach from them to the interior of the language field are represented by pencils of rays. Wherever the latter are crossed by pencils that have been cut off from their origins, a "center" for the relevant association element is created. For the acoustic field, the double-sided connections are not indicated, partly in order not to complicate the diagram, partly because of the lack of clarity that exists about precisely the relationship between the auditory field and the acoustic language center. — Dividing the connections with the optical field, also, spatially into two pencils permits taking into consideration the fact that eye movements are enlisted in a special way in the association process of reading. From Sigmund Freud, *Zur Auffassung der Aphasien: Eine kritische Studie* (Leipzig: Franz Deuticke, 1891), 83.

depends on a "functional effect over distance *(Fernwirkung)*[16] without an organic lesion of the language apparatus" (*AA* 82), as opposed to cases of verbal and asymbolic aphasia, in which there are lesions of the language apparatus. He wants to separate the two types clearly, and to that end has drafted the diagram, "which disregards the anatomic situation" (*AA* 83).

16. Freud liked the term *Fernwirkung* so much that he used the German in his French paper of 1893, "Des paralysies motrices organiques et hystériques." It is significant that Nothnagel also used it in 1887 (Nothnagel and Naunyn, "Über die Localisation der Gehirnkrankheiten"), and Bastian used an English equivalent ("Loss of Speech in Cerebral Disease").

That is, his intent with Figure 9 was the greatest possible abstraction. He uses the diagram to explain exactly what effects will result from which location of a lesion. In the case of "verbal aphasia," the effects depend on the relative closeness to one of the "centers" that frame the speech field. The more toward the center of the language field itself a lesion is located, the less it will affect one of the association elements, and the more it will depend on functional elements instead of localization. For the asymbolic type of aphasia, Freud cites Heubner's case as an "ideal" example, because the language area was completely severed from its associations. He points to the connection between the idea of the word and the idea of the object [*Wort-und Objektvorstellung*] as the weakest link in the speech function; that is, it is the most easily disrupted, an illustration of which is Pick's 1891 case. We may recall as well Grashey's patient who provided another example of this disturbance. In a different theoretical discourse, one could extrapolate that this disturbance might shed some light on the entire question of representation. When Freud drops the term *Vorstellung* from the illustration in his 1893 dictionary entry, however, it means that his conceptual framework there has excised questions of representation.

In connection with a discussion of echolalia, Freud once again brings in Bastian's three modifications as an analytic tool. After drawing further distinctions among the different manifestations of aphasia, he arrives at a discussion of the loss of parts of speech which returns to the starting point of his book, expanding the remarks he made there on grammar, and placing the grammatical phenomena into the explanatory context of the language apparatus. Without developing the idea beyond a suggestion, Freud, with this integration, has arrived at the cradle of what we might call the notion that grammar is hard wired—that there is a kind of symbiosis between grammatical structures and the language apparatus in the brain. He has carried Delbrück into the pathology laboratory:

Spontaneous speech is not abolished, no matter how marked the asymbolic-verbal aphasia is, but it is characterized by a poverty of parts of speech that have a narrow meaning. These (nouns, adjectives) were usually spoken in response to visual stimulation. In response to stimulation from other object associations which probably enter at other sites in the auditory field, the language field produces mutilated speech, or it transmits to the motor speech pathway all possible stimuli which do not require the more narrow object associations, such as particles, syllables (gibberish). (*AA* 86–87)

By using the term *narrow* to apply to nouns and adjectives, Freud breaks away from noun/object limits and turns to the more complex language theories of Delbrück and Ross.

In the course of the discussion that elaborates the connections he finds between the types of aphasia and his theory of the speech apparatus, Freud draws attention in a footnote to an article that gives him another opportunity to critique scientific methods. The article in question is the account of certain experimentally induced aphasic symptoms.[17] Freud responds that the experimental results differ from the actual clinical picture of the syndrome, which is that deprivation of perceptive acuity will cause an aphasic patient to develop illusions, whereas a healthy patient (such as the subject of the experiment) will react merely with uncertainty. He contributes the example of one of Ross's patients, who read the newspaper for hours without understanding it and wondered about the "nonsense" written in the papers.

Drawing once again on his leitmotiv, Bastian's modifications, Freud now takes the important step of introducing expanded applications of Bastian (with the concession that "we have already often discussed the three stages of decreased functional capacity that Ch. Bastian postulated for the centers of speech."): "We can accept these [stages] even if we disregard the centers of language in a physiological sense by saying that the visual, auditory, kinesthetic component of the language apparatus remains functional under such and such conditions" (*AA* 91) Making explicit the jettisoning of Bastian's centers allows Bastian (sans centers) to be joined with Hughlings Jackson: "The Bastianian modifications, in a certain sense, also constitute degrees of dis-involution, or functional retrogression." Freud next takes this amalgam as relevant for "every element of speech association activity," analyzing first the auditory, then the visual (reading and writing), then the motor elements. As do other aphasiologists, Freud places the "associative activity of the auditory element" (*AA* 92) at the heart of the entire language operation.

Meyer-Palmedo added a footnote at this point to indicate how far into the future Freud's ideas were affected by his aphasia work.[18] She quotes from a passage in *The Ego and the Id* (1923) in which Freud writes: "Verbal residues are derived primarily from auditory perceptions, so that the system Pcs. has, as it were, a special sensory source. . . . In essence a word is

---

17. Ernst Siemerling, "Ein Fall von sogenannter Seelenblindheit nebst anderweitigen cerebralen Symptomen," *Archiv für Psychiatrie und Nervenkrankheiten* 6 (1890): 284–299.
18. Freud, *Zur Auffassung der Aphasien*, 135.

after all the mnemic residue of a word that has been heard" (*SE* 19:20–21; *GW* 13:248). Strachey also refers to the aphasia book as the source of this conclusion (*SE* 19:20).

Freud notes that when the auditory element is no longer capable of making associations to symbols, the resulting asymbolia may be caused either by a localized lesion or, in a functional relation, by a more distant one; the two explanations have, at this point, come to enjoy a status of equality. In association with this evolution of theory, the aphasia book has undergone another kind of evolution. Its tone seems to have "softened" over the time of its composition: it has sloughed off the layers of defiance and eliminated dogmatic argument, finally blunting its rhetorical edge. Rhetoric and theory formation have, in this case, advanced in tandem.

The section on the visual element is of special interest because it includes Freud's explanation of the reading process as well as a self-observation on writing. Freud begins by noting that Bastian's third category, spontaneous (self-generated) activity (the most intact state of language centers), does not apply to the visual element because that element is not directly connected to object associations inasmuch as "our characters, unlike those of other peoples, are not direct symbols of concepts, but of sounds" (*AA* 95). At this critical juncture, when Freud is elaborating the final version of his views on aphasia, one of its important features, which is described in the combined discourse of brain and mind, proves itself to be a culturally specific phenomenon. After reviewing and disagreeing with Wernicke's theory of reading, and presenting his own views on the visual element in several aphasias, Freud arrives at a point where he uses a self-observation to support the claim by other aphasiologists that disturbances of writing are associated with motor disturbances rather than with reading disturbances. The proof is that practiced writers write independently of the images of letters: "Self-observation shows that except for foreign words, proper names, and words which one has only learned while reading, spontaneous writing does not rely on the visual element" (*AA* 97). Again with this observation Freud thinks beyond Grashey's focus on the individual letters of the alphabet. The series of self-observations Freud has interjected in his aphasia narrative are meant to authenticate the arguments he is presenting. From the vantage point of a greater distance in time, however, they can also be read as reminders of the fact that this theory is being developed at a particular time and place and by a particular person. Though from one point of view his observations may have wide application, they are, at the same time, the observations of a man educated in a certain way in a culture where a certain social class (or classes) had developed certain literate practices. Freud is, of course, an outstanding exemplar of such a culture. Can his individual reading and writing experiences be of wider relevance beyond those cultural specificities? Are they able to shed light on the organization of language in other human brains?

Freud points out that disturbances of reading ability can be present even when the patient has no trouble recognizing the letters of the alphabet. Many different kinds of lesion may be at fault because of the complexity of the process of association during reading. A disturbance may result from "an easy exhaustibility of the visual function" (*AA* 98), for which Freud gives the example of the condition named by Rudolf Berlin, "dyslexia." [19] Freud's presentation is worth noting for three reasons: (1) its distorts Berlin's report; (2) it provides the occasion for Freud to explain what reading is; and (3) it demonstrates again the pervasiveness of Jackson's influence:

> This case will be recognized by the fact that the inability to read is preceded by a briefly successful attempt to spell, and its interpretation will be that the damaged visual element, while capable of the simpler activity of associating the visual images one time with the auditory or kinesthetic element, is, however, incapable of multiple repetitions and correct sequencing of these activities which, in order to lead to reading, must in addition proceed with a certain amount of speed. This is a case of loss of the more complex ability while maintaining the simpler one. (*AA* 97–98)

Berlin—who deals with the theories of Wernicke, Exner, Kussmaul, Lichtheim, and Grashey—presents a series of case histories, the first one dating back to 1863, all of them characterized by the same peculiar symptom: the patient is able to read four or five words, then stops and turns away (or pushes away the reading material), sometimes with signs of disgust, and is unable to read further. One patient would faint when required to try to read more. Thus, contrary to Freud's statement, Berlin's patients are not trying to spell, and Freud's idea of maintaining a simpler ability does not apply. Nor does Freud's description convey any sense of Berlin's primary concern, that is, that the disturbance he describes as "dyslexia" is always a sign of a soon-to-be-fatal brain illness. Every patient manifesting

19. Rudolf Berlin, *Eine besondere Art der Wortblindheit (Dyslexie)*(Wiesbaden: J. F. Bergmann, 1887). Freud's first example is of a case by Bertholle (1881), cited by Désiré Bernard, "De l'aphasie et de ses diverses formes," in *Publications du Progrès médical* (Paris: Thèse de Paris, 1885).

this symptom died within a relatively short time, either of stroke, tumor, the effects of syphilis, or other brain illness. Berlin is concerned with the propriety of the name he has chosen and critically examines Greek etymologies to justify his choice, but above all, he is a committed clinician trying to diagnose and treat profoundly ill patients whose initial problem had not appeared serious (although it impressed Berlin sufficiently for him to hold on to the memory of the first patient of this kind for twenty-four years). At stake is how Freud reads sources. In this instance, his theoretical premises are served by a description that ignores the larger picture of profound disability and serious disease. In point of fact, the author of the study Freud used had very different questions in mind.

Freud is clearly fascinated by reading itself, even beyond its relation to brain damage in aphasia. He goes on to transfer his above remarks into the discourse of brain function, speculating in the uncertain territory beyond available evidence:

> Reading comprehension comes about only after transmission of the stimulus from the visual to the motor elements through association of the latter with the auditory elements. On the other hand, in the case of an auditory lesion, as well as of asymbolia, purely mechanical reading [capacity] can be retained. In other respects the explanation of reading disturbances—which I do not intend to consider in detail—causes several difficulties which can be disposed of neither by localizing factors nor by the assumption of the familiar functional changes. In complex cases sometimes some, sometimes other pieces of the [reading] function are retained, probably according to which of the elements that serve association in a particular direction have remained functional here or there in a large enough number. (*AA* 98)

Berlin explains the differences in terms of individual differences in localization of the reading function. Although he leaves open the question of whether an anatomic "reading center" exists, he does believe that in the psychic sense, "everyone has his own individual reading center" (63). Perhaps Berlin's conviction reminded Freud of another researcher who based his interpretations on individual differences; for at this point in his text (after discussing the motor element) Freud devotes two pages of text to Charcot's thesis that the nature of aphasic disturbances depends on individual differences in language development. This discussion is of considerable rhetorical interest in view of assumptions about Freud's attitude toward Charcot at this time.

Freud calls Charcot's theory "an interesting and important point of view" (*AA* 100), then proceeds to demonstrate its untenability. Freud's own point of view, as he explains it, requires that, among the speech elements, certain functional associations are favored over others, and these are the ones that developed over the course of learning to speak (which means that the auditory is the key element). Charcot's view, by contrast, sees all associations as possible and equally likely. Precedence is determined by individual practice or individual brain organization. In speaking, writing, or reading, one person will depend primarily or exclusively on the visual, another on the kinesthetic element; there is no general dependence on the auditory element. The consequences of this view, according to Freud, are that, for example, an individual who depended on the motor element would be nearly unaffected by the lost of visual and auditory elements, whereas loss of the motor element would rob him of all language capacity. Diagnosis of the location and extent of a lesion on the basis of loss of function would be impossible if the clinician did not know beforehand which associations the individual favored, and such information would be nearly impossible to acquire.

Freud engages in a dialectic with Charcot's theory—expressing appreciation while showing it to be wrong—which is unique in the aphasia book, and in which we can detect a case of conflicted and ambivalent feelings. The only way Freud finds to resolve the conflict is to call on his own canonical authorities, Bastian and Hughlings Jackson, although that call also turns out to be fraught with ambivalence. The rhetorical uncertainty of this section is apparent in his phrasing: "I need to acknowledge an interesting and important point of view whose introduction into the theory of aphasia we owe to Charcot, since its acceptance would require us to modify our explanatory efforts to an even greater degree" (*AA* 100). After discussing Charcot's view Freud writes:

> Nobody has so far wanted to completely dismiss Charcot's view. It remains to be seen, however, to what extent it has significance for the theory of language disturbances. Extreme claims, such as, for example, those by Stricker, for the predominance of the motor element for speech, were refuted by Ch. Bastian with the comment that he would first wait until a case was shown to him where a person had become word deaf after destruction of Broca's area. (*AA* 101)

(Broca's area controls the motor function of speech; word deafness is sensory aphasia.)

It is noteworthy that Salomon Stricker, in whose laboratory Freud had worked in 1878 and 1884, is mentioned just this one time and negatively. Jones mentions Stricker's unpleasant personality.[20] Gruesome animal experiments were common in his laboratory, which would explain his emphasis on the motor, as opposed to the sensory, element for speech. Stricker's monograph, to which Freud refers in a footnote, is intended for a broad audience, probably for that reason is written in the first person, and depends heavily on anecdotal self-observation.[21] By any standards it is a weak piece of work that draws broad conclusions from insufficient or poorly interpreted evidence. For example, Stricker maintains that all brain lesions found in autopsies of aphasic persons were found in the motor regions of the cortex (i.e., Broca's area)(26). He seems unaware of the limits of investigation and presumes that he is in possession of the final truth about the brain. His conclusions rest on experiments (including Munk's) on dogs and monkeys, the results of which, however, cannot provide insight into the human language function. From the observation that the brains of monkeys are "known to be analogous" (26) to human brains, Stricker takes a leap to the conviction that the language function is strictly a motor function. (Naturally, it would be impossible to test the theory of sensory aphasia by vivisection of animals.) Freud's reference to Stricker's theory shows how little respect he accorded it.

In view of Freud's reference to Bastian for support against Stricker, it is instructive to read what Bastian actually did remark. He refers to the "doctrines . . . of Stricker and Hughlings Jackson," which ". . . would also necessitate the view that an isolated lesion in Broca's region only should cause 'word deafness' as well as aphasia, which it certainly does not do. How can they explain this discrepancy?" ("Kinds of Aphasia" 986). Freud has protected his favorite, Jackson, by neglecting to mention Bastian's associating Jackson with this view and has created a bit of sarcasm out of an originally rather dry remark. Freud crafted his source material to suit his rhetorical purposes, one of which is to bring in Jackson as a final authority at the end.

Freud adds that there has been no pathological evidence found to support Charcot's supposition. Though "the possibility should not be excluded" that such individual specialization might play a role in the healthy speech apparatus, that would not be the case once it had been damaged

---

20. Jones, *Life and Work of Sigmund Freud*, 54.
21. Salomon Stricker, *Studien über die Sprachvorstellungen* (Vienna: Wilhelm Braumüller, 1880).

(*AA* 101). Freud's treatment is a rhetorical giving and taking, a sign of hesitation, as if he still felt ties to Charcot and were reluctant to make a complete break. The conclusion to this section is particularly odd:

> Certainly, however, it would be unjust to forget [Freud adds the preposition *an* to the verb *to forget*, which makes it less direct and softens its effect] Charcot's idea entirely and to let oneself be seduced into a schematic rigidity in the interpretation of speech disturbances. "Different amounts of nervous arrangements in different positions are destroyed with different rapidity in different persons," [quoted by Freud in English] says Hughlings Jackson. (*AA* 102)

Jackson's geometric increase in differences is not necessarily related to Charcot's theory, inasmuch as the theory Freud associates with Charcot emphasizes an individual developmental favoring of one capacity over the other, as opposed Jackson's remark on the individual nature of the destructive process. Nor does it do Charcot's idea a service to assert Jackson's final authority on the topic. Freud seems to be inclined to preserve some positive connection to Charcot, even at the cost of a breakdown in logic. This entire section constitutes a very personal review of ambivalent feelings whose undercurrent testifies to an intellectual tie already severed while remnants of emotional attachment remain.

Jackson's phrase seems to have impressed Freud for purposes beyond Charcot's theory and the aphasia book; for it recurs in German, in slightly varied form, four years later in "The Project," where Freud wrote about "the possibility, in the case of practical thought, of the most various pathways being reached at various times under various conditions by various individuals" (*SE* 1:377; *GW, Nachtragsband,* 467). (While Strachey chose "various" to translate *verschieden,* I would have chosen "different" in accord with the Jackson quotation.) Even in terms of individual formulations, then, Jackson remained an undercurrent in Freud's thought.

Freud gave his last five pages the supertitles "Summary," "Results," and "Closing Word." In the first part, a brief review of the history of aphasia study begins with Broca's discovery, followed by Wernicke's discovery and his theories, and Lichtheim's subcortical and transcortical aphasias. The consequence of these developments was that "the key to understanding language disturbances" was considered to lie in the "contrast between center and conduction aphasias" (*AA* 102). At this point Freud brings in Grashey, to whom he gives credit for a discerning analysis that departed from the theories of localization and introduced a functional explanation, resulting in the division of language disturbances into those caused by local lesions and those resulting from functional changes.

Then Freud switches to his own story: he wanted to test both the localization theory and the centers versus conduction pathways distinction. He touches on his findings in relation to Wernicke's and to Lichtheim's views, concluding with his finding that the supposed sub-and transcortical aphasias were actually cortical. On the basis of Heubner's case he was able to find a cortical localizing explanation for so-called transcortical sensory aphasia and to rename it "asymbolia." Next he wanted to find an explanation for the fact that lesions in the same location could cause "different clinical pictures" and was led to the assumption of functional changes. Here Bastian's "three pathological conditions of a center" provided the explanation for the nature of these changes (*AA* 103). His next step was to show, with the assistance of one of Bastian's modifications, that Grashey's case was actually to be explained by a localized lesion. Thus he arrived at a refutation of the prevailing hypotheses he had set out to examine. "Now it was our duty to arrive at a different conception [*Vorstellung*] of the structure of the language apparatus and to specify how topical and functional elements come into play when it has been disturbed" (*AA* 104).

After reviewing his critique of Meynert's theories, he presents a rephrased description of the language apparatus in anatomic and quasi-religious terms:

> Thus the language apparatus revealed itself to us as a coherent portion of the cortical area in the left hemisphere between the cortical terminations of the acoustic and optical nerves, and the fibers for motor control of speech and arms. The portions of the language field adjoining these cortical fields—with necessarily indeterminate boundaries—acquire the signficance of language centers in the sense of pathological anatomy, not of function, because their lesion prevents one of the elements of language association from connecting with the others, which does not occur when a lesion is centrally located in the language field. (*AA* 104–105)

At the heart of this description—where the connections are made—is indeterminacy. Freud's goal was to refute the easy associations and clearly defined boundaries projected in schemes such as Lichtheim's. As a result, he had to come up with a description that fails to offer the certainty suggested in his diagrams.

After reiterating his three categories of aphasia—"purely verbal," "asymbolic," and his own contribution, "agnosic" (*AA* 105)—he devotes a brief paragraph to the "psychological point of view" that defines "the word" once again, and its relations. Finally, he reviews the nature of the effects of lesions on the language apparatus. Within the categories completely or incompletely destructive, and location within or at the periphery of the speech field, the lesion that is incompletely destructive and located at the periphery can cause functional changes as described by Bastian's modifications. "If the lesion is centrally located, however, the entire language apparatus suffers functional disturbances that result from its nature as an association mechanism, and which we have attempted to enumerate" (*AA* 106). Here Freud's discourse has finally taken on a mechanistic metaphor such as those used by other writers.

Appropriately for the field of meaning encompassed by "mechanism," Freud's review imputes a unity and consistency to arguments that are, as we have seen, actually characterized by disjunctions, inconclusiveness on the central concept of "language," personal narratives of Freud's life experiences, and conflict among ultimately undecidable disciplinary discursive conventions. Contrary to his testimony, Freud's choices, finally, are mixed. Language and language disturbances remain an amalgam of several descriptive options, not clearly separated as he had expressly intended. In this "failure" can be detected not only an early version of the psychoanalytic reader of patients but also the early version of an integrated perspective on aphasia, which did not take hold in aphasia studies, although it might have benefited both patients and theory.

Freud concludes the book with a standard formula of modesty: what he has written will inevitably be unsatisfactory to the reader because he has tried to substitute for a convenient theory one that is less easy to visualize (even with illustrations) and less complete. He hopes, however, that it more accurately reflects real conditions and that highlighting the difficulties will lead to further clarification of the topic. After a two-sentence review, again, of earlier authors and Wernicke, he adds an ending that makes only the slightest of claims: "It appears to us that with these theories the significance of the factor of localization for aphasia was overestimated and that we would be well advised to pay attention once again to the functional conditions of the speech apparatus" (*AA* 106–107).

Where Exner and Westphal, for example, had launched initial explorations in medical terms, Freud developed a theory with broad and lasting implications. It is remarkable that in the concluding pages, Bastian is called upon three times to serve in a explanatory capacity. Heubner is mentioned once. Although Jackson is no longer mentioned, his ideas and his way of thinking were deeply ingrained in the aphasia book and continued to play a role in the development of psychoanalytic theory. Freud was able to combine the three by relating both Heubner and Jackson to Bastian. Out of Heubner's question, Bastian's categories, and Jackson's evolutionary theories, plus the material provided by other researchers (including those with whom he disagreed), Freud was able to develop an improved explanation for the dynamic relationship among the elements of the language capacity, with a scheme for its organization in the brain. Beyond these achievements, the aphasia book distilled the state of Freud's thought on matters that remained important to him and to which he returned in future writings. In those future writings, ideas that were stimulated by Bastian and Jackson, Delbrück, Grashey, and others are recast in new and evolving contexts.

6

FREUD IN ABSENTIA

As we have seen, researchers with a special interest in Freud have gone to the trouble of seeking out and examining the aphasia book, often to credit it with being an important document in the development of psychoanalysis. Despite this interest, the aphasia book does not appear to have entered and influenced the mainstream of aphasia studies, even though Freud had positioned himself to do just that with his ambitious research program and highly developed argument (and, when we include the two dictionary entries, publications on aphasia from 1888 to 1893). Henry Head, a leading figure in the field, wrote in his massive overview of 1926, *Aphasia and Kindred Disorders of Speech*, that in the late nineteenth century, "the time was ripe for a ruthless destruction of false gods," by which he meant it was necessary to refute the assumptions of Lichtheim and the other "diagram makers" who reduced every form of aphasia to pathways versus centers and simple correspondences between clinical manifestations and neural events.[1] One would expect Head to have turned to Freud's monograph as an early attempt to interrogate and advance aphasia theory, but he mentioned Freud only for having "employed the term 'agnosia' " (Head 105), despite the fact that

1. See Introduction, n. 11, above; here, 1:66.

Freud had raised fundamentally the same questions Head was raising. Lichtheim, whose theories have been proved wrong, remains "alive." His name appears in contemporary texts that include historical overview, and his theories continue to be interrogated.

Why was Lichtheim not dropped as a result of Freud's and later researchers' demonstrating the incorrectness of his views? Why, instead, did Freud himself fall by the wayside in aphasia studies? Others have been recognized who published only one article or monograph on the subject. Was Freud marginalized because he did not publish his own reports on aphasic patients? Was it because once he later became known for psychoanalysis, his previous publications were ignored? Was it because psychoanalysis made Freud's a less authoritative voice in medicine and neuroscience? Was his early work delegitimated as respectable science by his later work? Whatever the reason, the elision was abetted by James Strachey's choosing not to translate the entire aphasia book for the *Standard Edition*. Language, however, ought not to have been an obstacle. Wernicke, Lichtheim, and other German aphasiologists were read in the original. Up until at least the middle of the twentieth century, it was common for researchers to read one another's untranslated publications in French, German, and English and sometimes other languages as well. Most important of all, what happened to the questions Freud raised? I believe that the fate of Freud's ideas in the field of aphasia studies exemplifies the truism that selectivity and arbitrariness are built into any narrative of history, including history of science, and that the ensuing gaps, like typographic errors in common words or politically inspired erasures in the record of the past, tend not to be perceived, even by well-intentioned viewers.

One of the most distinguished aphasiologists in the United States, Harold Goodglass, published in 1993 a history and survey of the present state of aphasia theory.[2] Because the book is a recent overview of the field by an author of stature who is also interested in the historical record, I have chosen to use it as an example of the absence of Freud. Although the name "Freud" never appears in the book, I propose, nevertheless, that Goodglass is a "Freudian" aphasiologist by virtue of his assuming a standpoint compatible with Freud's of over a century before. If it can be determined that my interpretation is accurate, then one or all of several possiblities are indicated: (1) The fundamental division in approaches to aphasia that Freud's book marks for the late nineteenth century is still

2. Goodglass, *Understanding Aphasia*.

alive today. (2) Ideas (or perhaps attitudes) survive and may be transmitted without traceable sources. (3) Origins tend to be elided; some texts ancestral to Goodglass's book do mention Freud,[3] but the transmission did not continue into the present time, though the transmission of some of Freud's sources did.

Goodglass's book includes references to authors and publications Freud used: Bastian (1869, used by Freud), Jules Joseph Dejerine (1891, 1892, 1901; Freud used a different article by the same author), Exner (1881, used by Freud), Finkelnburg (1870; Freud used only Spamer's citation), Freund (1889, used by Freud), Hughlings Jackson (1866, 1874, 1878, 1915, some used by Freud), Kussmaul (1881 [first edition 1877], used by Freud), Lichtheim (1884, German original used by Freud), Pierre Marie (1906), Pick (1913, 1923, 1931), Albert Pitres (1898), and Steinthal (as originator of the term *apraxia*). That is, Goodglass's book skirts near, but finally around, Freud. As was typically his fate, Freud remains an outsider, irrespective of the quality of his work and the evidence on which it was based.

As one would expect, theorizing in the Goodglass book arises out of concepts about brain and language not available to Freud. Some examples are *modality*, *models*, and *networks* in the neurosciences. In contrast to Freud's time, research in aphasia now requires experimental verification and the testing of competing theories. Neuroanatomy has been significantly refined since Freud's time; for example, Freud's word-object connection has been anatomically localized (under different names).[4] In spite of the vast differences in time, place, discourse, methods, technology, and neuroanatomic precision, however, Freud's fundamental theoretical stance on aphasia can be found again in Goodglass's presentation. The issues and problems Freud and the other aphasiologists of his time faced, continue to be contentious today, for example, the nature of "conduction aphasia" (Lichtheim), whether or not there is a "naming center" (which Goodglass disputes), and others. Goodglass writes: "At no time has there been complete consensus on how the various manifestations of aphasia should be classified" (209).

3. A prominent one is Kurt Goldstein, who praises Freud's book in his *Language and Language Disturbances* (New York: Grune and Stratton, 1948).
4. On this topic Goodglass writes: "It appears, then, that the anatomic channels through which the various sensory components of conceptual representation communicate with the language system occupy a region low in the parieto-occipito-temporal region where lesions are likely to produce either a severe two-way dissociation of name from concept, a naming difficulty selective to a single sensory modality (particularly visual), or dissociations of a

Many nineteenth-century categories of aphasic disturbances have been carried over to the current time. For example, Goodglass's description (49) of "optic aphasia" (designated initially by Freud's source, C. S. Freund) essentially matches the description of that syndrome in Freud's text. In fact, it is remarkable, in view of advances in neuroanatomy, how many of the earlier descriptions have been retained. In addition, not all methodology in current use is of recent vintage. Goodglass reports on "the collection of speech error data from normal speakers in everyday discourse" (35) as one type of experimental foundation—one that had also been advocated, for example, by Berthold Delbrück in 1886 and later utilized by Freud and his sources for *The Psychopathology of Everyday Life* (1901).

At the outset, Goodglass acknowledges, as Freud did in 1891, the limits of knowledge claims: "It would be rash to claim that we are anywhere near understanding, at the neural level, the processes by which language is carried out in the normal and damaged adult brain." Despite enormous progress in neurolinguistic studies since Freud's time, the same goal eludes investigators now which eluded Freud and Hughlings Jackson. Nevertheless, it is possible according to Goodglass to describe certain "regularities" "between lesion sites and symptoms produced" which produce a "plausible but only partial account of the gross neural circuitry of language" (xi). Freud also felt he was able to describe such regularities in "localizing" terms but that a different theory was required for those aphasias for which the prevalent localizing theory could not account. Goodglass critiques a standpoint with which he himself has been associated: the "currently most widely used system of syndrome terminology—the revised 'classical' taxonomy promoted by Geschwind, Goodglass, and others from the Boston school of aphasiology . . ." (5)—a typology that is "an updating of that of Wernicke, as it was passed on among European scholars from the latter part of the nineteenth century . . . [and] . . . has become dominant in the European and American literature" (209). His criticism of that typology (like the criticism of Exner, Westphal, and others in Freud's time) is "that the number of instances where the syndrome configuration is at odds with the observed lesion is sufficient to undermine confidence in the localizing value of the syndromes" (5).

Goodglass provides a detailed critique of the inadequacy of classification

---

single sensory modality from the rest of the conceptual representation (e.g., visual agnosia)" (49). This explanation provides an anatomic underpinning for the *Vorstellungen* of the word and the object in Freud's parlance.

by syndrome for purposes beyond providing "a shorthand summary of the most prominent features of a patient's language disorder" and "communicating between clinicians" (216). This had been the major unrecognized problem in Freud's time: there were no agreed-upon standards of testing, labeling, or reporting. Case histories were transmitted, translated, reported, and used in various theoretical contexts without the possibility of verification or even the confidence that one set of questions, observations, and notations was consistent with any other. Only rarely was the inadequacy of a report so obvious that it was commented on. From today's perspective, problems remain in the discourse of syndrome determination and description. Goodglass discusses several: (1) "mixing of features from unrelated domains" (e.g., channels affected, linguistic character, phenomenological impression); (2) "inconstancy and lack of precision . . . in feature specification," where the problem itself appears to differ little from the form it took in the nineteenth century ("The use of subjective standards for judging the presence or absence of symptoms that vary on a continuum makes for great difficulties in documenting agreement between clinicians, except in a handful of classical, prototypical cases"); and (3) "inconstancy of anatomical criteria" (i.e., the link between syndromes and "their supposed neural basis") (217).

The discourse remains problematic for the same reasons Freud diagnosed and supported, using, for example, the postmortem studies by Heubner and Giraudeau. Goodglass presents evidence that "sheds doubt on the notion that . . . [conduction aphasia] . . . is primarily a disorder of repetition, and . . . on the anatomic interpretation of a disconnection of an auditory language center from a motor speech planning center" (143). He disputes, just as Freud did, the validity of the diagrams of Lichtheim and others and their postulation of the meaning of "centers" versus "pathways." Nonetheless, Goodglass consistently refers to the "anatomical-connectionist model" (19) that originated with Lichtheim as the "classical model," which becomes the "classical typology" (20) and is thereby invested with the kind of higher legitimacy accorded anything named "classical." Goodglass hints at what might lie behind unacknowledged allegiance to a theory and thus indirectly sheds light on the nature of Freud's project and his achievment:

> The syndrome label carries an additional load of implications to one who has been indoctrinated with the classical anatomo-functional model of language based on centers and connecting pathways. To such an individual, the syndrome label carries more than the expectation that the lesion

has an increased likelihood of lying in a particular zone. It means that a particular anatomo-functional change has taken place that must be the result of one of a small number of anatomic possibilities. (216)

Freud in his time resisted "indoctrination" by a theoretical complex so pervasive and convincing that it has survived to prevail in critical minds of our time. Perhaps, to take on established views, took not only a powerful mind and an iconoclastic bent but also a deep-seated personal agenda.

Goodglass maps aphasia according to the same assumptions Freud used in his description of the "language apparatus" in which the nature of an aphasic disturbance was related to the proximity of the involved lesion to brain sites that control the corresponding sensory faculty. For example, "auditory comprehension" is related to the "primary center for audition." In aphasia of "motor articulatory processes" the lesions are "adjacent to the cortical area for the control of oral musculature," and "deficits involving letter and word recognition" involve "lesions bordering on the visual association areas" (Goodglass 3). Goodglass's discussion of recovery from aphasia—which "can be rapid and complete in the case of a small lesion or of a lesion on the periphery of the language zone" (9)—entails the same theoretical suppositions Freud applies to his discussion of the relative severity of aphasic lesions according to their location more toward the center or the periphery of the "language field." Freud also theorized that recovery from left-hemisphere damage to the language area would occur in the case of those sensory capacities that were also represented in the right hemisphere. Goodglass postulates with regard to word deafness that it "can appear only when the Wernicke's area homologue in the right hemisphere is totally unable to process word meanings from auditory input" (125). Goodglass believes that differences in the organization of language functions "may be established by different brains" and that these individual differences "place limits on our expectancy of discovering a distinct lesion difference for every variation in patterns of dissociation among language functions" (46). Taking into account the obvious difference between the use of the term *function* today and Freud's meaning in his aphasia book, we may ascertain that Goodglass, who does not cite Charcot among his sources, is accepting Jackson's version of individual differences, which is the version also accepted by Freud. The theory of individual differences supplies one neurological explantion for Freud's view on "functional" consequences of lesions. Another current explanation for Freud's view is supplied by the assumption of neural networks so closely interwoven that damage at any point in the system would have consequences for the rest (Goodglass 46). All together, then, in Good-glass's account, the two pillars of Freud's theory reappear: his critique of the assumptions of schematic localizing (the Lichtheim model) and his proposal for a language zone that explains aphasia in neuroanatomic terms.

Language itself is an area of some compatibility but also significant differences. Freud was grappling with definitions and distinctions that have, of course, been greatly refined in the intervening years. Goodglass distinguishes among three types of naming of "structural lesion sites in the cerebral language system": in terms of functional anatomy (channels of "sensory input or motor output"), in psycholinguistic terms ("naming" and "using grammatical forms"), and in terms of "pathological adaptive symptoms" ("nonfluency and paragrammatic speech") (4). Although the same distinctions had not been made in Freud's time, he was, nevertheless, acutely aware of the need for such discursive distinctions and tried to establish them within the limits available to him. Hughlings Jackson's theories on language and aphasia, which Goodglass cites with regularity for their historical importance, entered, of course, into Freud's delibera-tions. Goodglass cites Jackson's view of aphasia as the loss of ability to "propositionize" and calls it defining aphasia by "psychological intent," as opposed to the second defining principle, which attends to the "grammati-cal or linguistic function of particular words in the message" (6). At these two extreme lie the views of Jackson and Delbrück. Missing from Good-glass's account is the evolutionary context of late-nineteenth-century theo-rizing: it was built into Jackson's theory of the progressive loss of language capacity and into Delbrück's because linguistics (philology) was a historical discipline. Goodglass does, however, include a footnote reference to the-ory that is straight out of Jackson's evolutionary views, in particular one adopted by Freud: what is best learned and most often repeated or used is least vulnerable to aphasia, which means that in the case of polyglots, the languages learned later would be lost before the native language. This time, there is neurological evidence:

> There is evidence to support the idea that the representation of knowl-edge that is highly overlearned is vulnerable in a more restricted zone in the brain than is knowledge that is less well practiced. Ojemann and Whitaker (1978)[5] found that word finding in the first language of a

5. G. Ojemann and H. A. Whitaker, "The Bilingual Brain," *Archives of Neurology* 35 (1978): 409–412. Ojemann has gathered further evidence for the conclusion that the first language learned is more compactly organized in the brain than later ones, as he reported in "Cortical

bilingual speaker could be disrupted by cortical stimulation in relatively few points, in comparison with the wider distribution of points that disrupted word finding in the second, less well practiced language. (221)

Goodglass credits successors to Freud with Freud's insights.[6] He writes, "The classical typology of the aphasias was passed along to the clinicians of the twentieth century with minor modifications of the original Wernicke-Lichtheim model," and he credits Dejerine, in a 1901 publication[7] (ten years subsequent to Freud's book) with not accepting the "purity of the syndromes predicted by the Wernicke-Lichtheim model" or "the notion of transcortical aphasia, as predicated by that model" (Goodglass 20). As we have noted, Freud's case against transcortical aphasia was one of the strongest he made and an integral part of his theory. Goodglass writes, "The names most prominently associated with the reaction against models based on anatomic centers and interconnections are those of Marie (1906) and Head (1926)" (21). Von Monakow (1914)[8] is credited with recognizing "the depressing effect of a cerebral lesion on functions that depend on structures remote from the lesion site" (Goodglass 23)—the foundational theory of Freud's book. Henry Head is called "the successor to Hughlings Jackson" (23), who brought Jackson's views back to general attention after they had been long neglected. One is inclined to ask Was Freud's work deliberately suppressed at some early date in the century?

Goodglass is an author who pays special attention to the history of the field and, in the case of Jackson, takes pains to give him credit for his observations, which have come to be "virtually axiomatic for contemporary clinicians" (Goodglass 22). He also gives fullsome credit to Finkelnburg for the concept of asymbolia, which Freud had recast as an interruption in the relationship of the word to the idea of the object. Freud renamed Finkelnburg's asymbolia "agnosia" (*AA* 80), which another of Goodglass's sources refers to as "Freud's term."[9] Goodglass discusses Roman Jakobson's views at length without mentioning that one text, Ja-

---

Organization of Language," *Journal of Neuroscience* 11 (August 1991): 2281–2287, here 2282. Goodglass points out, however, that there is variation in language loss which cannot always be predicted by practice or use (10–11).
6. I do not intend to be judgmental here; I am using Goodglass's text as an example of rereading in the history of science, *not* as an example of historical error.
7. Jules Joseph Dejerine, *Anatomie des Centres Nerveux* (Paris: Rueff, 1901).
8. Constantin Von Monakow, *Die Lokalisation im Grosshirn* (Wiesbaden: Bergmann, 1914).
9. Theodore Weisenburg and Katharine E. McBride, *Aphasia: A Clinical and Psychological Study* (New York: Commonwealth Fund, 1935), 101.

kobson's 1956 monograph, comes out of a combination of Jackson's views and Freud's (see Chapter 1 at n. 27). It is certainly not to be expected that every account of historical antecedents include a complete genealogy, but this elision is of particular note because Goodglass writes that he was "strongly influenced" by Jakobson's views (29).

Goodglass credits the authors of a 1961 examination of aphasia with proposing "that there were five autonomous components of language that could be damaged: visual-to-oral transmission, aural-to-oral and aural-topographic transmission, and matching to either oral or visual stimulation." [10] This is a variation on theories illustrated in diagrams such as Grashey's (Figure 1 above), with the difference that the intervening concept of the "word" has been dispensed with. Goodglass describes the "flow charts" produced by cognitive psychologists which are "made up of boxes that represent separate processing operations and arrows connecting them that represent the path of information flow. In some cases, such as oral reading, there may be several concurrent, alternative pathways reaching an output product through different possible processes. Aphasic symptoms of particular types are expected if a particular pathway is disabled" (36). Unlike Goodglass, the designers of flow charts generally do not historically contextualize their way of imaging theory, although it assumes, almost without interruption, a nineteenth-century imaging tradition. [11] In contrast to Freud, who produced a flow chart of his own along the lines of Grashey's, Goodglass distances himself from the reductiveness of flow charts: "The labeled constructs . . . remain at the black box level, being specified no further than required for the internal logic of the model. . . . The human cognitive apparatus is capable of many more and many more subtle ways of perceptually analyzing the visual input and generating associations than these labeled boxes convey" (169).

Freud did not develop his aphasia theory on the basis of sophisticated linguistics. He was incorrect to focus on the word and the letter of the alphabet. They were arbitrary choices, based on historically contingent assumptions, not on supracultural neural findings. Focusing on letter recognition in testing creates special obstacles for patients, as Goodglass writes:

10. Goodglass, *Understanding Aphasia*, 30, citing J. M. Wepman and L. V. Jones, *The Language Modalities Test for Aphasia* (Chicago: University of Chicago Press, 1961). Goodglass also cites earlier work by Wepman in which Wepman "proposed" "jargon aphasia," a term that, as we know from Freud (*AA* 23), was in use at the time among British authors, such as Ross, who used it in his 1887 book.
11. Goodglass (170) reproduces a flow chart that looks like an amalgam of diagrams by Spamer, Wysman, and Grashey.

Letter recognition and letter naming is a skill imposed by a convention of modern civilization—one for which there is no evolutionarily based special mechanism. . . . Letter-name learning places a demand on visual-verbal associative capabilities that is unprecedented and unmatched by any other task in language learning. Not only are letter forms composed of a small set of abstract lines and curves in different, meaningless combinations, but their names are short, phonologically impoverished syllables that have no significance except as labels for the equally meaningless visual forms. (243)

It is obvious that theory dissociated from real language use will result from conceptualizing aphasic disturbances and testing patients in terms of the letter of the alphabet. A distorted interpretation of patients' abilities will also result. Beyond that, the view of "the word" prevalent among aphasiologists in the late nineteenth century ignored the fact that "the 'meaning' carried by a written word is not an indivisible concept, but one having multiple layers that may be differently affected by aphasia," Goodglass points out (158). For example, a patient may be able to distinguish the category to which a word belongs but not its more specific meaning. A patient's ability to read is influenced by the concreteness of words as well as their emotional intensity, according to Goodglass. This observation replicates Jackson's theory and is related to Freud's anecdote about being in life-threatening situations and imagining a piece of paper with relevant words floating before his eyes. Freud invested "concrete" words with a greater positive valence than "abstractions" (see *Interpretation of Dreams*). In early psychoanalysis the origins of hysterical symptoms were encoded in concrete and emotionally loaded words that called for a reader with the qualities of an insightful aphasiologist.

Had Freud taken into consideration Delbrück's ideas on aphasia and aphasia testing, more linguistically meaningful theory would have resulted. For example, Delbrück stressed the intactness of the sense for word order in a sentence, even in severe cases of aphasia. Goodglass writes that "the use of word order is resistant to damage both in the production and interpretation of sentence meanings" (102). The "canonical" sequences of parts of speech convey meaning. Thus "syntactic decoding" is responsible for more of the difficulties aphasics face than is "impaired lexical comprehension" (117). Like Delbrück, Goodglass points to the importance of considering the national language in which the patient is tested: "In the case of individuals who are bilingual, the expectations of meaning interpretations that are derived from word order or from noun animacy may result in different interpretations in the two languages of the same patient, depending on which language she or he is tested in" (103). Reporting the work of C. Heeschen,[12] Goodglass presents an example of the type of errors made by agrammatic patients whose language is German. They are different from the choices made by an English speaker with the equivalent aphasic disturbance: "There are certain morpho-syntactic regularities that are extremely resistant to agrammatism in German. One of these requires that the infinitive form of the verb appear at the end of the sentence" (112). Goodglass, in contrast to Freud, would have been in tune with Delbrück's analysis. Why did Freud tune out the linguistic analysis? Was it because only a reductive version of language could be utilized in his neurological and psychological models? It remains remarkable that he did not *directly* address the conventions on language prevalent among aphasiologists the way he addressed the neuroanatomic conventions.

Beyond linguistics, the notion of "multiple layers" of meaning in a word not only is of clinical significance for aphasia but reaches also from aphasia theory into psychoanalysis. Goodglass discusses the fact that a listener may respond to, without ever being consciously aware of, meanings of a word other than the contextual one. Those other meanings, therefore, must lie "below" the level of consciousness. Freud takes up this feature of language in later texts. In contradiction to Freud's view (with reference to John Stuart Mill) in the aphasia book that contrasted the "closed" *Vorstellung* of a word with the "open," and thus unlimited, *Vorstellung* of an object, Goodglass writes about the many more possibilities to be found in a word than in an object, and in so doing he contradicts Freud on aphasia but describes Freud's program in, for example, *Jokes and Their Relation to the Unconscious:*

> By being liberated, in a sense, from the baggage of the original object concept [the equivalent of *Vorstellung*] to which it refers, the word as a linguistic element gains the unlimited flexibility of other words. It can be deliberately used in a nonsensical sense, retrieved for listing as a member of all sorts of categories defined by any of its semantic features, its phonological features, or the features of its orthographic form. It may be redefined to give it a technical meaning or spun-off for metaphorical meanings, in addition to its conventional meaning, and may become a

12. C. Heeschen, "Agrammatism versus Paragrammatism: A fictitious opposition," in *Agrammatism*, ed. M.-L. Hean (New York: Academic Press, 1985).

subject for metalinguistic word games, such as puns. . . . In comparison with the uses of the object name as a word, the original nonverbal concept of its referent is an awkward and lumbering mental entity. (241)

Far deeper than the overt treatment of language in the aphasia book is the unacknowledged language theory hidden between the lines. Freud's rhetoric, his metaphors and anecdotes in the aphasia book, his real-life passion for language games, and his later exploration of language in the *Jokes* and the *Dreams* books exemplify Goodglass's description, bringing together finally, in a roundabout way, complex aphasia theory and complex language theory.

Goodglass's summary indicates that in the field of aphasia, however, Freud was tilting at windmills:

The nineteenth century view, fostered by the center-and-connection models of the "diagram makers," was that there was an invariant relationship between the destruction of a center or connecting pathway and a complex of resulting deficits and spared abilities. In this view, each syndrome was a disease entity that pointed to its source, just as a medical disease entity might point to a causative microorganism. This view has persisted to some extent, in spite of the decades of experience with the fuzzy boundaries between the syndromes and the variability of anatomic lesion sites. (218)

Already in 1891 Freud was a specialist in "fuzzy boundaries" and "variability." The complex of ideas with which he was deeply engaged was carried over from his time, yet his work itself was left behind—a ghostly shadow of an unrecognized presence in the twists and turns in the historical narrative of aphasia studies.

INDEX